Praise for *What It Is Like to Go to War*:

"Karl Marlantes has written a staggeringly beautiful book on combat—what it feels like, what the consequences are, and above all, what society must do to understand it. In my eyes he has become the preeminent literary voice on war of our generation. He is a natural storyteller and a deeply profound thinker who not only illuminates war for civilians, but also offers a kind of spiritual guidance to veterans themselves. As this generation of warriors comes home, they will be enormously helped by what Marlantes has written—I'm sure he will literally save lives."   —Sebastian Junger

"Marlantes is the best American writer right now on war and the extreme costs to society of sending young men and women off to combat without much of a safety net for them when they land back home. . . . With *What It Is Like to Go to War* a second Marlantes book resides on the top shelf of American literature."   —Anthony Swofford, author of *Jarhead*

"To say that this book is brilliant is an understatement—Marlantes is the absolute master of taking the psyche of the combat veteran and translating it into words that the civilian or non-veteran can understand. I have read many, many books on war and this is the first time that I've ever read exactly what the combat veteran thinks and feels—nothing I have ever read before has hit home in my heart like this book."
—Gunnery Sergeant Terence D'Alesandro,
3rd Battalion, 5th Marines, U.S. Marine Corps

"The passion and self-revealing pain of *What It Is Like* make it a must-read for anyone interested in war . . . Marlantes is top-notch in describing ground combat and its morally brutalizing effect on warriors. . . . With an intellect as sharp and critical as Marlantes's, and a temperament not afraid to display confusion or remorse, *What It Is Like* is more than worth the effort of any reader."   —*Los Angeles Times*

"*What It Is Like to Go to War* is a well-crafted and forcefully argued work that contains fresh and important insights into what it's like to be in a war and what it does to the human psyche."   —*The Washington Post*

"In this thoughtful, literate work of self-exorcism, Marlantes tells tales of incredible bravery as well as brutality."   —*People*

"*What It Is Like to Go to War* offers profound insight on how we must prepare our youth who become our warriors for their hard and uncompromising journey through war's hell and back home again."   —*Vietnam Magazine*

"[Marlantes's] research and rationale form a voice of reason with a reason to be heard. . . . Those who support the troops will read this book and will better understand what it is like to go to—and come back from—war."
—*Air Force Times*

"A precisely crafted and bracingly honest book."   —*The Atlantic*

"A gripping, first-person plea to consider the impact on the human spirit of being a soldier."   —Huffington Post

"Wrenchingly honest . . . Digging as deeply into his own life as he does into the larger sociological and moral issues, Marlantes presents a riveting, powerfully written account of how, after being taught to kill, he learned to deal with the aftermath."   —*Publishers Weekly* (starred review)

"Marlantes knows what he writes . . . Raw, unsettling honesty pervades the work."   —Time.com

"A valiant effort to explain and make peace with war's awesome consequences for human beings."   —*Kirkus Reviews*

"At his best, and he is often at his best, Marlantes succeeds in that greatest of writers' skills, allowing the reader to realize what he or she unconsciously knew but could never articulate. *What It Is Like to Go to War* is the brave and illuminating work of a courageous and humane man."   —*The Times* (UK)

"Part memoir, part primer for the modern warrior, and part exorcism of past ghosts, *What It Is Like to Go to War* is brutally honest, clear-eyed, and necessary. . . . a powerful book that should be required reading for those going to war— and the leaders who send them."   —*Financial Times*

"With war such a part of contemporary American life, this book is deeply important, as timely and urgent as contemporary on-the-ground reporting from Afghanistan and Iraq."   —*The (Minneapolis) Star Tribune*

"A sound debunking of anything smacking of the glory of warfare—but written with compassion, honesty, and wit for men and now women who fight and for all of those who care about them."   —*St. Louis Dispatch*

"A gutting look into the psyche of a soldier, adding flesh to the often flat and stereotyped personage. Humanizing, empathetic, and wise, this reading experience will light corners in the human experience often judged dark."   —*Library Journal*

"With unflinching honesty, best-selling author Karl Marlantes tells us *What It Is Like to Go to War* in his compassionate, powerful narrative on Vietnam. Marlantes does not shy away from recounting experiences that, outside the arena of war, are horrifying or embarrassing. . . . He tempers the brutal truths of fear, power games, and courage with a thoughtful prescription for our soldiers' well-being; caring for our soldiers and their families differently will benefit society as a whole. Marlantes sets a new standard for understanding the experience of war." —Amazon.com

"[Marlantes] examines with lacerating frankness his own sentiments and experiences at the forefront of battle, in Vietnam more than forty years ago. . . . Every modern British officer should read this book, and consider what they can learn from it. Today, too many young men return from our wars to lose a personal battle for the mind. Marlantes describes the nature of this struggle with exceptional force, and even brilliance." —*The Sunday Times* (UK)

"A mesmerizing account of his combat experience, filled with self-analysis and raw introspection that should serve as a touchstone for those about to go to war. . . . A straightforward, firsthand account about the brutality of war written with a warrior's passion and a large dose of unfiltered truth." —*The San Antonio Express*

"A slim spiritual guide . . . Marlantes's book is a sincere plea for better soldiers and veterans." —*Seattle Weekly*

"Fierce and brilliant . . . Marlantes writes unforgettably about soldiers not as they should be, or as we'd like to think of them being, but as they are. . . . The book draws heavily on his Vietnam experiences—but also on the fact that he's thought carefully about them ever since." —*Reader's Digest* (UK)

"There's a Vietnam combat sequence in Karl Marlantes's book that is so thrilling and well choreographed that if the author hadn't been there to witness it you'd have thought it could only have come from a movie. . . . Marlantes is a born storyteller and his new book more than delivers on its title." —*The Mail on Sunday*

"Cathartic . . . I remember learning about *how* to go to war, but there was little discussion about what it was *like* to go to war and its place in the human experience. . . . A compelling testimony for the contemporary warrior." —U.S. Naval Institute

ALSO BY KARL MARLANTES

Matterhorn

WHAT IT IS
LIKE TO GO
TO WAR

KARL MARLANTES

Grove Press
New York

Excerpt from *Seven Pillars of Wisdom* by T. E. Lawrence, copyright © 1926, 1935 by Doubleday, a division of Random House, Inc. Used by permission of Doubleday, a division of Random House, Inc.

Excerpt from *The Collected Works of W.B. Yeats, Volume I: The Poems, Revised* by W. B. Yeats, edited by Richard J. Finneran. Copyright © 1940 by Georgie Yeats, renewed 1968 by Bertha Georgie Yeats, Michael Yeats, and Anne Yeats. All rights reserved. Reprinted with the permission of Scribner, a Division of Simon & Schuster, Inc.

Excerpt from *Egil's Saga* reprinted by permission of Everyman's Library, London.

Excerpt from *The Mahabharata* reprinted by permission of Bharatiya Vidya Bhavan.

Almost all call signs, names, nicknames, and their origins have been changed to protect the privacy of the individuals and their families.

Printed in the United States of America
Published simultaneously in Canada

ISBN-13: 978-0-8021-4592-5

Grove Press
an imprint of Grove/Atlantic, Inc.
841 Broadway
New York, NY 10003

Distributed by Publishers Group West

www.groveatlantic.com

12 13 14 15   10 9 8 7 6 5 4 3 2

The nation that makes a great distinction between its scholars and its warriors will have its thinking done by cowards and its fighting done by fools.
—Spartan king, quoted by Thucydides

Any fool can learn from his mistakes. The wise man learns from the mistakes of others.
—Otto von Bismarck

This book is dedicated to the Marines I served with in Vietnam, those who came home and those who didn't, and to all combat veterans who fought and are fighting now with noble hearts—all.

CONTENTS

PREFACE

I wrote this book primarily to come to terms with my own experience of combat. So far—reading, writing, thinking—that has taken more than forty years. I could have kept my thoughts in a personal journal, but I took on trying to get these reflections published so that I could share them with other combat veterans. Perhaps, in some way, I can help them with their own quest for meaning and their efforts to integrate their combat experiences into their current lives. I also want to share my thoughts and experiences with young people who are contemplating joining the military or who are about to enter combat themselves, sort of like providing them with a psychological and spiritual combat prophylactic, for indeed combat is like unsafe sex in that it's a major thrill with possible horrible consequences. Finally, this nation is now engaged in three wars simultaneously, two with both air and ground forces and one from the air only. I am quite certain these are not the last. All conscientious citizens and especially those with the power to make policy will be better prepared to make decisions about committing young people to combat if they know what they are about to ask of them.

The violence of combat assaults psyches, confuses ethics, and tests souls. This is not only a result of the violence suffered. It is also a result of the violence inflicted. Warriors suffer from wounds to their bodies, to be sure, but because they are involved in killing people they also suffer from their compromises with, or outright violations of, the moral norms of society and religion.

These compromises and violations are not generally discussed and their impact on a warrior's mental health and soul is minimized or even ignored entirely, not only by current military training but by society at large.

The book is not intended to fix or improve military training. I was a U.S. Marine in the Vietnam War and believe that the Marine Corps prepared me then, and still does prepare our young Marines, to fight our country's battles exceedingly well, as do all the other branches of the United States military. In fact, today's young warriors are far better prepared than we were in the Vietnam era, at least technically and tactically. This book, rather, focuses on those aspects of combat that can't adequately be prepared for by institutional training programs, no matter how lengthy or thorough. The preparation for these aspects of combat must be done by the individual, in the quiet places, alone, in communion with his or her own heart and soul. It would probably be better if such soul-searching were done before an individual volunteers for military service, but I am well aware that eighteen-year-olds are not known for introspection. This is one of many reasons why young people, particularly young men, make the best warriors. However, imminent maiming and death do help motivate young warriors to contemplate these more serious aspects of their profession. So if by reading this book before entering combat a young warrior can be helped to better handle the many psychological, moral, and spiritual stresses of combat, then the book will have been worth writing. In addition, if the ideas discussed here help citizens and policy makers attain a clearer understanding of what they are asking of their warriors and of their own role in sending them into the moral quagmire and sacrificial fire called war, then the book will have succeeded, if not beyond my hopes, perhaps beyond my expectations.

1

TEMPLE OF MARS

Warriors deal with death. They take life away from others. This is normally the role of God. Asking young warriors to take on that role without adequate psychological and spiritual preparation can lead to damaging consequences. It can also lead to killing and the infliction of pain in excess of what is required to accomplish the mission. If warriors are returned home having had better psychological and spiritual preparation, they will integrate into civilian life faster and they and their families will suffer less. But the more blurred the boundary is between the world where they are acting in the role of God and the world where they are acting in an ordinary societal role, the more problematical the reintegration becomes.

The sun had struggled all day behind monsoon clouds before finally being extinguished by the turning earth and the dark wet ridges of the Annamese Cordillera. It was February 1969, in Quang Tri province, Vietnam. Zoomer lay above my hole in monsoon-night blackness on the slick clay of Mutter's Ridge, the dark jungle-covered ridge paralleling Vietnam's demilitarized zone where the Third Marine Division and the North Vietnamese Army had struggled together for two years. A bullet had gone through Zoomer's chest, tearing a large hole out of his back. We kept him on his side, curled against the cold drizzle, so the one good lung wouldn't fill up with blood. We were surrounded and there was no hope of evacuation, even in daylight. The choppers couldn't find us in the fog-shrouded mountains.

I heard Zoomer all night, panting as if he were running the 400, one lung doing for two and a body in shock. In and out. In, the fog, the sighing sound of monsoon wind through the jungle. Out, the hot painful breath. Zoomer had to go all night. If he slept, he'd die. So no morphine. Pain was the key to life.

To help him stay awake, and to calm my own fear, I'd crawl over to him to whisper stories.

I grew up in Oregon, where as a teenager I worked with my grandfather Axel on his fishing boat at the mouth of the Columbia River. One night in June 1959 a dull thunk startled us into alertness as a heavy body slammed into the four-football-fields-long gill net. The body's weight made the cork line, which floated on the surface and from which the net hung like a curtain, sink beneath the cold salt water. We approached the large gap in the cork line quietly, me steering the thirty-foot fishing boat in the dark, Grandpa Axel in the bow with the rifle, worried that it was a sea lion. A sea lion could destroy the net, which next to the boat itself was Grandpa's most valuable investment. My spine prickled when I saw the plated body of a seven-foot green sturgeon slowly undulating, eerie and ghostlike, beneath the dark water.

It took everything both of us had to haul the sturgeon into the boat, several hundred pounds at nine cents a pound and not much tearing of the net. Grandpa Axel was pleased. He and I heaved the sturgeon into the built-in fish box that temporarily held the salmon until we could put back in to Scandinavian Station. That was where we unloaded and weighed our catch, bobbing on the swell beneath the crane that hoisted the fish boxes up to the waiting ice, Grandpa impatient to get back to fishing, me happy to be idle.

That night when we hauled in the sturgeon, we still had plenty of room in the fish box, so we continued fishing. The sturgeon lay there, alive, its wet scales reflecting starlight. It seemed an ancient thing from before the dinosaurs, breathing there, too primitive and rugged to die quickly like the more complex and finely tuned salmon. I kept going over to watch it.

In—*Spiritus*. Out—*Sanctus*. Those were the words that came to me as I watched its gills pumping the alien air. In comes the spirit, out goes something holy, life perhaps, but I realized then that the "in" and the "out" are somehow the same thing and everything is touched by the holy when in the presence of death.

I watched Zoomer pumping air, hanging on to life with that same primitive doggedness of the sturgeon for all that night and most of the next day before the fog lifted enough to get in a medevac bird. Others died, like the salmon, but Zoomer kept pumping, enduring the shelling with the rest of us, waiting for the fog to clear, waiting for the helicopter that would take him home. It came. As the fog closed in again, just minutes after the helicopter got Zoomer out alive, I realized that the mystery of life and death had once again played out before me and that once again I was in a sacred space and, other than in my role as a walking weapons guidance system for the United States of America, totally unprepared to be there. The Marine Corps taught me how to kill but it didn't teach me how to deal with killing.

I first became conscious of this wartime sacred space, this temple of Mars, several months before Zoomer won that race with death. It was Christmastime 1968. I was the commander of a Marine rifle platoon. A rifle platoon at full strength consisted of forty-three Marines, but that winter we struggled against malaria, jungle rot, dysentery, and the North Vietnamese Army to keep our strength above thirty. Although I could radio in my position down to six grid points, I no longer knew where the hell I was spiritually. That more innocent, and certainly more spiritually connected, fourteen-year-old on his grandfather's fishing boat hadn't yet had his instinctive links to the spiritual world sawed away by eight years of high school and college and, finally, severed by military training.

Our company of three platoons had just secured the top of a mountain for a new artillery firebase, high in the cordillera where Laos met the old demilitarized zone that divided North Vietnam from South Vietnam. We were far from help and, after attrition from disease and firefights, my platoon was down to twenty-five. After nearly a month of continual moving through the jungle, eating only canned food, without the ability to wash properly or change clothes, some of the Marines were so covered with ringworm and jungle rot that they worked naked to lessen the discomfort. Rain and swirling fog delayed the hoped-for move of the artillery battery. Then, after only two of the normal complement of six 105mm howitzers had arrived, and a limited amount of ammunition, the rest of the regiment got into a fierce fight in the lowlands about 30 kilometers to our east and needed every Marine, weapon, and helicopter they could get. The regimental commander took a calculated risk and ordered my single undermanned platoon and some volunteers to stay behind to guard the howitzers and their crews and sent the rest of the company to reinforce the lowlands operation.

I was left in charge of the firebase. I alone would make all the decisions and count my mistakes with lives and pain. With the regiment stretched and the weather bad, there would be virtually no chance of reinforcements or resupply if the NVA attacked, for we were well inside the enemy's traditional operating area and well outside our own. If I blew it, or our luck was bad, we'd probably be overrun before help could reach us. I was afraid I would die. I held the lives of others in my hands. I had entered the temple of Mars, where not only were humans sacrificed, including me, but I was also the priest. This priest, however, had only been to a seminary called the Basic School where he learned the ritual moves but none of the meaning.

We patrolled hard and ceaselessly in terrain so steep and difficult we often had to use ropes to get up and down the cliffs. On the radio we pretended to be a company so the enemy wouldn't know how vulnerable we were to attack. At night no one slept longer than an hour at a time. We placed our nighttime listening posts far from the lines, well down the southern approach on a hill so steep I could stand facing it and touch dirt by putting my hand straight out in front of me. The north side was a 1,600-foot cliff. Given the difficulty of getting back to the lines at night, we all knew our listening posts would probably be sacrificed to warn the rest of us.

One night, small teams of NVA soldiers tried infiltrating past our listening posts to probe our main defenses for weak points and determine the layout of our lines. One of those teams blundered right into a listening post and the three Marines called in fire from the two 60mm mortars that had been left to us by the company commander. On the second volley one round fell short, wounding all three kids in the listening post. Nine Marines and a Navy corpsman volunteered to go get them, six to carry the wounded and four to fight. I waited by the radio, sick with dread, as the rescue team stumbled through the dark jungle dragging the wounded back up the muddy slopes. One of the wounded Marines kept screaming obscenities until someone gagged him with a sock. When they were safely inside the lines I saw bits of his brain spattered on the inside of his jungle hat. If we were lucky enough to get them all out alive, I knew at least one kid would never function normally again.

We did get the wounded out alive because of the heroism of a helicopter crew from Marine Air Group 39 who flew through the mountains in total darkness as we guided them in over the radio by the sound of their engines and blades. They burst into sight only feet from us, barely avoiding crashing, our enlisted forward air controller, whom we called FAC-man, screaming over the radio that they were right on top of us. We had outlined the landing zone on top of the mountain by putting lighted heat tabs in our helmets. The zone was so small the CH-46 could get only its rear wheels on the ground, with the front of the bird hovering over the edge of the cliff.

The bird left us in the dark and we immediately sent out new listening posts. The next morning the ceaseless patrolling continued, as did the fog, both from the monsoon and from the endless ache for sleep. I, however, was dealing with a lot more than lack of sleep. I had come upon, for the first time and, sadly, not even close to the last time, the terrible feeling of responsibility and guilt for the death and wounds of my men. The mortars, like everything else on the hill, were under my command. When I examined the mortars the next morning, I discovered one of them had a slightly loose tripod leg that I should have discovered in my routine weapons inspections beforehand. It had probably shifted after the recoil of the first round, causing the next round to fall short. In combat, inattention to details can kill people.

No other birds got in after that brave medical evacuation because the monsoon had shut down all flying in the mountains. Two days before Christmas the fog lifted just enough to allow a single chopper to work its way up to us, a dangerous journey, squeezing beneath the cloud ceiling just a few feet above the jungle-covered ridges. Along with food, water, mail, and ammunition came the battalion chaplain.

He had brought with him several bottles of Southern Comfort and some new dirty jokes. I accepted the Southern Comfort, thanked him, laughed at the jokes, and had a drink with him. Merry Christmas.

Inside I was seething. I thought I'd gone a little nuts. How could I be angry with a guy who had just put his life at risk to cheer me up? And didn't the Southern Comfort feel good on that rain-raked mountaintop? Years later I understood. I was engaged in killing and maybe being killed. I felt responsible for the lives and deaths of my companions. I was struggling with a situation approaching the sacred in its terror and contact with the infinite, and he was trying to numb me to it. I needed help with the existential terror of my own death and responsibility for the death of others, enemies and friends, not Southern Comfort. I needed a spiritual guide.

Many will argue that there is nothing remotely spiritual in combat. Consider this. Mystical or religious experiences have four common components: constant awareness of one's own inevitable death, total focus on the present moment, the valuing of other people's lives above one's own, and being part of a larger religious community such as the *Sangha, ummah,* or church. All four of these exist in combat. The big difference is that the mystic sees heaven and the warrior sees hell. Whether combat is the dark side of the same vision, or only something equivalent in intensity, I simply don't know. I do know that at age fifteen I had a mystical experience that scared the hell out of me and both it and combat put me into a different relationship with ordinary life and eternity.

Most of us, including me, would *prefer* to think of a sacred space as some light-filled wondrous place where we can feel good and find a way to shore up our psyches against death. We don't want to think that something as ugly and brutal as combat could be involved in any way with the spiritual. However, would any practicing Christian say that Calvary Hill was not a sacred space? Witness the demons of Tibetan Buddhism, ritual torture practiced by certain Native American tribes, the darker side of voodoo, or the cruel martyrdom of saints of all religions. Ritual torture or martyrdom can be either meaningless and terrible suffering or a profound religious experience, depending upon what the *sufferer* brings to the situation. The horror remains the same.

Combat is precisely such a situation.

Our young warriors are raised in possibly the only culture on the planet that thinks death is an option. Given this, it is no surprise that not only they but many of their ostensible religious guides, like the chaplain with the booze, enter the temple of Mars unprepared. Not only is such comfort too often delusional; it tends to numb one to spiritual reality and growth. Far worse, it has serious psychological and behavioral consequences.

To avoid, or at least mitigate, these consequences, warriors have to be able to bring meaning to this chaotic experience, i.e., an understanding of their situation at a deeper level than proficiency in killing. It can help get them through combat with their sanity relatively intact. It can help keep them from doing more harm than they need to do. It is also a critical component in their ability to adjust when they return home. This "adjustment" is akin to asking Saint John of the Cross to be happy flipping burgers at McDonald's after he's left the monastery. When one includes drug and alcohol overdoses, single-person car crashes, fights in bars, and a whole host of other self-destructive behaviors in addition to so-called normal suicides, the number of veterans who have killed themselves at home after the war was over is disturbingly large—and largely ignored.

You can't force consciousness or spiritual maturity. Teenage warriors like to fight, drink, screw, and rock and roll. You can, however, put people in situations where consciousness and spiritual maturity can grow rapidly, if those people know what to look for. It's called initiation.

Joseph Henderson, who died in 2007 at the age of 104, was one of the pioneers of Jungian analysis and a world authority on initiations. He once explained to me that there are two broad categories of initiation experiences. The first kind prepares the individual to fulfill an adult role in his or her society. Traditionally it was where the boys learned to accept the danger and responsibility involved in hunting and the girls learned to accept the danger and responsibility involved in childbirth. The second kind goes beyond societal roles and is of a spiritual nature. It is about accepting one's mortality. It is about facing death. To fully mature as individuals we need to undergo both kinds. In our culture individuals now must do initiatory rites on their own. Some do and some don't. A lot of people in our culture simply never grow up.

There is no longer one simple initiation rite of the kinds with which we are most familiar, those of the hunter-gatherer cultures such as the hunger and terrifying dreams of the Native American vision quest or the pain inflicted on young Aboriginal boys and the terrifying sounds of the bullroarers, secret ritual instruments forbidden, upon pain of death, for the noninitiated even to hear. In our culture we mostly undergo a series of partial initiations and we undergo them unconsciously and without guidance.

Boot camp was an initiation of the first kind, societal. I arrived at Quantico, Virginia, on a bus from the Port Authority in New York, to be met by screaming drill instructors in the middle of a muggy June night. There I was run through a succession of supply huts collecting gear, sweating in my civilian clothes, got my hair cut off, and finally fell exhausted into bed. In what seemed like five minutes I was shocked awake by sudden glaring lights splitting the humid darkness, a crashing metal garbage can being kicked down the squad bay by a rampaging madman, people being dumped—thin mattresses and all—onto the clammy concrete floor, and bewildering shouting and cursing as we desperately tried to pee, shave, shit, and get dressed in far too little time.

I survived the hazing and harassment, the drills and the spills, but the incident that actually altered my consciousness, that prepared me for the societal role of a Marine instead of a high school kid, occurred because I slapped at a mosquito during a talk by the drill instructor while we were out on a night field problem. He had me strip down to my shorts and marched me into a nearby swamp where he ordered me to stand at attention. My unprotected body was soon covered with mosquitoes.

The drill instructor would return to check on me periodically, asking if I'd had enough. I'd shout out the requisite "No, sir!" and he'd leave. By the time a half hour had gone by, it hurt. After around forty-five minutes I was covered with red welts. I could feel blood trickling down my body. I could feel the mosquitoes inside my shorts biting my testicles. But I had decided this was a test I wasn't going to fail.

I remember the drill instructor standing in front of me on his fourth trip back, eyeball to eyeball, looking right inside me. This time he didn't ask me if I wanted to quit. After a while there was an almost imperceptible change in his eyes. His head nodded just a fraction. Then he ordered me back into my clothes, shouting at me for being so stupid as to stand naked in a swamp filled with mosquitoes.

From that moment on I knew that this frightening black man had accepted me into his group, which he often referred to as "my Marine Corps." From that moment on I started thinking of myself differently. I felt proud. I was a Marine. I still feel proud to be a Marine. But there was one very critical issue that was missing from this particular passage of mine—the spiritual. I did connect with something larger than myself, the Marine Corps, but that is a long way from connecting with something larger than myself such as humanity or God.* My loyalty was to the U.S. Marines, and to Marine ancestors, not the ancestors of my people, who in the modern world are all people.

The uninitiated often think that Marine boot camp is stupid or even sadistic. Clearly, getting bitten on the testicles by mosquitoes wasn't training me to shoot straighter or attack smarter. But before society sends high school kids to do our killing in battle, those kids have to transform the way they think of themselves, or they are not going to be very effective killers. Worse, they will be more likely to endanger others. Lacking discipline on an ambush or losing concentration on a listening post by slapping a mosquito,

---

*I recognize that the word *God* often connotes the image of some white-bearded father figure up in the sky someplace, but short of sounding completely silly by using such expressions as *the Unexplainable* I don't know any way around this problem. I don't find it any more enlightening or sophisticated to write *the Universe* or *the Cosmic Energy* than to write *God*.

or even scratching a mosquito bite, can get you and everyone else killed. At the very least, lack of discipline under extremity will make the whole organization less effective at killing. And killing is what we are asking these kids to do. This isn't done without a major psychological transformation, unless we're already dealing with a criminal mind, and it has to be done quickly. Our society invented boot camp to do this. Boot camp doesn't turn young men into killers. It removes the societal restraints on the savage part of us that has made us the top animal in the food chain.

Part of my own spiritual initiation was that awareness of death on Axel's fishing boat, but spiritual initiation got a major booster shot the last weekend before graduation from boot camp. This was the first time we were allowed liberty; we got twelve hours to go off base. Most of us were headed for Washington, D.C., the nearest big city.

Come Saturday morning we weren't just feeling cocky; we felt invincible. We were fifteen pounds heavier and lean as snakes. We were Marines. My particular invincible band left Quantico for Washington on the noon bus: four of us, including Perkins. Perkins was a wiry kid, cocksure and quick and with a short fuse. We'd been in town a couple of hours, bathing ourselves in the air-conditioning in Benny's Rebel Room and drinking cold beer, the result of very poetic interpretations of the birth dates on our driver's licenses, when Perkins said, "Let's go over to the Cap 'n' Guys." I looked at my two other friends. They looked at their beers. The Cap 'n' Guys was reputed to be the toughest bar in D.C. No one, however, wanted to tell Perkins no. So we all went out into the blinding afternoon and walked the several blocks to the Cap 'n' Guys.

Three very sour-looking guys wheeled on their bar stools when we pushed in through the glass door, rattling the dirty venetian blinds. Two other guys were talking at a back table. They were all in their late twenties or early thirties, a little overweight, old men to our nineteen-year-old minds, some even starting to show beer bellies. Shit. This didn't look like such a tough bar.

We ordered four pitchers of beer and took them with us to a back booth where the condensation puddled on the Formica tabletop, making our glasses stick just slightly every time we lifted them to drink.

We had about half-emptied the pitchers when Perkins walked down to the jukebox and punched up a dollar's worth of music. He was walking back to our booth when one of the sour-looking trio at the bar turned on his stool and said, "I don't like nigger music."

Perkins, white and southern, said quietly, "It ain't nigger music. I'm playing it." He slid into the booth next to me. I started to hear the dim sound of warning bells through the fine alcoholic haze.

"I said I don't like nigger music, jarhead." The man's two friends were now turned our way, as well as the two guys at the back table. Jarhead was what you called Marines if you didn't want to be friendly.

The warning bells were now going full blast. I cut in and said, "It's only a dollar's worth. Sorry."

Perkins gave me a "What the hell are you doing?" look. I poured him some beer. The three guys turned back to their drinking, apparently mollified.

We tried to resume talking, but this unanswered threat in the air inhibited us. Finally, I said in a low voice, "Let's go back to the Rebel Room."

"They're a bunch of fat turds," Perkins hissed. "You going to let them run us out of here?"

"They're not running us out. We're just leaving."

I gulped the rest of my beer and set the glass down firmly. Three of us got up, but I had to climb over Perkins, who scowled at the Formica. We were squinting in the bright light again when he pushed out through the door onto the street. There, Perkins talked about pride. He persuaded my two friends to go back inside with him. I headed for Benny's Rebel Room alone, feeling bad about my lack of pride.

I hadn't even sat down with my onion rings when one of the guys who had stayed with Perkins came running into Benny's saying Perkins had been beaten up. Perkins had gone back inside and punched up another dollar's worth of "nigger music." He had then ordered two more pitchers of beer and, when he walked over to the bar to wait for them, had apparently deliberately chosen to be sloppy with his elbow. The one who didn't like nigger music said some more unkind things about Marines. Perkins said something back, not very original, and picked up the two pitchers from the bar. The man started pushing Perkins lightly with his fingers on his chest, backing him across the floor, slopping bits of beer from the pitchers onto Perkins's freshly ironed civilian shirt.

It was Death Before Dishonor time for Perkins. Pure ego. He threw the beer in the guy's face. Lack of recognition of his own mortality.

Fighting on television lasts long enough to entertain people. Fighting in bars doesn't have the same purpose. Perkins was on the floor in about two seconds, writhing in agony from kicks to his kidneys, blood streaming from his face where the guy had stomped him. The other two guys had trapped my two friends in the booth. One of them had a switchblade out.

The Marines surrendered.

We got Perkins into a cab, and as I sat in the back with his bloody head on my lap on the way to Quantico I had a feeling of anxiety and foreboding. Even Marines can get hurt, even if we're in better shape than our opponents. Suddenly the war we were training for got real. I kept watching the trees go by outside the cab window and the grass on the median strip. Grief welled up in me. I knew I had strong odds of never seeing trees and grass again, just ordinary grass on a freeway median strip—so extraordinarily beautiful. Even today, when I walk on grass I feel as if I'm walking on someone's skin.

We were just able to get Perkins cleaned up enough to stand formation that evening. The drill instructor looked into his pulpy face long and hard. "You lost, didn't you, maggot."

"Yes, sir!" roared Perkins.

That night, while other platoons had the evening free in their squad bays to get ready for Sunday's graduation, clean gear, write letters, our whole platoon was out running and doing push-ups, punishment for losing. We ended up on the obstacle course sometime near midnight doing push-ups in the dark until, one by one, we dropped from exhaustion. I remember lying in the dust, gasping for air, when the brilliantly polished boot of the drill instructor toed me over. "Get on your feet and tell me what happened."

I told him.

"Jesus Christ, the Cap 'n' Guys. Perkins I can understand, but I thought you had more brains. And you let him go in there? Shee-it, Marlantes." He assigned me fire watch that night (no sleep) for being stupid and for not keeping Perkins out of trouble.

At the level of turning boys into shock troops for American society, the drill instructor had to teach the lesson that no matter how tough things got, there was more in you. You never quit.

He also had to teach that if one is hurt, all are hurt; so Perkins ran with us the whole time. We had to help him, but he made it through, and we all felt that Marine pride again. I learned about thinking *before* I got into a fight. I also learned that smart people, no matter how fit, don't go looking for fights with seasoned bar fighters.

The drill instructor did his job well. We soon forgot all about the Cap 'n' Guys and were once more invincible shock troops knowing that there were no defeats, just temporary setbacks, and no pain too great to keep you from winning. These are critical lessons that any reasonable society would want to inculcate in its shock troops and also a large part of the reason society uses eighteen- to twenty-two-year-olds to do its fighting. This age group combined with these societal initiation rites produces good fighters. Months later, in Vietnam, I was in situations where any reasonable person would have quit, but I had become a Marine and Marines aren't reasonable people. Quitting is unthinkable and pain is just weakness leaving the body.

These, however, are societal, not spiritual, lessons; a drill instructor's job isn't spiritual guidance. What had hit me in the cab going back to Quantico was beyond the initiatory rites for which a drill instructor is responsible. So when the shit hit the fan I wasn't spiritually prepared. When I did eventually face death—the death of those I killed and those killed around me—I had no framework or guidance to help me put combat's terror, exhilaration, horror, guilt, and pain into some larger framework that would have helped me find some meaning in them later. Maybe if the right person had shown up for me that Christmas in Vietnam, he might have started me on an inner journey that could have saved me and my family a lot of grief. It would have been a relief to me to talk about my terror. That particular visitation by the chaplain was like somebody visiting a dying friend and talking about the weather. We don't talk about death in our society. Even the chaplains. Even when it's all around us.

War, however, blows away the illusion of safety from death. Some random projectile can kill you no matter how good a soldier you are. Escaping death and injury in modern warfare is much more a matter of luck—or grace—than skill, and this is a significant difference from primitive warfare. In a combat situation you wake up from sleep instantly aware that this could be the last time you awake, simultaneously grateful you're alive and scared shitless because you are still in the same situation. Most combat veterans keep this awareness—that death is just around the corner. We know that when we drive the freeway to work we could be dead within the next hour. It's just that the odds have changed greatly in our favor from when we were in combat. It's the difference in the odds of getting killed that makes combat a noticeable experience of one's mortality and going to work on the freeway an unnoticed one.

Noticing is another word for awareness or consciousness. Understanding that combat will be a dark and terrible initiation *before* one goes into combat will help provide some structure and meaning to this soul-battering experience. A large part of treating PTSD is simply getting the veteran to remember and talk about what happened to him. The more psychic structure or framing that is brought to the experience of combat, the easier it will be to cope with the experience afterward. It can help provide a bit of meaning in an often meaningless situation. As it is, young warriors' minds and souls are going to be battered and overwhelmed. Killing someone *will* affect you. Part of you *will* think you've done something wrong. It's drilled in from babyhood. If, however, you're prepared ahead of time for it, you'll suffer less because this knowledge and structure will add a thin layer of armor. Why put on the armor after the war? This is what I did.

I remember, even five years after I got home, laughing with combat veteran friends about all this bullshit about bad dreams and weird behavior as a result of combat. I was just fine. This is because I'd shoved the whole experience deep into my unconscious. Funny how I just did high-adrenaline jobs for years, constantly on the move. My oldest daughter has pointed out to me, more than once, that in one eight-year period she attended twelve different schools.

It is bad enough that we send our youth off to fight our wars ill prepared for the spiritual and psychological consequences of entering combat. Add to this the fact that combat is becoming increasingly intermingled with the ordinary civilian world. With cell phones, Facebook, Twitter, air travel, and remote-control weaponry, the battlefield is less clearly defined and the bloody consequences of what modern weapons do can be completely masked. Consider the bomber crews that fly from the United States and back to bomb Iraq or Libya, telling their spouses and kids they'll be gone a little longer than usual that day; or the young woman pushing a button to launch a cruise missile from a naval vessel on a serene sea hundreds of miles from the "target," known to his mother as Alim; or the pilots doing nine-to-five jobs at computer consoles in Nevada killing people in Iraq and Afghanistan with drones and commuting to and from their homes like any other commuters. Imagine the psychic split that must ensue from bringing in death and destruction from the sky on a group of terrorists—young men who have mothers and a misplaced idealism that has led them into horrible criminal acts, but nevertheless young and brave men—and then driving home from the base to dinner with the spouse and kids. "Have a nice day at the office, hon?"

Death becomes an abstraction, except for those at the receiving end. We must come to grips with *consciously* trying to set straight this imbalance of modern warfare. What is at stake is not only the psyche of each young fighter but our humanity.

I'm not against hot turkey at Thanksgiving. I would have loved some. What I'm arguing is that the chances of transforma tive psychological experiences are decreased enormously when you wage war with all the comforts of home. You have no easy way of knowing when you are in the sacred space of Mars and death or coming home from it. In World War II it usually took months to both go to and come back from war. In Vietnam we put people on airplanes and had them returning from combat in some cases in only a matter of hours. Today a soldier can go out on patrol and kill someone or have one of his friends killed and call his girlfriend on his cell phone that night and probably talk about anything except what just happened. And if society itself tries to blur it as much as possible, by conscious well-intended efforts to provide "all the comforts of home" and modern transportation and communication, what chance does your average eighteen-year-old have of not becoming confused?*

My own R&R was typical of this confusion of two worlds and the lack of psychic and temporal space between them.

---

*I am not saying that the infantry today has it easy. Certainly the communications with home have changed, but the field conditions, such as filth, cold, heat, fatigue, and lack of sleep, have not changed since the infantry was using rocks. However, the trend is clear. Robots are already being deployed for fighting in cities. And soon they will be able to be controlled from Nevada.

We were in the mountains north of Khe Sanh providing security for an artillery battery that was supporting two infantry companies in combat to our west, right on the Laotian border. The two companies ran into more trouble than they could handle alone and we were dropped in as close as we could to join the fighting.

I was scheduled to go on R&R the next day. I was pissed.

I had been in-country a long time. I still had fear, but after seeing so much dying a numb fatalism had masked it. Honestly, the foremost thing on my conscious mind was not the impending combat but that we'd soon be in the shit and I'd have to miss my R&R to Hong Kong, a destination for which quotas were often jammed and for which I had waited a long time.

We had to move hard and fast to reach the other companies, so we climbed a steep ridge where the jungle was still on fire from napalm. Bare trunks oozed boiled sap and smoke. All the leaves had been burned away, exposing us to a fierce tropical sun that oppressed us with white heat through the acrid greasy air. We were soon covered in black soot. It was in our throats, lungs, and eyes. We were under strict water discipline because when working up a ridgeline you're above the streams. We waded in ashes over our boot tops. The suffocating air smelled like oil. Sweat mixed with soot and glued our shirts and trousers to our skins. The water in our plastic canteens felt hot to the tongue.

Late that morning we reached the fighting. I lost more friends.

By midmorning the next day the skipper said I could make my R&R if I could find some way out of the bush on my own. I helped pack some wounded up to an LZ* hoping to get a ride

---

* Helicopter landing zone, usually a circle hacked out of the jungle or elephant grass with machetes and knives.

in with them on a medevac chopper. The LZ was taking sniper fire and occasional mortar rounds. Unless the wounded were declared emergencies, the highest priority, no one was going to fly in for them, much less take some grunt out on R&R.

I sat there, stuck and despondent, trying to imagine Hong Kong, fuming because the company with the mission of eliminating the NVA snipers and mortars hadn't gotten its goddamn job done.

Then one kid got hauled in who was bleeding very badly in places the corpsmen couldn't stop, so the priority for the medevac got pushed up. Fifteen minutes later a lone Huey* worked its way up the steep ridgeline, the heat and altitude-thinned air making climbing difficult. As the chopper flared in I heard tubing, the popping explosions mortars make as the shells leave the tube to start the high arc to their destination. I had a feeling where that destination was going to be.

I wasn't going to be deterred. As the shells started exploding around the chopper, I helped pile all the wounded aboard, dragging them underneath the rotor blades, shoving the last Marine in like some mad train pusher in Tokyo. Then I just stood there, dumbfounded. There was no room left for me. I faced a wall of wounded men nearly falling out of the side opening of the Huey.

The corpsmen and stretcher-bearers ran for their holes and the chopper's rotor blades started picking up speed. The last Marine I'd pushed into the chopper had one arm in a sling. Since we'd sat together on the hill bitching, waiting for a bird, he knew I'd miss my plane out of Da Nang. R&R is sacred time to

---

*The workhorse medical evacuation helicopter of the U.S. Marines and U.S. Army in Vietnam. Huey comes from HUE-1, helicopter, utility, evacuation.

a grunt in quite another way. He shouted out, "Grab my hand. Ride on the skids."

I jumped for the door, trying to find the long metal landing skids underneath the Huey, locking my left arm with the wounded man's good arm. The bird was already in the air, the pilot unaware I was trying to get on. He was too busy figuring out how to get the overloaded chopper off the mountain and not get shot out of the sky. I managed to grab something in the door frame with my right hand. My M-16 was dangling from that arm by its sling and my legs were kicking empty space as the chopper tipped forward, heading for the edge of the landing zone. I knew the drill. With heavy loads in low-oxygen mountain air the pilots had to put the birds into a steep fast fall, falling downhill with the slope of the mountain instead of rising upward off the landing zone. This way they hoped to pick up speed in order to get sufficient lift and get safely airborne. Over the side we went in a rush, my body and legs dangling out of the chopper's side. I scraped the top of a splintered tree, painfully bruising my ankle.

The chopper made a tight banking turn, tipping to the right, and the Marine trying to hang on to me started to slip out of the open doorway into space. My own legs swung out away from the body of the chopper. Another wounded Marine managed to wrap an ammo sling around my helper's legs to stop him. Finally other wounded passengers tied their canteen belts around both of us, taking the strain away. I rode the entire distance to the hospital with my feet dangling over the jungle. When we touched down, since my feet were below the skids, I touched down before the chopper. Hermes landing with winged feet—and with trousers crusted from dried diarrhea and cum.

Six hours later, new clothes, new haircut, I was in an air-conditioned club in Da Nang called the White Elephant. No need for winged feet here; there were plush carpets on the floor. There were also American women in miniskirts and American men in short-sleeved white civilian shirts or starched and pressed uniforms. Ice tinkled in heavy glasses. For excitement, people rolled dice to see who would pay for drinks.

I sat at the bar squeezing pus from jungle rot and infected leech bites onto a paper napkin printed with the logo MACV, Military Assistance Command Vietnam. I felt a growing anger. Today, I know the anger had to do with the profanity of people carrying on drinking and schmoozing while my friends were, at that moment, dying. It also had to do with a tint of puritan anger at the decadence of it all and the fact that I was doing exactly the same thing they were. To numb all the conflicting feelings, I proceeded to drink too much.

Drawn by false courage and desire, I tortured myself further by moving as close as I thought wasn't rudely obvious to a Red Cross woman and her date, an overweight man who worked for AID.* They were talking about buying cars without paying duties. There was a German woman who'd set up an agency for Mercedes-Benz and was making a fortune. Then I heard the AID man tell the Red Cross woman he was getting hazardous duty pay for being in a combat zone.

This was months after my encounter with the chaplain. By this time in my tour I wasn't cool about anything. I was still a long way from enlightenment, but you don't have to be Jesus Christ to know when someone is pissing on the church floor. The rage came boiling out. I wanted to kill him for profaning and demeaning the words "combat zone." I made a fuss.

---

*Agency for International Development.

I was escorted from the club by a tight-lipped manager and a couple of Army MPs who took down my name, rank, unit, and serial number, all of which I lied about. I never thought until this moment that all they needed to do to catch the lie was look at my dog tags. I've never been accused of being calculating. A few hours later I was on a Boeing 707 with stewardesses serving Cokes* and peanuts in little plastic cups. Three hours later I was getting drunk in the Venus bar in Kowloon, trying to decide which prostitute I wanted to take back to my hotel room.

At the very end of my tour I cajoled a clerk who'd been in the bush with me before he was badly wounded and given a desk job into losing the record of my R&R to Hong Kong. I could then take a second one to Sydney, which I did, with the same bizarre juxtaposition of worlds. Two days after being in combat, I was in Australia, where I stole a car because I wanted to go to a party and there was no transportation. It never even occurred to me that I was stealing it. I needed it and figured that when the party was over I'd bring it back. I was unbelievably lucky, because the man I stole it from was a combat veteran of the North African campaign and didn't press charges. Three days earlier, I had been killing people. Taking someone else's car to a party without asking was nothing. Three days after stealing the car, I was back in combat.

The definitively contained battlefields that George Patton experienced in World War II got blurred in Vietnam and today are becoming increasingly merged with the civilian world. In the past, combat was an initiatory experience traditionally differentiated from normal life. Today, those who engage in killing through high

---

*Few on the aircraft were old enough to drink alcohol legally.

technology take no personal risk, so the initiatory experience is basically nullified. It's a job. Even for those who do risk their lives and confront their own deaths on a more traditional battlefield, modern communications increasingly blur the battlefield with normal life. While on the one hand everyone is glad to be able to strike their enemy with impunity, and ten minutes later call home and have a Coke, there is a psychological and spiritual price to pay. When it comes time to leave the world of combat behind for the world of "ordinary life," it is going to be more difficult to do the more we blur the two worlds together. How can you return home if you've never left?

2

KILLING

Killing someone without splitting oneself from the feelings that the act engenders requires an effort of supreme consciousness that, quite frankly, is beyond most humans. Killing is what warriors do for society. Yet when they return home, society doesn't generally acknowledge that the act it asked them to do created a deep split in their psyches, or a psychological and spiritual weight most of them will stumble beneath the rest of their lives. Warriors must learn how to integrate the experience of killing, to put the pieces of their psyches back together again. For the most part, they have been left to do this on their own.

I'm occasionally asked, "What's it feel like to kill someone?" Sometimes I'm not asked what killing someone feels like; I'm told. "It must feel horrible to kill someone." And, infrequently, but harshly enough to sting, I've been judged. "How could you ever kill a fellow human?"

When people come up to me and say, "You must have felt horrible when you killed somebody," I have a very hard time giving the simplistic response they'd like to hear. When I was fighting—and by fighting I mean a situation where my life and the lives of those for whom I was responsible were at stake, a situation very different from launching a cruise missile—either I felt nothing at all or I felt exhilaration akin to scoring the winning touchdown.

I used to hesitate to say this, worried it would only further fuel the accusation that we Vietnam veterans were the sick baby killers we were being told we were. Maybe some veterans did feel horrible and sick every time they killed another man, just the way many people think they ought to. I'm also sure some of the people telling me they'd feel horrible and sick could very well feel that way if they ever had to do it. But they didn't have to. I did. And I didn't feel that way. And it makes me angry when people lay on me what I ought to have felt. More important, it obscures the truth.

What I feel now, forty years later, is sadness.

There was one particular NVA soldier whose desperate fearful eyes I still vividly recall, standing out like black pools in an exploding landscape of mud and dying vegetation. With my mind's eye I can still see him rising from his hole to throw a hand grenade at me. The wild desperation, the animal cornered, looking for a way out, and there was no way out. The panic. The lips pulled back showing his teeth. His friend crumpled over next to him, dead. He was a teenager, like my radio operator.

My platoon had just broken through a line of bunkers that circled a hill. The fighting was fierce. What now lay before us was a band about 30 meters wide of interconnected fighting holes and trenches that circled the top of the hill. Fire would suddenly come from one side or the other or directly above us. The hill was so steep we could see only pieces of the system at a time, the uphill positions always hidden from our sight.

Ohio, my radio operator, and I kept moving upward. Fire teams of three or four individuals would go after each position as it was discovered. Our turn was announced by Ohio, screaming, "Chi-comm!"* I looked directly uphill and saw the dark shape

*Chinese communist grenade, the same design as the Russian and German World War II "potato masher," a round canister filled with high explosive and steel ball bearings on top of a wooden stick.

of the grenade tumbling in an arc against the silver-gray cloud cover, coming right toward us.

We scrambled *up* the hill to try to get underneath the arc, hoping the grenade would hit behind us and bounce a little farther down the steep hill before exploding. We buried our faces in the mud; pulled up our legs, trying to stuff ourselves into our flak jackets; and waited for the explosion. It went off below us without hurting us. We both pulled grenades out and tried to do the arc in reverse. Again we buried our heads against the clay as the two explosions pounded our eardrums. We looked up. Out of the smoke above us two more Chi-comms came tumbling through the air.

This exchange went on three times.

It seems incredible that it took me three times to figure out that one time the unseen grenade throwers above us were going to get lucky. It probably occurred to me because I was down to one grenade. Immediately after the explosion of the third Chi-comm, instead of throwing another grenade back, I took off around a small nose on the hillside. It immediately hid Ohio and me from each other's sight. I scrambled up the muddy hill, falling on my elbows and knees, churning with my legs. I remember seeing Ohio's grenade sailing over my head a little to my right and hoping he'd given it a good throw. With the grenade in midflight I caught a glimpse of the hole. A dead NVA soldier was crumpled forward in it, his upper body sprawled over the lip of the hole. I threw myself flat as Ohio's grenade exploded next to the hole. Shrapnel, rocks, and dirt whammed over the top of me.

I looked up as the stuff was still coming down, settled the stock of the rifle into my shoulder, and waited for the other NVA soldier to stand up to throw his next grenade. I had switched the selector on my M-16 to single shot instead of automatic. Don't ask me why. Somehow in my addled brain I decided to take this guy with one clean shot. The fighting hole was in plain view about 15 feet above me. There was the dead crumpled soldier. Apparently one of our grenades had connected. I didn't feel anything. Thinking of nothing else, I waited for that unseen grenade thrower to pop up.

Then he rose, grenade in hand. He was pulling the fuse. I could see blood running down his face from a head wound. He cocked his arm back to throw—and then he saw me looking at him across my rifle barrel. He stopped. He looked right at me. That's where the image of his eyes was burned into my brain forever, right over the sights of my M-16. I remember hoping he wouldn't throw the grenade. Maybe he'd throw it aside and raise his hands or something and I wouldn't have to shoot him. But his lips snarled back and he threw it right at me.

As the grenade left his hand I pulled the trigger, trying to act as if I were on the rifle range. And just like on the rifle range I "bucked my shot." I jerked the trigger instead of squeezing it and, anticipating the recoil with my shoulder, caused the tip of the rifle to lower just slightly as the shot went off. The bullet struck the lip of the hole in direct line with the kid's chest, spraying dirt right into his face and body.

My feeling? I felt *embarrassed* that I'd bucked my shot and it wasn't a clean hit. I felt chagrined that I had been foolish enough not to put my rifle on full automatic. I knew instantly that, had I not switched off automatic to play Deadeye Dick, the continuous recoil of automatic fire would have ridden the front of the barrel upward, putting several bullets in a straight line right up through the kid's chest and head.

I fired off two or three very hasty unaimed follow-up shots as I was rolling and moving because the grenade was now bouncing right over the top of me, about to explode. My first shot, right in line, almost certainly went into his body. So too could any of the three other wild shots. I'll never know for sure if any of them actually killed him, because Ohio came tearing around from the right side of the nose and, with *his* rifle on full automatic, sprayed the soldier with half a magazine, diving for the dirt himself as the Chi-comm went off just below me down the steep hill.

My feelings then? It felt pleasurable and satisfying to see Ohio ripping that kid apart on full automatic. I was alive! That certainly felt good. Another obstacle was out of the way of achieving our mission. That felt good too. But it also felt just plain pleasurable to blast him. Take *that*, you (choose a name that describes anything but a fellow human). In combat you are already over some edge. You are in a fierce state where there is a primitive and savage joy in doing in your enemy.

Jane Goodall once talked quite movingly about watching her little tribe of peaceful chimpanzees declare war on another tribe and savagely and ruthlessly exterminate it.* Up to that point in her studies of chimpanzees she had concluded that chimps were somehow above humans in this regard. But in a dispute over territory she watched what can only be described as atrocities— chimps being savagely dragged on the ground, clubbed, whirled by their limbs to smash their skulls—not in order to just drive them away from the territory but in order to exterminate them. I'm afraid I know how the winning chimpanzees felt. There is a very primal side to me. I suspect we all have this, but are so afraid of it that we prefer to deny its existence. This denial is more dangerous than acceptance because the "killer," that mad primitive chimpanzee part of us, is then not under ego control. It's why a good Baptist can get caught up in a lynching. It's why a peace advocate can kill a policeman with a car bomb.

*Radio interview, April 1, 1993.

My radioman and I both survived the explosion, although I was hit with small bits of shrapnel in the back of the legs. They felt like bee stings, hot and many. I was so pumped up with adrenaline they didn't even slow me down. When I looked up after the explosion, the Vietnamese kid was dead. My feeling? I felt relief. "Phew, no more grenades." I churned up the steep slope to take on the next position and quickly forgot even that feeling. I didn't even think about the incident until years later.

I now have all sorts of feelings. Suppose it was one of my sons, Peter or Alex, trapped, filled with fear as these huge American Marines, known to be ruthless, even crazy, came relentlessly from out of the jungle, swarming up the hill, killing his friends in their holes around him. Then two are just below him. Desperately, he tries to lob a grenade into the unseen dip in the hill where the two Marines disappeared. Two grenades come flying back from unseen hands, exploding around the hole. Again, he and his friend each toss a grenade. Again, two come back. The cycle repeats. One of the grenades kills his friend and stuns him, bloodying his face. Now he's totally alone. To leave the hole is to die. To stay in the hole is to die. Death is coming in a crummy hole hundreds of miles from his family, and he has never made love with a woman and he will never know the joys and trials of a family of his own. Then, there is the enemy, lying in plain view just below the hole, rifle ready, his brown eyes staring at him over the barrel, the eyes the only living color in a face that is a pallid mask of dried clay smeared with smoke smudges, terrible and gaunt with exhaustion and fighting.

"Throw the grenade! Try and save yourself, Peter!" But two rifles spit white-orange light. Peter is dead . . . my son.

My feeling now? Oh, the sadness. The sadness. And, oh, the grief of evil in the world to which I contributed.

What is different between then and now is quite simply empathy. I can take the time, and I have the motivation, to actually feel what I did to another human being who was in a great many ways just like my own son. Back then, I was operating under some sort of psychological mechanism that allowed me to think of that teenager as "the enemy." I killed him or Ohio did and we moved on. I doubt I could have killed him realizing he was like my own son. I'd have fallen apart. This very likely would have led to my own death or the deaths of those I was leading. But a split occurred then that now cries out to be healed.

My problem was that for years I was unaware of the need to heal that split, and there was no one, after I returned, to point this out to me. That kid's dark eyes would stare at me in my mind's eye at the oddest times. I'd be driving at night and his face would appear on the windscreen. I'd be talking at work and that face with its angry snarl would suddenly overwhelm me and I'd fight to stay with the person I was talking with. I'd never been able to tell anyone what was going on inside. So I forced these images back, away, for years. I began to reintegrate that split-off part of my experience only after I actually began to imagine that kid as a kid, my kid perhaps. Then, out came this overwhelming sadness—and healing. Integrating the feelings of sadness, rage, or all of the above with the action should be standard operating procedure for all soldiers who have killed face-to-face. It requires no sophisticated psychological training. Just form groups under a fellow squad or platoon member who has had a few days of group leadership training and encourage people to talk.

There are other feelings associated with killing. On this particular assault the battalion staff and another company being held in reserve had set up on a hill about a kilometer to our east. Normally upon seeing the first Marine break through the last defenses on an assault, something I experienced only three times, I had the same wonderful feeling—an explosion of relief that made me want to run forward with savage joy. We'd won! We would be safe. The organism, we, me, would be here tomorrow. But this time we were being watched, and when we finally broke into the open across the top of the hill we heard cheering coming from the battalion headquarters group and the company placed around them for security.

I turned murderously angry.

This seems odd, given that I was feeling savage joy myself just moments before. I think the anger came from the fact that we and not they had paid the price for this victory—and it was very steep. Human sacrifice had been turned into spectator sport. I now don't blame those who were cheering. They were unconsciously responding to a built-in psychology, no different from that of any spectator vicariously getting the "touchdown feeling." I probably would have done the same. But then I was enraged about it. I'd very nearly died. Some of my friends and my respected enemy had indeed died, while others would be maimed for life. It felt wrong that the guys on the other hill should be enjoying the same feeling they'd get watching a football game back home. I felt profaned. I felt something sacred had been stolen from me, my friends, and my enemy—our very real sacrifice. I felt had.

I'm aware that our bodies, the result of millions of years of evolution, do what they do. They have certain evolved responses. The choice before us is whether we are ever going to have the self-discipline and awareness necessary to guide these responses into productive channels or continue to allow them to overpower our sense of decency.

People who actually fight and win battles are in fact unlikely to cheer when they get the touchdown feeling, no matter how powerful it is. I never once heard anyone cheer who was actually involved in fighting. This is because the predominant feeling, when you win in battle, is numbed exhaustion.

One night Grandpa Axel and I pushed it just a little too far. We were catching fish, lots of them. And a storm was coming. Just one more drift . . . just one.

We laid out several hundred yards of gill net in the darkness. The water was moving in short harsh chops, the wind freshening. The net always seemed miles long to me, even in good weather, since I was that part of the two-man crew called the "boat puller." Grandpa Axel was the part called "the captain." A gill-net boat is about thirty foot long, open in the bow, with a cabin in the back and sunk in the middle of the cabin a four- or six-cylinder Marine or old tractor engine, depending upon the relative wealth of the fisherman. In a boat this size you don't actually pull the net into the boat. The net is far too heavy. You actually pull the boat along, sliding it *under* the net, to get the heavy water-laden net into the boat—hence the name boat puller.

We got the net laid out, tied the boat to one end of it, and sat drifting, waiting for the salmon. *Punk. Punk.* You could hear the satisfying sound of the cork line going under the water as a fast-moving salmon hit the net.

The rain started coming hard. Visibility closed. *Punk.* More money. Sockeye salmon were getting thirty-three cents a pound. Every *punk* was a buck or two. *Punk.* It was like a money machine. *Punk. Punk.*

Suddenly a large swell lifted the little boat, tipping it dangerously close to the gunwale because the bow was tied to the net. The wind came slashing down on us with a cold rain and the already dark night went totally black except for the dim white of the little battery-powered mooring light on top of the cabin. You could no longer hear any *punks*. You could hear only trouble.

Being only fourteen, I hadn't been through a lot of bad weather. Axel had. Even then, I noticed a grimness, a set of jaw, when he came limping forward to untie the bow from the net. The limp was a measure of that man. He'd been poling logs several winters earlier when the fish weren't running and slipped between two giant log rafts, crushing both legs. He swam to shore, then crawled nearly two miles to his car. He drove himself, using a stick shift with a clutch, to the hospital, where they amputated one leg just below the knee. Did I really learn to ignore pain in boot camp?

When Axel got worried, I got damned scared.

We started hauling in the net. The boat was corkscrewing like a bucking horse. We'd climb up a near-breaking swell, a curl of white water on top, and I'd almost be pulled overboard, trying desperately not to lose my grip on the net. Then we'd crash down, and I'd haul as fast as I could to keep the boat from going over the top of the net and tangling the prop. Axel was cursing in Swedish, untangling fish from the net, throwing them anywhere he could except out of the boat.

We both knew that the wind was driving us onto the rockbound lee shore only a few hundred yards beyond us, a shore we couldn't see or hear in that howling air. Rain and cold spray from the waves slashed almost horizontally into our faces. The boat would plunge downward and hit a swell with a shock, and water would come smashing over the gunwales, sloshing at our feet, making the boat wallow, inviting even more water in the next time.

Axel ran aft to get the pump going and try to maneuver the boat so I could haul in the net faster while he also tried to slow the boat's drift toward the shore. I was left alone, afraid I'd be pulled overboard if I hung on to the net and afraid to let go of the net because it was what was saving me from a wave that could take me overboard. Axel rejoined me, rushing between hauling in net and trying to steer using the auxiliary controls just beneath the bow. I hauled, net and salmon tangled together into a huge jumbled pile on the deck. We fought the foaming stallions for what seemed hours.

Finally, the last of the net came in over the side. We didn't know how close to shore we'd drifted. Axel scrambled to the back, gunned the engine, and headed on a compass bearing away from shore.

I collapsed on the wet net, chest heaving, staring upward into black nothing that sprayed water on my face. The boat bucked and heaved through the swells, but I was too exhausted to care. I just lay there on that wet seaweed-smelling net, flopping salmon dying around me, and stared into wet black nothingness. Totally exhausted. Feeling lucky to be alive.

Winning a battle feels like that. Only you don't get to flop on the net because you're fourteen and Axel is there to take care of you. You have to set up defenses immediately in case there's a counterattack. And it's not salmon that are dying around you.

Killing in war isn't always the morally clean "it was them or me" situation which we so often hear about and which I have described. The more technically sophisticated we get, in fact, the less common this situation will become, and the more problematic the morality. The more common situation in the future will be that of people quite distanced from the actual killing they are doing, their own lives not remotely in danger. I've never done this sort of killing, but I do have some perspective on it, having killed from the air, albeit where I could still see the damage I was doing, unlike the crew of a B-52 or a submarine.

Late in my tour, after being wounded two times, I'd been attached to division intelligence as an air observer. A five-man-Marine reconnaissance team had been discovered by an NVA unit in the mountains that border Laos just south of Khe Sanh. In the ensuing fight one member of the team had been badly wounded and now the team was trying desperately to escape but was severely hampered because of having to carry the wounded man. The Marines were a good 20 kilometers from the nearest friendly unit and out of artillery range. My pilot and I were already airborne in a little single-prop O1-Charlie spotter plane when division diverted us to answer the team's call for help.

When we made contact with the team, I directed the Marines toward a clearing on a hilltop I had spotted. From there we would try to get a chopper to lift them out. Packing their wounded teammate on slippery slopes, they made slow progress. They would have to turn to fire on their pursuers every so often, then scramble upward some more, only to turn and fight again. Because they were outside artillery range, all we could do was scramble some Marine A-4s* from Da Nang, well over 100 miles to our south, hoping that they'd arrive in time and the constant clouds and rain showers wouldn't make it impossible for the fast-moving jets to be effective. To fill in for the missing artillery and jets, in the meantime, the pilot would bring the O1 right over the team's head and I'd lean out of the little plane's window and shoot at the pursuing NVA with my M-16. I'd watch my tracers dropping earthward as if the ground were sucking

*The primary attack aircraft used by the U.S. Navy and U.S. Marines during the Vietnam War.

them into itself, trying to place them into the winking bright points that I knew were NVA automatic rifles firing back at us. I felt good helping. I also felt curiously excited. What from the air looked like winking lights I, in fact, reacted to like winking lights. I focused on them as indicators of the origin of the fire, not as automatic weapons fire that was trying to kill me. It is like becoming so present focused that you are pure observer. You know from experience that to allow the mind to get involved with future, nonpresent issues like "this could kill me" will only make it more likely that you will be killed. (By this time I'd been in Vietnam nearly a year.) I was actually more apprehensive that we weren't going to be able to pull this one off and would lose the team. The time for debilitating fear is before and after the mission. There was no time now. I was trying to keep map coordinates going to the pilot, warning him when we'd get too close to cloud-hidden peaks that I was trying to locate through reading my map, talking to the Marines on the ground, trying to direct them around obstacles that they couldn't see and which would slow them down, talking on another frequency to the division recon staff in Dong Ha, who kept wanting to know what was going on, and trying to spot the pursuing NVA and shoot them with my M-16 from the shot-out windows of the airplane. Meanwhile the pilot was talking to the now scrambled Marine jets on another frequency; talking to the incoming evacuation bird on yet another frequency; trying to keep the plane spinning around only a couple of hundred feet off the ground to help maintain my M-16 fire directed at the pursuit, while at the same time trying to keep us from crashing into the numerous unseen peaks, guessed at by me, that surrounded the smaller hill the team was climbing; planning the approach paths of the attacking aircraft when they arrived; and doing the math to figure out how much time was left before we ran out of fuel—oh, and not stall the airplane. In combat your mind is *jammed.*

Eventually the team reached the summit and set up a hasty perimeter defense. Between us, we now concentrated on keeping the NVA at bay until help arrived.

The NVA had spread halfway around the perimeter and were closing in, peppering us and the small recon team with automatic weapons fire. Everyone in the air was worried; everyone on the ground was scared.

Two Marine A-4s arrived from Da Nang armed with "snake and nape."* Clouds obscured the hill, sometimes for minutes at a time, making it nearly impossible for the jet pilots to locate the target and making the helicopter rescue a real problem. We went in low. I remember everything going gray white as we entered a swirling low cloud and wondering if we'd hit the ground before we could see again. It seems remarkable to me now, but I simply trusted we would. That was the pilot's job, not mine. I leaned out of the window with my rifle ready to fire. Like a sudden curtain going up on bright daylight the green-gray ground rushed up at us. We were coming in parallel to the front of the team's defense on the same heading we'd given to the jets and my pilot fired one of our phosphorous smoke rockets into the enemy that ringed the team, marking the target for the much faster and higher-flying A-4s. He twisted the plane over to port and downhill trying to get it safely back into some altitude. I remember seeing pieces

---

*"Snake" is short for snake-eye bombs, bombs with pop-out tail fins that slowed their descent to enable more accurate delivery and the escape of the faster-moving jet in tight conditions like this. "Nape" is napalm, jellied gasoline, a horrific incendiary substance invented during World War II that sticks to its targets, such as human flesh, and is used in flamethrowers and bombs. The name derives from *na*phthene and *palm*itate, the primary jellifying ingredients.

of burning phosphorous flying through the air leaving brilliant white smoky arcs from where the rocket had exploded among the enemy soldiers. I didn't think about the burning phosphorous on their skin.

Almost immediately, braving the same intermittent clouds, the two A-4s, guided by my pilot over the radio and the brilliant white smoke of our burning phosphorous, were on top of the now running NVA soldiers. They delivered their snake on the first pass and blasted out large open patches in the jungle just below the team. I could see the stunning waves of concussion shaking trees in concentric circles, as if a huge rock had been thrown into a dark green pond. We then directed the two jets back in with their napalm and lit everything on fire.

In those smoking clearings I could see the charred burning bodies of the NVA who'd died or were still dying. Some were crawling for the cover of the unblasted jungle, trailing smoke from their clothing and skin.

My feeling? I had been elated! I shouted to the team, "We got Crispy Critters all over the hill!" Crispy Critters was a popular breakfast cereal at the time.

If, back then, I had been who I am today I would have felt differently. There would have been no elation. But back then I was just like the battalion staff that had cheered our victory on the hill. I identified with the reconnaissance team, whose lives were very much in doubt. Psychologically I had become identified with the threatened group, and the advancing enemy was no longer human. I didn't kill people, sons, brothers, fathers. I killed "Crispy Critters." It could have been krauts, nips, huns, boche, gooks, infidels, towel heads, imperialist pigs, yankee pigs, male chauvinist pigs . . . the list is as varied as human experience. This dissociation of one's enemy from humanity is a kind of pseudospeciation. You make a false species out of the other human and therefore make it easier to kill him. The touchdown feeling combined with dissociating the enemy was in full glorious effect.

We directed in one more pass of snake and nape, but this one was hardly necessary. The NVA were now content to fire at the aircraft from the cover of the surrounding jungle rather than go after the team. The first flight returned to base. We got a second flight of A-4s up and kept them on station until a very brave chopper pilot from MAG-39 got into the zone.* Everyone on our side made it out safely. We were delighted.

I'm still delighted. Do I delight over this out of some sort of depravity? Some sort of warping in my childhood? I don't know. I may just be built this way. I can feel that old excitement as I write this. How similar I am to others I also don't know. Few will ever have to run the test. I suspect I am not very different. All I know for sure is that, at the time, I didn't feel sickened or horrible about it. I was doing a good job of saving some fellow Marines.

And how do I feel now? I can still indulge in the excitement—and it is indulgence. It sells billions of dollars worth of entertainment. But I can also bring some consciousness to this past action of mine, and when I do, I find myself amazed at the many *other* feelings lying hidden there that this excitement masks and helps us deny.

Primarily it's a matter of identity and age. I am now in relation to both the team and the enemy. I now think of what was "the enemy" as human beings, so I find it hard to crow about burning

---

*It's not just for daring the fire that I call these chopper pilots brave. In peacetime a pilot would be considered totally crazy to fly in those mountains, with their tricky winds and clouds obscuring the instant death called hillsides. Marine Air Group 39 (MAG-39) flew out of Quang Tri.

them to death. I'm also very aware of the genuine cost being paid by those NVA soldiers and that reconnaissance team for me to get those feelings of excitement and pleasure.

I'd still do the same thing, only I would be aware of a horrible dilemma. I would be much more reluctant to use napalm now, knowing I could get the job done a lot more humanely with bombs. But scrambled aircraft arrive on station loaded with what they're loaded with. Once I had decided to be in that situation, I couldn't then decide that the team should sacrifice itself for my misgivings about using napalm. I wouldn't let the team down. I would have chosen to be on their side, totally. I don't believe in pulling punches during a fight to the death. But there would certainly be no excited calls over the radio, no Crispy Critters language. I'd hope that I'd remember to respect my enemy's pain and agony.

Could I empathize like this while up in the airplane? Unlikely. Empathy comes with years, and most fighters are very young. This is why politicians and generals need to see these kids as *their* weapons and use them with care and consciousness. Ideally, I would hope that, in spite of the adrenaline, I'd at least stay conscious of a terrible sadness while I burned these people. But burn them I would.

The ideal response to killing in war should be one similar to a mercy killing, sadness mingled with respect. A few years ago I came across a sick seagull on the beach. Dogs were harrying it. Both its wings were broken. Still, it defended itself, bravely slashing with its beak to try to keep the barking dogs away. People kept walking by, not wanting to look at it. I chased the dogs off and wrung the bird's neck. I felt no elation, only regret for the events that led up to the situation, and a sort of wistful "Why me, Lord?" as I did what no one else wanted to do.

When my German shepherd, Sancho, grew old, he got overly protective of the front porch. My kids would bring in their little friends, who would occasionally trip on him. Sancho started to snap and snarl, something he'd never done with kids when he was younger. (I can relate.) One day he snapped and snarled at a three-year-old who was trying to get out of the car. The mother freaked out, grabbed her child, and slammed the car door. Later she phoned to tell us that she wasn't coming over anymore. It's hard to blame her. Sancho weighed 134 pounds. We tried everything we could think of. Took him around kids on a leash. Talked to behavior experts. Moved his food away from the front door. Had him checked out for hearing problems, eye problems. I lay down next to him in the little mudroom where he slept one night and talked to him, tears in my eyes, asking him to change. He didn't change. One day Alex, my youngest son, then three, tripped and fell on him. He snapped at Alex, biting him on the cheek.

I took Sancho to the vet and lay next to him with my arms around him as she injected him with sodium pentothal. I made a tombstone out of concrete and we buried Sancho down by the trees at the edge of the field.

As I said, it is unlikely young soldiers will feel about killing in war the way I felt, decades older, on a beach with a seagull or at the vet's with my dog. It just goes against the nature and level of development of the mostly young people who will do our nation's killing. Still, I think we fall far short of our potential. We don't even strive for it with the youngest, and we can definitely instill a great deal of this sensibility in the older professional noncommissioned and commissioned officers. Even then it is difficult because the oldest people who are likely to be directly involved with killing the enemy, or directly supervising those who kill, are still usually in their twenties or early thirties. My company commander in Vietnam was twenty-three.

In war, we have to live with heavy contradictions. The degree to which we can be aware of and contain these contradictions is a measure of our individual maturity. You can't be a warrior and not be deeply involved with suffering and responsibility. You're *causing* a lot of it. You ought to know why you're doing it. Warriors must touch their souls because their job involves killing people. Warriors deal with eternity.

My first encounter with knowing this consciously came during an operation where the company was dropped by itself into a barely known area of thick jungled mountains just below the extreme western part of the DMZ.* Three days into the op we'd stumbled into an NVA outpost. The NVA triggered a command-detonated mine that had been lashed to a tree at waist height, killing our point man. He always kept a picture of his girlfriend, who was a year younger than he and still in high school, in his breast pocket for good luck. The piece of shrapnel that stopped his heart went right through her face. Somehow, when I pulled the picture from his pocket and looked at it, it stuck with me, this beautiful, young face obliterated by the same random piece of steel that had stopped her lover's heart.

A series of firefights ensued while the NVA tried to keep us at bay. We kept probing forward in the jungle to get at what they were protecting. Normally, with nothing at stake, the NVA would have pulled back to escape the inevitable artillery fire we would call in.

---

*The demilitarized zone that separated North Vietnam from South Vietnam.

Two hours of off-and-on firefights and several artillery missions later, we came to the edge of a very steep drop-off above a small beautiful valley. We followed a steep zigzag path to the bottom, where we found underground bunkers containing tons of ammunition, food, and other supplies and half a dozen large thatched-roofed open-air sheds that served as meeting places, mess halls, and so on. There was a pretty little stream running right through the center of the camp. There were smaller bunkers with the sleeping pads and personal items still lying around and hastily abandoned cook sites with half-prepared food. In the bunker I occupied were two bowls of half-eaten rice and a still-smoking bamboo water pipe neatly placed on the floor, as if the occupants had stepped outside for a pee or something. The whole thing gave me the impression of a macabre bamboo Brigadoon just waiting for the hundred-year return.

My lessons in eternity weren't over yet. That night, all was completely hidden in a creeping fog that you could feel but not see. We had our own ambush teams out on all the approaches, waiting in the cold darkness. I'd just relieved Doc Southern, one of our two platoon corpsmen, for radio watch. He hung around, obviously unable to sleep in that spooky atmosphere, wanting to talk, which suited me just fine. Our other corpsman, Brailier, was asleep in the captured bunker next to us. Brailier was a quiet kid, very near the end of his tour. Even though he was only twenty, I always sensed something very deep in him, deep and troubling perhaps. In the course of our quiet conversation that night I asked Southern about Brailier. Was he always this way?

Doc Southern looked out the opening of the bunker and started to talk, very quietly, his soft voice mixing with the fog that hung just outside the black hole.

"I was just new to the platoon," he said, staring into the past. "We was out northwest of Con Thien. We'd been in the shit off

and on for a couple of days. There was this point-to-point firefight. No one got hurt but this one gook. He was a mess. M-79
shotgun round right in the stomach. You could hardly tell what
pieces were what. The spine was pretty much gone, so he'd been
a basket case for sure if he did live. But the problem was he was
still alive. And we didn't know if he'd be dead in twenty minutes,
or two weeks, or two years.

"The louie* kept asking Brailier, 'Is he going to die? Is he
going to die?' We was all anxious to get the fuck out of there. Shit
was still happening and, like I said, we was in the middle of fucking
nowhere and the company had to move on. It meant we'd have to
leave a squad back to protect the LZ if we was going to medevac
the gook. And believe me, no one wanted to be that squad, not
no one, not then."

I could well understand the lieutenant's need to know if the
NVA soldier was going to die anyway. If he was alive, then ethics
said medevac him, but that risked losing the chopper crew and
the squad protecting the zone, and for what? Death in a day or
two anyway? A life as a basket case? It's very hard to say when
one becomes morally and legally responsible for a prisoner's life,
given that such decisions often involve risking the lives of your
own people. Leaving him there to die, however, could mean days
of agony for the wounded man, and that was really not much different from murder. But to murder a prisoner outright was certainly wrong and could send the lieutenant to jail for a long time.

Doc Southern was going on, still looking into the blackness. "I remember looking up at Brailier and the louie. I was
holding in pieces of this gook's pancreas and stomach, trying to
get him ready for the chopper if that's what they decided to do,

*Lieutenant; the platoon commander.

and trying to ease the pain. He was in a real bad way. You get to know when it really hurts, and this guy hurt, sir.

"There was this moment. You know. This moment. Then Brailier said, 'He's going to die.'

"That's all the louie needed and he started rounding up the squads and moving them out and I packed up my gear and started off after them." He stopped talking for a moment.

"Only Brailier went off by himself for a few minutes. I don't know if he was praying or taking a piss, but he came back and shot the man right through the head."

We didn't say anything for a long time. I never asked Brailier about it.

So ask the now twenty-year-old combat veteran at the gas station how he felt about killing someone. His probable angry answer, if he's honest: "Not a fucking thing." Ask him when he's sixty, and if he's not too drunk to answer, it might come out very differently, but only by luck of circumstance—who was there to help him with the feelings during those four long decades after he came home from war. It is critical for young people who return from combat that someone *is* there to help them, before they turn to drugs, alcohol, and suicide. We cannot expect normal eighteen-year-olds to kill someone and contain it in a healthy way. They must be helped to sort out what will be healthy grief about taking a life because it is part of the sorrow of war. The drugs, alcohol, and suicides are ways of avoiding guilt and fear of grief. Grief itself is a healthy response.

3

GUILT

War is the antithesis of the most fundamental rule of moral conduct we've been taught—do unto others as you would have others do unto you. When called upon to fight, we violate many codes of civilized behavior. To survive psychically in the proximity of Mars, one has to come to terms with stepping outside conventional moral conduct. This requires coming to terms with guilt over killing and maiming other people.

T. E. Lawrence wrote in *Seven Pillars of Wisdom:**

Some of the evil of my tale may have been inherent in our circumstances. For years we lived anyhow with one another in the naked desert, under the indifferent heaven. By day the hot sun fermented us; and we were dizzied by the beating wind . . . The everlasting battle stripped from us care of our own lives or of others'. We had ropes about our necks, and on our heads prices which showed that the enemy intended hideous tortures for us if we were caught. Each day some of us passed; and the living knew themselves just sentient puppets on God's stage . . . The weak envied those tired enough to die . . . Gusts of cruelty, perversions, lusts ran lightly over the surface without troubling us; for the moral

*Originally published in 1922.

laws which had seemed to hedge about these silly accidents must be yet fainter words. We had learned that there were pangs too sharp, griefs too deep, ecstasies too high for our finite selves to register. When emotion reached this pitch the mind choked; and memory went white till the circumstances were humdrum once more.

What now looks wanton or sadic seemed in the field inevitable, or just unimportant routine.

When I was in Vietnam killing people, I never felt evil or guilty of sin—and I was raised a Lutheran, so I definitely would have known a guilty feeling when I had one. However, when I returned to the States I got the message. *Somebody* had done something quite bad in Vietnam and it must have been us, since we were the only ones there.

One day my wife talked me into attending a fairly typical 1970s encounter group therapy weekend. This was mostly because I wouldn't talk about *anything* emotionally laden, not just the war. At the retreat I was asked to role-play talking to the mother and sister of the NVA soldier I'd killed when he threw the hand grenade at me. You'll recall our eyes had locked. I recognized he was human. I was conscious, right then, that he was young and terrified—like me. Then he tried to kill me and I killed him. I know today that I did far worse things, burning men with napalm, shelling men with "Willy Pete," shells that spewed burning white phosphorous that was impossible to put out and that burned deep holes right through men's bodies. But this one was the tough one because most of my other kills were made when I was in the frame of mind that I was killing someone from another species. It was more like killing animals, bad enough, but not horribly guilt provoking. They were the enemy. This time I killed a human.

I was asked by the leader of the therapy group to apologize to this imagined mother and daughter for killing their son and brother. Part of me was angry that I was asked to do this in front of a group of near strangers. Of course, I could have declined, but I didn't; once a Marine always a Marine. Within a minute of starting the apology I broke down wailing like a frightened child. Out came a torrent of terrible memories and remorse. This was the first time I felt any emotion about having killed. It was about ten years after the action. I sobbed and ran snot for hours that day, walking and running alone in the woods, my childhood place of solace. My ribs ached. The crying started again the next day, and would start again days and even weeks afterward and go on for hours at a time. Even at work the faces of dead friends and mutilated bodies on both sides would come unbidden to mind. I'd have to make excuses to go outside where no one could see me shaking, throat aching to hold back the sobs, walking down a city street or hiding in some corner of a parking garage. It went on like this for months, until I quit my job. I got into something new and everything went away, until next time. This pattern went on for nearly three decades.

The group was well intentioned but woefully ignorant, as was I, of post-traumatic stress disorder, or PTSD. I never joined another therapy group again. Although the exercise got me "in touch with my feelings," it was a damaging experience because no one was there to help me figure out how to handle those feelings in a healthy manner. It not only triggered extreme PTSD emotional symptoms, such as constant unstoppable crying, but also crystallized one of my enduring problems with the war, guilt. Did I really need to apologize?

About five years and two jobs later, still groping, I was fortunate enough to have dinner with the lecturer and mythologist

Joseph Campbell. I'd seen him in the bar of the hotel where we were both staying and, overcoming my fears of rebuff, I asked if I could buy him a whiskey. Although he was certainly well known to people interested in the study of mythology, this was long before he became a popular figure, so my offer perhaps wasn't the intrusion it might have been later. He said how could any good Irishman refuse a whiskey.

What followed was dinner, more whiskey, and lots of wonderful talk. We got into the Vietnam War. I talked about my feelings of guilt.

He said, "Look, you just found yourself on one side of the world of opposites. You think the other guy's side was all right and yours all wrong?"

I had to admit both sides were no angels.

"Don't you see the other guy's fate put him on the opposite side from you?"

I nodded.

"So there you are. Now, what you had to do was fill out your side of the bargain with a noble heart. It's your intentions and your nobility in how you conduct yourself in this world of opposites that you've got to think about. Did you *intend* right?"

My eyes teared. I could only nod my head in assent.

"Then, phew." He dismissed my problem with a wave of his hand. Absolution.

Reconciling the moral conduct we are taught as children with the brutal actions of war has been a problem for warriors of good conscience for centuries. The *Mahabharata,* the classic Indian epic, which was written down and first preserved around AD 400 but has its roots centuries earlier in the mythologies of the Indo-Aryan invaders and the people they conquered, speaks directly to this dilemma. Much of it takes the form of a beautifully written poetic dialogue called the Bhagavad Gita between

Arjuna, a human warrior, and Krishna, a god who has taken the human form of Arjuna's charioteer.* Arjuna, the warrior hero of the myth, is drawn up in his chariot before the enemy hosts. The battle is impending. On the enemy side he sees his own relatives and many friends. No one wants to fight kith and kin, and any conscious warrior of the future is going to be a person who sees all humanity as brothers and sisters.

Arjuna cast his eyes on the grand spectacle. He saw the heroes ready for battle, and he saw there all those who were dear to him. They were grandfathers, teachers, uncles, brothers, sons, dear friends, comrades. He was overcome with compassion for all of them. His voice shook with grief and he said: "Krishna, I feel an awful weakness stealing over me . . . Krishna, my head is reeling and I feel faint. My limbs refuse to bear me up . . . I look at all these who are my kinsmen and I feel that I cannot fight with them . . . I do not want to win this war . . . For the passing pleasure of ruling this world why should I kill the sons of Dhritarashtra? They have been greedy, evil, avaricious, covetous. I grant all that. But the fact remains that they are my cousins and it is a sin to kill one's own kinsmen. I would rather turn away from the war. It will even be better if I am killed by Duryodhana. I do not want to fight." Arjuna collapsed on the seat of his chariot. He had thrown away his bow and arrows and was overcome by grief.

---

*Krishna is the eighth avatar (or incarnation) of Vishnu, the preserver, part of the Hindu trinity along with Brahma, the creator, and Shiva, the destroyer. Kali, the mother goddess in her destructive form, is Shiva's wife. Krishna, as preserver and protector, represents that which maintains the world, including order. This is an important aspect of Krishna, an aspect which used to belong to our very early Western war gods but which we lost.

At first Krishna tries to buck up Arjuna by appealing to his reason, explaining how critical the situation is. This fails. Then he appeals to pride, chiding Arjuna for letting his feelings get the better of him. This fails too. Finally, Krishna taunts Arjuna about his manhood. This is, traditionally, where most men rose to the challenge, at least prior to Vietnam and the women's movement. Arjuna is not swayed.

"How can I aim my arrows at Bhishma and Drona?" Arjuna asks Krishna. "I cannot do it. Krishna, you know that I am not a coward. This is not weakness. It is compassion for the enemy." Arjuna sat silent, refusing to fight.

Even two thousand years ago it was understood that appeals to manhood and social duties were not sufficient to kill our brothers on the other side. Krishna presses forward, this time appealing to religion, usually a surefire persuader. "Believe me," Krishna says, "the eternal soul is imperishable. No one can comprehend it . . . You do not kill and your victim is not killed . . . Weapons cannot hurt the soul; fire cannot burn it; water cannot wet it. It is eternal and it is the same forever. Once you realize this truth there is no need for you to grieve."

Religion of course is still exploited to get men to kill their brothers. But saying it's okay to kill my own brother because, just maybe, the universe is a vast recycling plant had about the same effect on Arjuna that it would on any of us today—none.

Realizing that this whole line of argument will go nowhere with Arjuna, Krishna finally gets down to what I consider to be the only argument and what is, indeed, the point of the whole story. He appeals to the fact that we humans are caught in existence and we must make choices. That is, when we are confronted by the very real existence of forces for good or for evil, we must choose sides. Krishna states in the *Mahabharata*, "It is not right to stand by and watch an injustice being done. There are times when active interference is necessary."*

However, the warrior has to be very careful about whom the politicians make out to be devils. We have to choose sides with limited information and limited self-knowledge. Many decent Germans ended up sacrificing everything fighting for a government that was murdering millions in concentration camps and saying it was defending their fellow countrymen against the onslaught of Bolshevism and "international Jewry." For myself and many other Americans, a generation later, we ended up fighting for a government that was napalming villages to defend the shoppers back home against the evils of "international Communism." These "devils" begin to look suspiciously similar—and spurious. It is precisely along these lines that I became appalled at the rhetoric that came out of Washington in support of going to war in Iraq and Afghanistan. I supported going after Osama bin Laden and Saddam Hussein, but most terrorists aren't devils—they're just horribly ignorant people who got riled up casting our side as devils. Turning warfare into crusades only invites clouded judgment and fierce self-righteous opposition that may otherwise have crumbled. It also evokes crusades on the other side and vengeful retaliation. People can eventually judge rationally whether or not they're on the wrong side of a political fight about human rights and values and it would just be better to quit fighting; people generally cannot judge rationally when it's a religious fight.

Krishna tells Arjuna that there are two paths to realization, the path of knowledge by meditation and the path of work for men of action. These same two paths are identical to those

*I am paraphrasing or quoting directly from the *Mahabharata*, Udyoga Parva, trans. Kamala Subramaniam, 1988.

portrayed in our Western mythology, for example the story of the knight Parzival, which is part of the Grail legend. There the fisher king's brother represents the path of knowledge. He is a monk and religious contemplative whom Parzival meets just before reentering the Grail castle. Parzival himself shows us the path of action, the same path put forward by Krishna to Arjuna.

Krishna says to Arjuna: "Remember, no man can be still, even for a moment. He has to do work. It is a law of nature that man should work . . . By not working you cannot live. Even the bodily functions need work to sustain them.

"How then can one escape the bondage of work? By performing a sacrifice for the general good. That is the secret of work well done. Work should be done so that others may benefit by it and not you. Dedicate all the work to me, and fight."

When you dedicate the work to Krishna it means that you get your ego out of the way, that you do it for some reason other than personal gain or pleasure. It also means acting in the name of a universal spiritual, ethical, or political principle. Dedicating the work is precisely what I and many others did not do in Vietnam.

Those few who do dedicate their actions in this way, no matter which side they fight on, will very likely fare better in the guilt department than those who do not. For example, it is likely that the young Canadian, British, American, and other NATO or coalition troops who fought in Afghanistan or Iraq will have less guilt the more they believe they were fighting to stop a clear terrorist threat or overthrow a brutal dictatorship or religious reign of terror. They will suffer less than those of us who fought in Vietnam for a less clearly defined cause. Sadly, as the two present wars drag on, the original clearly defined missions and reasons for being there have become less clear. The less clear the justifiable motives, the more difficulty returning veterans will have with guilt.

Unfortunately, when you dedicate your actions to Krishna you can be wrong. Terrorists, for example, who have dedicated their actions to Allah will have no guilt about these actions, no matter how horrific. Until they realize they were lured into a misunderstanding of the most basic tenants of Islam, there will be even less of a moral brake on unnecessary violence. The same goes for crusading Christians. So Krishna's answer, "Dedicate all the work to me, and fight," helps warriors deal with guilt and doubt only if they never come to believe they made a mistake about what they were fighting for. Because of this, it behooves the warriors to pay close attention before they start.

Even though it is unrealistic to believe one will be able to stay continually engaged in combat at the detached level of Arjuna, an idealized character, and even though Krishna's advice has snares, such as being caught up in an ideal that one later regrets, it is the best way I know to minimize the guilt about killing in combat. Try to achieve this ideal when entering into the fray in the first place. One can only hope the chosen transpersonal reasons are good ones; but if they are not, there will still be less guilt if you kill for these wrong transpersonal reasons than if you kill for selfish ones. The more one kills for personal reasons, such as anger, revenge, fame, career, or political advancement, the heavier will be the guilt.

While Campbell and the *Mahabharata* are certainly correct in saying that if we perform with a noble heart and dedicate our efforts to some higher good we minimize the suffering of guilt afterward, this unfortunately will not eliminate the suffering of mourning. Guilt is different from mourning.

In virtually all warfare, other than a direct confrontation with terrorists or with totally uncoerced professional soldiers when there are no bystanders around, the warrior must understand that almost all those he kills, civilian or military, will probably not be there by their own choice. Even with that wonderful moment of absolution from Joseph Campbell, I still carry considerable emotion over killing conscripted young men ultimately no different from my own sons. But I have grown to understand that in the cases where I killed to help or save my fellow Marines I don't feel guilty. I feel sad. The warrior of the future will simply have to take on this pain and perhaps realize before doing the killing that it will be a cost worth paying. Look at depictions of Abraham Lincoln's face at the end of his presidency and you'll get some idea of what I mean. I don't think he felt guilty about fighting to save the Union or end slavery. He mourned the dreadful cost. If I were able to choose, I'd choose sadness over guilt.

On the surface, Campbell's and Krishna's answers about having to act in the world of duality, into which you had no choice about being born, seem to let people off the moral hook. "Well," one might say, "if it's all just a cosmic game and a matter of chance where you end up fighting, then what the hell?" Once you understand this answer more deeply, however, rather than being let off the moral hook you end up with it firmly set in your mouth. That moral hook is conscious awareness. If it wasn't something you were aware of previously, you have just now had the hook set. It will hurt. You now know that you are on one side and your enemy is on the other. You are conscious that you have a choice to make about killing that other person. You have to choose to do *something*. Even refusing to think deeply about it is choosing to do something. You must decide to pursue action with a noble heart or not. Doing nothing is an action. You can't get out of this.

I don't know whether or not George Bush went to war with a noble heart. Only George knows. I do know that he knew, as did we all, there was a risk that a sick man with a lot of power and money could help destroy tens of thousands of Americans. Because he, and we, knew about the torture and rape cells, he had to choose whether or not to allow torture, rape, and horrible deaths to go unchecked. Whatever his true motives, it is clear that the president chose to do what the United Nations chose not to do. Those diplomats had the same problem he and all of us had, and I only hope they all took the problem seriously.

I know that more than twenty people are dead directly as a result of my behavior, but the people they killed are dead too. Saying I was right and they were wrong, or vice versa, isn't going to make me feel better, or their mothers and sisters, or the mothers and sisters of the ones they killed. I understand why Jesus said, "Let the dead bury their dead."* It's the future killing that counts now. All any of us can do is wrestle with our own noble and ignoble intentions so that when we are asked to consider life-and-death issues, we'll do it honestly.

In the divine play of opposites the warrior knows only one thing for certain, that a side must be chosen. Once a side is chosen, the actions have to be dedicated to what is beyond the world of opposites. Even by remaining neutral you help one side or the other, because withholding help is helping the other side win. By not helping one side or the other, you influence the outcome.

*Matthew 8:22

Jesus put this very succinctly when he said, "He that is not with me is against me."*

Having chosen a side, we cannot do so thinking we are knights in shining armor. As I have clearly indicated, I supported the decision to go to war to kill or capture Osama bin Laden and remove Saddam Hussein from power. What scares me is the attitude we chose to do this with. And I mean we. There was just as much self-righteous knight-in-shining-armor idiocy going on with those opposed to the Iraq war as with those who supported it. Going on a crusade to eliminate evil, whether you think it is Saddam Hussein and his Baathist cronies or George Bush and his oil cronies, is very different from reluctantly and sadly eliminating evil because it is a loathsome task that a conscientious person sometimes has to do. When the dog gets rabies it is a sad event, especially for the dog, yet the dog still must be killed. Killing the dog and crowing about it on TV is wrong. So is calling the man who put the dog down an animal hater and picketing his front lawn. Being a knight in shining armor only results in our unrecognized dark side roaring out of control. Donald Sandner puts it as follows: "If man is to sacrifice the intensity of his animal nature he must also sacrifice his divine pretensions."† A warrior must try his or her best to be on the "right" side but shouldn't naively expect to choose wisely all the time. None of us, from the president on down, has complete information. Even if we did have it, how many of us are able to step outside our upbringing and bring only clear intellect, devoid of cultural prejudices, to bear

---

*Matthew 12:30.

†Donald Sandner, "The Split Shadow and the Father-Son Relationship," in *Betwixt and Between: Patterns of Masculine and Feminine Initiation*, ed. Mahdi, Foster, and Little, 1987.

on the decision. Any cause, no matter how well intentioned, may indeed be in vain. Think of the noble fighters in the communist revolution in Russia, the early Baathists in Iraq, the wonderful humans who fought for the Confederacy. Think of the difference between a young German who went to war for his fatherland and another young German who went to war to rise in rank and power in the new Reich. Although both lived to see their cause exposed as a lie, the former has far less to deal with than the latter.

There is no foolproof formula for choosing the right side; there are only guidelines. The warrior operates in extreme zones. The more removed a situation like combat gets from everyday life, the less applicable the guidelines get. This is why we must rely so much on character rather than rules when discussing and experiencing extreme situations like war.

Warriors will always have to deal with guilt and mourning. It is unfortunate that the guilt and mourning reside almost entirely with those asked to do the dirty work. Choosing to fight for the right reasons can assuage this guilt. Mourning can lessen it. But all warriors or erstwhile warriors will need to understand that, just like rucksack, ammunition, water, and food, guilt and mourning will be among the things they carry. They will shoulder it all for the society they fight for.

4

NUMBNESS AND VIOLENCE

The ethical warrior must avoid getting crushed between falling in love with the power and thrill of destruction and death dealing and falling into numbness to the horror. Numbness is learned in our society from an early age. The numbness protects us. We want it. The warrior of the future, however, will have to break away from the conditioned numbness, opening up to all the pain, and at the same time recognize the danger of opening up to the rapture of violent transcendence.

I have a friend who was a Navy A-4 pilot with two carrier tours bombing North Vietnam. These were some of the toughest bombing assignments ever experienced in the history of air warfare. Combine these missions with night landings on a tossing carrier deck and you begin to appreciate that, truly, these pilots were brave men.

The time my friend spent flying these missions has left a deep imprint in him, but like most Vietnam veterans he hardly speaks about it. He carries on, a successful businessman, an active contributor in his local community, his wife an active member of a local church. We occasionally go up in his Cessna. He knows I understand he is simply playing when he suddenly rolls the Cessna over, comes down close to the deck, and "strafes" somebody on a bicycle, or when he talks about distance to target instead of the next airfield. He can let this stuff out with me because I don't judge him about it. He knows I've felt it myself.

I happened to have a lunch appointment with him on April 16, 1986, the day after the United States first bombed Libya. I asked him what he thought about it, expecting the usual, reasoned businessman's answer. He put his fork down on the white tablecloth. His jaw was working as he stared down at his plate, completely silent. Then he looked up at me, moisture making his eyes gleam. "Goddamn, I wish I was there!" That's all he said.

What do we do with these feelings? He has them. I have them. Where can we place this energy?

Many people's initial reaction to this story is that something is wrong with this guy. "Doesn't he think about hurting innocent people?" I actually believe he does, but later. It certainly isn't his initial reaction. And that's why I tell the story. There's a deep and honest part in this ex-Navy flier that he's not afraid to let out, at least in front of me. It lies close to the surface in him. Imagine the conflicting forces and pressures that are in play every day as this guy goes dutifully to the office, with his wife to church, and to his kids' ball games.

These same unconscious conflicting pressures are there, in varying degrees, in all of us. But most of us, unlike my friend, keep them well hidden. It's easier to discharge these unwanted tensions by condemning people like my friend than it is to live consciously with them.

The least acknowledged aspect of war, today, is how exhilarating it is. This aspect makes people very uncomfortable. Not only is it politically incorrect; it goes against the morality taught in our schools and churches. The hard truth is that ever since I can remember I have loved thinking about war—and I wasn't the only one. I played it in the woods with my friends. I read about it, and people wrote what I read. I saw it in movies, and people filmed what I saw. As a college student I played strategy board games—and people designed and sold those games. In Vietnam there were times when I swelled with pride at the immense destruction I could deal out. There is a deep savage joy in destruction, a joy beyond ego enhancement. Maybe it is loss of ego. I'm told it's the same for religious ecstasy. It's the child toppling the tower of blocks he's spent so much time carefully constructing. It's the lighting of the huge bonfire, the demolition of a building, the shattering of a clay pigeon. It's firecrackers and destruction derbies on the Fourth of July. Part of us loves to destroy. Nietzsche says, "I am by nature warlike. To attack is among my instincts."*

Richard Ellmann, the great biographer of Yeats, has the right answer. He says this feeling is just the other face of creativity, in Jungian terms, the shadow side of creativity. "The urge to destruction, like the urge to creation, is a defiance of limits; we transcend ourselves by refusing to accept completely anything that is human, and then indomitably we begin fabricating again."† What's scary is that it is far easier to take the path of transcendence through destruction than to take the path of transcendence through creation. And the destructive path gets easier as technology improves, while positive creating, whether spiritual, artistic, or commercial, is just as hard as it ever was. Corporations that took decades to build can be "raided" and

*Friedrich Nietzsche, *Ecce Homo,* trans. R. J. Hollingdale, 1979.
†Richard Ellmann, *The Identity of Yeats,* 1964.

"unbundled" in weeks. Books that take years of toil and sacrifice to bring to fruition can be burned in minutes.

The easier the path of destruction gets, the more likely we'll be to take it. This is another reason why warriors, above all, must fundamentally be spiritual people, that is, people who are on a different path to start with. Kierkegaard says, "It is not good works that make a good person but the good person who does good works."* It's probably why Bushido† required the samurai to practice daily a meditative art form, such as the tea ceremony or writing haiku. It is through meditative practices that you observe your own mind. You can't be a good person until you observe how bad you are. It is only when the evil is conscious that it can be countered. Torturers during the Inquisition thought they were doing good.

The poet Yeats wrote, "All things fall and are built again, and those that build them again are gay."‡ He failed to say that those who destroy them have a real good time too.

Transcendence through violence. I've experienced it. For some reason the incident I remember most seems hardly worth repeating. Perhaps because of its very banality, I remember my feelings of a godlike transcendence more vividly in this instance than in other, more spectacular circumstances.

I was temporarily commanding the company and had to reach a platoon of mine that was holding a key bridge on Route 9 in territory we didn't control. It was about 12 kilometers from our company position. The platoon holding the bridge had been hit the night before and I had to get out there for purposes of

---

*Provocations: Spiritual Writings of Kierkegaard, 1999.

†Literally, "warrior way," the code of the Japanese samurai.

‡William Butler Yeats, from "Lapis Lazuli."

leadership and to assess for myself the morale of the platoon and its commander and whether they had what they needed to take another attack. I couldn't get a chopper, and convoys weren't running because of the attacks, so I decided to take a jeep and fill it with ammunition. In addition to the driver, to help me make it through I took one of the platoon sergeants and one other volunteer.

The driver, the son of a Marine colonel, had gone immediately after high school to Japan to study martial arts in a Zen monastery. After several years he joined the Marine Corps as an enlisted man. He was fiercely Zen, into not only the technical aspects of the martial arts but the spiritual as well. He would take notes of mistakes he made during the day, and then review them at night so as not to make the same mistakes in the future—things like assuming a strange rock on the path was safe without knowing for sure it wasn't a booby trap. The platoon sergeant was a professional, one of those men who make the Marines so good at what they do, a hard background, a hard player on leave, and a hard fighter. He showed up with an M-60 machine gun that we rigged in the jeep, his own M-14 (he didn't like M-16s in open terrain),* several dozen LAAWs,† and all the ammunition we could load on for the fight that night. The other Marine, a nineteen-year-old squad leader who'd been in-country for nearly ten months, and I

---

*The M-14 was the standard NATO rifle in use before the adoption of the M-16. It was much heavier than the M-16, with a heavier bullet, so it had greater range and accuracy, neither of which was needed in jungle warfare but both of which were greatly desired in open space. At that time the M-16 was also considered unreliable. It had improved, but only after needless deaths. A small act of tiredness during the design phase? A small favor granted to a defense contractor? A small bureaucratic slip about powder composition? Small things, magnified terribly by war.

†Light Anti-Armor Weapons, handheld antitank missiles like little bazookas.

were competent and experienced. I was particularly good by this time in calling in artillery fire and I made sure I was in contact with all the artillery within range: a Marine 105mm howitzer battery just north of Camp Carroll and two Army batteries, one firing 155s and the other firing the even larger long-range 175s out of LZ Stud.

We set off from the safety of our fortified position, weapons ready, eyes searching our assigned sectors of observation. As we sped down the dusty road into danger I had a most incredible feeling of power. It was like being in a chariot of the gods. We were armed and we were *good*. I actually wanted someone to try to stop us, just to see how bad we'd mess him up.

Luckily we reached the bridge without incident.

I'm asking the reader who has never experienced this feeling to try very hard to understand it and then balance it against the war feelings more legitimized by moral society, such as horror. I am well aware of the price of the feelings I'm talking about—dead friends, dead enemies, waste, pain, sorrow beyond imagining, sorrow even after forty years—and I see no end. In fact to remind myself of the sorrow and balance myself against this feeling of transcendent power I keep on my filing cabinet a picture of a fourteen-year-old girl from Mozambique, a stunted skeleton with drum-tight skin, hair gray, eyes swollen nearly shut, the starved result of war.

Yet it is exceedingly difficult to keep this image in my mind, even with all the moral weight of society behind it. The realm I enter now, the transcendent realm one reaches through violence, is one that society says it condemns but in fact celebrates everywhere, on film, on television, and in the news. It is because of this split that these feelings are so very dangerous. This split is like the wicked fairy who isn't invited to the wedding but who will get her due. It is the darkness that haunts the lynch mob that in the daytime is dispersed as lawyers, doctors, and church aldermen. But that darkness hovers ghostlike in the soft trees and shadowed alleys between the buildings. And at night it is all crazed power and torture, a thrill deeper than any ever imagined in the sleepy daytime.

The next time you're with a group of around forty people, perhaps at a meeting, maybe on a city bus, imagine them all with the lean hard bodies of eighteen- to twenty-year-old men. Arm them all with automatic rifles, rockets, and grenades. Add three machine guns and a supply of bullets backed by the industrial might of America. Understand that these armed young men will do, without question, absolutely anything you ask. Now add the power to call in jet aircraft that shake the earth with engine noise alone and can spew jellied fire over entire football fields, make craters big enough to block freeways, and fire lead so thick and fast that it would pulp the body of a cow in an eyeblink. Add to this artillery with shells as thick as your waist and naval gunfire with shells the weight of Volkswagens. And you're twenty-one or twenty-two and immortal. And no one will ever ask a single question.

This is just a platoon commander, the lowest-ranking officer in an infantry unit, which itself has the lowest level of sophistication in weaponry. In today's combat environment this lowly lieutenant can call in bombs from B-52s flying so high they are unseen and Tomahawk missiles fired from some 500 miles at sea, all with the accuracy of a rifle at 200 yards.

Try to get into this frame of mind. Try, because the world needs you to. If you say you can't, I will counter by saying you're tragically cut off from a very deep part of yourself—tragic for all of us, not just you. I loved this power. I love it still. And it scares the hell out of me.

For those who don't know it, but at least suspect they might love it, I have hope. Those who won't know it, those I fear. They are the ones who will kill a commie for Christ, even an eight-year-old. They are the ones who will spit on a veteran, even a medic. They are the ones who will send letter bombs to bankers, even the fathers of small children. They are the ones who will kill their sons' spirits and drive this immense energy so deep in their sons that when it returns, as it must, it will be in such a great rage that the gates of reason will be shattered like a boot going through a pane of glass.

When I returned from the war I would wake up at night trying to understand how I, this person who did want to be a good and decent person, and who really tried, could at the same time love an activity that hurt people so much. The easy path was to just say I hated it over there and be done with it, which is a posture I often took with no intellectual or social qualms. But the honest answer was that I hated only parts of it. Knowing I loved it *and* hated it, I concluded I was mildly psychotic, just another little something to hide from everyone, sort of like shell shock.

A wonderful teacher, John Mackie, my philosophy tutor at Oxford, evaporated the problem for me by asking me one day why I assumed there was only one person inside me. I remember bicycling up the Woodstock Road breaking into laughter every so often with the sheer relief of it all. Thinking you might be crazy can drive you crazy.

About a week after this tutorial with Mackie, Vicki, one of my housemates, lent me a book about Carl Jung, which I stayed up the whole night to read. We are legion, says the Bible. We have a shadow, says Jung. There's a part of me that just loves maiming, killing, and torturing. This part of me isn't *all* of me. I have other elements that indeed are just the opposite, of which I am proud.

So am I a killer? No, but part of me is. Am I a torturer? No, but part of me is. Do I feel horror and sadness when I read in the newspapers of an abused child? Yes. But am I fascinated? I read the whole article, every gruesome detail.

I've seen myself mildly bullying my own children just for the hell of it. My own children! We call it teasing, all good fun. Except to the child. After all, *I'm* not crazy. *I* wouldn't want to bully my kids. But that crazy part of me just loved purposefully baffling them sometimes or loved to keep them just a little bit longer in a wrestling hold when they wanted to stop.

Once we recognize our shadow's existence we must resist the enticing step of going with its flow. This is the way of Charles Manson and terrorist cells. This is also the way of filmmakers who suddenly get into its dark power and splatter it all over the screen in slow motion. This is the wrong way to relate to it. In the Grail legend, Parzival meets his dark and powerful half brother Feirefiz in battle and is unable to beat him. When they take off their helmets they decide to join forces rather than keep fighting. Parzival had many years earlier been kicked out of the Grail castle because he didn't ask the terribly wounded fisher king the question of compassion, "What ails you Uncle?" Now, after years of trial trying to find his way back, he takes Feirefiz with him to return to the castle and the healing of the kingdom. He doesn't join with Feirefiz, misusing their combined power to go off killing every knight within sight, to win glory and riches. But oh could they.

I was attending an event where we were encouraged to recite poetry that was meaningful to us. I was all full of this tenth-century Viking warrior poet Egil Skallagrimsson, who wrote about something with which I could identify. I waited eagerly to recite the poem. Late one evening I jumped up and let it go.

> *My mother told me men*
> *must and would buy me a good*
> *fast ship and finest oars*
> *to fight with Viking men;*
> *to stand tall in the prow,*
> *to steer the vessel well,*
> *to hold for harbour and*
> *hack down man after man.**

Robert Bly was there. When I finished he looked down at the floor. Then he asked me to say it again. I said it louder and more forcefully. He asked me to say it again, only softly. I did. Then he said, "How sad."

I was crushed. I said, weakly, "It's about shadow," but I knew that something had gone wrong. I was reveling in that power, instead of recognizing it, knowing it, and using it consciously. Bly's comment snapped me into recognition of this. I had done the same thing that day long ago in the jeep, identifying with the power. It is probably why my psyche has stayed with this image so long.

Even tenth-century Vikings talked about and took pride in weapons technology. That poem I recited is seven-eighths about boats and one-eighth about hacking people down. What we saw on television during the two Gulf wars was the same, psychologically, as "a good fast ship with finest oars." The "finest" means I'm better than you are. Technology in weapons makes us feel superior to that rejected "other" that I projected onto the poor sonsabitches I was itching to cream if they dared ambush me on the road that day.†

---

*Poem translated by John Lucas, in Christine Fell, trans. and ed., *Egil's Saga*, 1975.

†Combine this with the completely sufficient reason that it also means I'll have a better chance of surviving than you will and you've got overwhelming pressure to always increase weapons technology. If stopping war is a goal, attacking weapons development is a losing strategy.

Weapons are tools. Tools are an extension of ourselves. Tools make you more effective. They are ego enhancing. Ask any good carpenter how he feels about a really good tool. We enhance our feelings of self-worth if we have good tools. This probably accounts for a great deal of the sale of tools to guys who work all day at desks. How often is the household vacuum cleaner some cheap old wreck but in constant use, usually by the wife, while outside in the shop is the husband's $1,300, three-horsepower table saw that's used once or twice a year? If a fine tool is little used I have to assume it was bought to shore up the buyer's low self-esteem. If a crummy inadequate tool is used constantly I have to assume it's because of low esteem for the job. This is one reason why our cities are falling to pieces, physically and socially, while we have military hardware that glows in the dark and does handsprings.

Still, it's far too easy to say that unbalanced expenditures on weapons systems are simply the results of ego-enhancing little-boy posturing on the part of a bunch of military brass and their congressional cronies. It has this component, yes, but just as with the carpenter the job does indeed get done better with a fine tool. Those who procure weapons for our military have a moral obligation to get the best and finest. Unlike the carpenter, the people who use the tools aren't the ones doing the buying; they are the ones doing the dying. I never once got upset with a weapon that was "too expensive" or "too sophisticated." I got upset only with weapons that didn't work.

The critical psychological issue about weapons technology is the ability to distance the user from the effects. A constant martial fantasy is the "clean kill." To kill someone with an almost effortless eloquent blow of the first two knuckles of the fist is aesthetically more pleasing than to bludgeon him to death with a rock. How much more pleasing, then, with a fine rifle? A precision-guided bomb? A ray gun that simply makes people disappear? One of the major horrors of war is the blasted bodies, rotting parts, and bloated intestines, and the stench. In Vietnam I used to fantasize about a laser beam so fine you could slice an airplane's wing off with no more than a hairline cut—or a man's head with no blood at all.

This clean-kill fantasy avoids the darkness. It allows the hero trip without any cost, so of course we fantasize about it. And as we get more and more technologically advanced there are more and more policy makers tempted to live out this fantasy. Even the language is getting neat and tidy, as in "surgical strike." There is nothing very surgical about maiming Gadhafi's children, the children of Baghdad, Taliban fighters, or Iraqi soldiers. Managing the blood is a major problem in surgery.* I don't mind the activity nearly as much as the hypocrisy.

Numbness and hypocrisy aren't learned in boot camp. When it comes to inurement to violence, boot camp is just a finishing school.

I had an insight into inurement one day when I came off the train in Calcutta during a business trip and was faced with a beautiful little girl who had had both of her hands cut off to enhance her ability to beg. A cup was tied around her neck. I could hardly move. The world lurched. I stuffed something into the cup and stumbled out of the train station in horror. Yet the local people walked by her with seeming indifference. We in the United States react to violence the way the citizens of Calcutta react to such scenes of cruel poverty. We have identical nervous systems. Calcuttans are as bombarded by images of cruel poverty

---

*If not controlled blood obscures what the surgeon needs to see as well as weakens the patient.

as Americans are bombarded by images of violence. Although we often criticize them for their indifference, we are actually responding in the same way. To our shame, however, the Indians aren't inventing the poverty for purposes of entertainment.

Getting used to the extremes of violence in combat is just another level up from our everyday training. The circuitry is all in place, having been wired long years before. All that's happening is an increase in voltage. The problem is, however, that the voltage has been steadily and rapidly increasing in all of the entertainment fields. From the first shock of performers destroying their guitars onstage to the common and daily sadomasochistic fare of MTV and the like; from the stabbing in the shower in *Psycho* (1960), where we saw virtually nothing but a shadow, to the Roman-circus savagery of what is lightly stamped PG today, our psychic wiring is getting sized upward for higher and higher voltages. The score was roughly 100,000 to 127 in the first Gulf war and we loved it. Of course for Gulf I the reasons for going to war, to repulse an invasion and brutal bullying of an ally and friend, made it easier to get self-righteous. Self-righteousness is one of the best ways invented to fall into the rapture of violence: witness the terrorists who are waging holy war and taking "justified revenge." The wars in Iraq and Afghanistan, however, have forced us to face much more ambiguity about using violence, and the country is getting increasingly more divided on the matter as the wars lengthen.*

---

*I've watched my own position change. I initially supported both wars to eliminate weapons of mass destruction under the control of a sadist in Iraq and al-Qaeda's base and its leader in Afghanistan. When one mission turned out to be based on a false assumption and the other mission failed, I'd have brought the troops home. From the very start, however, I abhorred the "war as Olympic Games" coverage by the media and the self-righteous attitude of the administration.

Even the motivation for inurement to violence is the same in war as in everyday life, that is, ego survival. We mistakenly assume that bodily survival has a higher precedence than ego survival. This is simply not generally true. Ego will happily destroy body for its own sake. Look at overweight executives headed for heart attacks on the way to getting their pictures in *Fortune* or anorexic models suffering slow starvation on their way to getting their pictures in *Vogue*. Protecting the ego is the general case.

In war, as in normal life, there are still far more cases where the body is not threatened but the ego is. For those in positions of authority, and farther from the action, ego survival is the key factor. If pilots begin to weep whenever they're on a bombing run they might soon find that their proficiency would start to drop. Such pilots will hardly be the ones chosen to become squadron leaders. If becoming squadron leader is an ego need, then the ego will override the compassionate response. It's no different for the lieutenant trying to become company commander, the colonel trying to make general, the White House staffer trying to get a cabinet post, and the politician trying to ensure reelection.

Since many people strive for positions of power as compensations for needy egos, it is hardly surprising that the corridors of power are filled with people for whom the compassionate responses will be short-circuited as a matter of course. War simply draws out in stark relief the immense power of our need to be accepted by our peers, which causes us to conform to society's rules of conduct rather than respond with compassion. In so-called normal life we do these things every day, but we don't see the results quite so clearly and therefore don't relate to the remorse. This is because no one grabs us by the scruffs of our necks and shoves our faces into the messes we've created while shoring up our images.

When I first joined my company it was operating alone in the high mountains that formed the Vietnamese border with Laos. Our job was to disrupt the Ho Chi Minh trail and find and destroy supply bases and hospitals.* The company had set up on a hill temporarily and I was asked to take one of my squads out on a security patrol to screen the company position. It was my first combat patrol and I was determined to look competent. I was also nervous as hell. So, I assume, were my troops.

We'd been out several hours, moving ever farther from the company through beautiful untouched jungle, when we heard noise down in a very steep draw. We took cover, silently forming a hasty defense. After a few minutes of tense listening, the squad leader and the artillery forward observer, a young lance corporal who was extremely good at map reading, which was why he was directing artillery fire, turned to me with slight smiles on their faces. "It's a gook transportation unit," the F.O. whispered.

I was an NFG† for sure, but not stupid. So I knew some kind of joke was at hand, though I couldn't figure it out. "Okay, I'll bite. There's no roads for miles around here."

"Elephants. The gooks use them for packing gear."

"They do?"

"Sure they do."

Well, this made sense. I'd read about that back in the world. I tried to ponder what significance this might have for the patrol

---

*Supply bases replenish matériel. Hospitals replenish soldiers. Allowing the unhindered resupply of both increases the deaths and casualties on our side. Directly attacking wounded soldiers (e.g., indiscriminately bombing a hospital) is immoral but it is not immoral to take away hospitals through infantry action directed against troops who are guarding them. Once a hospital is taken, unevacuated patients should be cared for.

†New Fucking Guy.

and me when the artillery observer said, "It's a legitimate target. I usually call in a fire mission.* Okay, sir?"

I didn't want to look soft or indecisive. This was my first patrol, my debut, my coming out. So I ended up looking totally soft and indecisive and said, "You sure it's a legitimate target?"

"Sure. We do it all the time. The gooks use them just like trucks." And with that I said okay. My first fire mission in Vietnam was against an unseen "gook transportation unit"—a herd of elephants.

When the first shells came crashing in I heard the screams and the tearing and crashing of the brush by the maddened elephants. I called off the mission. I was so ashamed I didn't even take the patrol into the draw to see the damage. In the intensity of war we see the ordinary small evils driven by trivial causes, such as not wanting to look incompetent or soft, magnified into horrors, such as the wounding of innocent animals.

For all practical purposes, most of us have already been raised with this "short-circuit training" that enables us to override the more complex neurological wiring of compassion with the simple and direct short circuit of trivial concerns and immediate needs and wants. So how do we mortals overcome this short-circuiting of compassion?

There's a physical method and there's a ritualistic method.

The physical method is pretty simple. It requires that we make a conscious attempt to use other senses besides the visual whenever we are faced with making decisions that could result

---

*A fire mission occurs when an observer sees a target, radios back to the artillery battery the exact map coordinates, and adjusts the first few shells onto the target. He then gives the order to "fire for effect," meaning lob as many shells into the target as one thinks necessary to destroy it.

in killing or carnage. Our nonvisual senses haven't been dulled like our visual ones. A congressional junket to a combat zone is one junket this taxpayer would feel good paying for—as long as it doesn't stop short at headquarters. Unfortunately most of them do because most junketing members of Congress are there so that they can tell people back home they've been there and not to actually see the results or failures of their votes. Walk through a burned-out village where the dogs haven't been fed and you *hear* them eating the dead. If this doesn't snap through your conditioning, then *smell* human meat rotting. *Listen* to the wailing of the orphaned child and go mad with it because you can't get it out of your ears until you either walk away or do away with the child. Pick up chunks of body and *feel* the true meaning of dead weight. These senses aren't filtered and dulled by visual media. These channels are much more directly open to the heart. This is another reason why computer-game warfare has no natural checks on its violence.

The second area is that of ritual. Upon reading Homer's *Iliad* I was struck with how much time the ancient warriors spent in ritual. If they weren't offering something to a god or goddess, they were burning some dead comrade along with his armor. In the *Táin Bó Cúailnge,* the Irish equivalent of the *Iliad,* virtually every encounter is preceded by some ritual marking of stones utilizing the ogham,* placing of stakes in streams, placing of heads on stakes. During combat tours time must be carved out in which to reflect. I wish that after each action the skipper could have drawn us all together, just us. In ten or fifteen minutes of solemn time we could have asked forgiveness and said good-bye to lost friends.

Compassion must be elicited consciously in warfare. Our natural tendency is to think of the enemy as an animal inferior to

---

*Alphabetic system used by the ancient Irish.

us. This serves to help warriors accomplish very ugly tasks, but it brings on unnecessary suffering if not constantly checked. It takes time to respond with compassion. During combat, when you are actually fighting, you have to use this time for saving your own life. Your already learned survival mechanisms will cut out the compassionate response and you'll proceed to save your skin. But you don't fight all the time in a combat zone. You don't even fight all the time in an actual battle. There is time to be snatched, but unfortunately the way we go about fighting now is that you are most likely to get another sensory input of violence, and have to short-circuit the response to that, before you've unblocked the previous delayed response. Do this enough and the circuitry gets jammed completely and you become inured to violence as long as more violence keeps happening. Many years later all the jammed wiring starts coming loose. Rituals must be reinstated, on the battlefield, on the bloody street, immediately, to keep the jamming to a minimum.

Ego loses control when emotion (body) reigns. When you're sobbing, the body, not the mind, has control of the organism. The ego is a mind thing and it doesn't like this.

In a later chapter on atrocity I will tell of an incident when some of the kids in my platoon cut off the ears of some enemies we'd killed and pinned them onto their bush hats and helmets. I punished the kids who did this by making them bury the bodies. During the burial, which I assumed to be a totally mechanical task, two of the kids started crying.

Why don't we bury our enemies with ceremony?

Certainly, immediately after a battle we must set up for the counterattack. The bodies just get shoved aside as best they can be. I've used them for temporary sandbags on occasion. I'd still do it. But there always comes a time when you can spare a moment for ritual. It can come when you are set up and your security patrols are out and functioning, or you're being relieved by the next unit, or when, as it so often did, the order comes to abandon the hill so dearly gained.

Even if the graves are dug with bulldozers, the people who killed these people should file by and throw a handful of dirt on the bodies. They or the leaders should say a prayer, out loud, thanking these dead on both sides for their fully played part in this mysterious drama. We should allow people to curse the dead for murdering their friends, and then, if the younger ones can't, the older ones, officers and NCOs, should be trained in conducting the rituals of forgiveness and healing. Something like:

> Bless these dead, our former enemies, who have played out their part, hurled against us by the forces that hurled us against them. Bless us who live, whose parts are not yet done, and who know not how they shall be played. Forgive us if we killed in anger or hatred. Forgive them if they did the same. Judgment is Yours, not ours. We are only human.

There will be those who fear that doing such things will undermine the killer instincts of the troops. Well, if the war is a stupid one it probably will. If it's not, I wouldn't worry. Imagine the young NVA soldiers doing it to the young American soldiers laid out before them and ask yourself if in any way such a ritual would have weakened their resolve. Think of Russian soldiers pushed all the way back to Moscow doing it over the frozen bodies of young Germans. Now take those same Russians and have them do it over the bodies of dead Finns whose country they had just brutally invaded. Such rituals will indeed have consequences—all of them healthy.

5

THE ENEMY WITHIN

Under ordinary circumstances the repressed and despised parts
of our personalities manifest themselves as small human foibles
or weaknesses in character that foster only petty acts with minor
harmful consequences. In the crucible of war those same weaknesses
and petty acts can lead to consequences of immense horror and evil.
The warrior must recognize the moments when circumstances mirror
the ugly unwanted parts of his or her psyche. This is the only way
to minimize the evil consequences of ignoring these parts. To do this
requires recognizing and accepting one's own despised parts, a form
of heroism not taught in boot camp.

In 1968, while still in Vietnam, I recorded in my journal the first instance of a recurring nightmare that, along with similar dreams, took me over twenty years to lay to rest.

Somehow the gook* and I were left isolated right next to the river. I had only my kabar† and it looked as if he was unarmed. He saw me and we went at each other. My kabar was dull from chopping branches, so instead of slashing I tried to stab him in

---

*North Vietnamese soldier. I apologize for the use of this word, but that's where I was when I was in Vietnam.

†A large knife carried by Marines.

the throat. I hit him someplace but didn't stop him and then we were locked together and rolling into the muddy tepid water. I found out then he wasn't unarmed. In his right hand were two razor blades. He got me right across the wrist in a slash, and in the warm water I could feel my blood draining, mixing with the warmth around it, robbing me of energy, of life. I stabbed him in the Adam's apple and felt the hard resistance like a carrot. The knife was too dull to tear his throat, so I pulled it out and stabbed again and again in a mad race against the blood mixing, mixing in the warm brown water. Finally I could see no longer. My mind whirled. My body twisted and spun after my blood, joining it in a dance of entropy, cooling and spinning to the universal semi-warmth of the river.

The doc pulled me out and I awoke on the bank with an IV tube in my arm.

This dream is not about Vietnam. It's about what got me to Vietnam. I've been fighting that "gook," the enemy inside me, in one form or another, for most of my life. It represents the parts of me I despise. Not only don't I want other people to see them; I also don't want to see them myself. These are my weak parts, my indecisive parts, my violent parts, and probably a few parts so deeply buried I can't name them. The enemy, however, pops up in various forms in dreams. Sometimes he's a shiftless vagrant. Sometimes he's a frightening murderer or a crazy person.

Sometimes real people, not just dreams, catch this enemy within, acting like an unrecognized reflection in a mirror. Rather than realize it's my own reflection, I prefer to think that what I see is really them. This causes troubling encounters. For example, if I see fat people I immediately think badly of them. I myself was a bit fat as a child. I got over that through waging a fierce war against that fat little boy, training hard, running a lot, playing the toughest sports. But I still like to eat ice cream and lie around, so the fat little boy is still with me, stuffed inside where I don't have to think about him anymore. I can have a negative reaction to a fat person, but when I start to remember that fat little boy I used to be, my reaction becomes more neutral. Eventually it took certain painful war experiences, represented and played out in the repeating dream I just described, to finally make up a nightmare strong enough to get my attention and make me realize that something wasn't altogether sound at home. There was indeed an enemy within.

Everyone has his or her equivalent of "the gook inside." It's what Carl Jung called the shadow. People who say they don't have one have an even bigger one.

That NVA soldier and I were fighting by the Ben Hai River, the dividing line between North and South Vietnam. This is the dividing line between this world, the world where everyone, especially me, expects I'll be good at football and get a powerful high-paying job, and the other world, the world where I hide, and then forget, the parts of me I despise.

Although we all have shadows, we all have different ones. My own shadow has many masks. I'm a strong man—my shadow is a weak effeminate whiner. I'm a hard worker—"Sarge" visits me in dreams, a lazy, marijuana-smoking deserter and lover. He's got two sensuous sleek women friends. I'm not afraid to take on a challenge—my shadow constantly fears failing. What better way to fight these shadows than to join the Marines and prove to myself that they don't exist? After I left the Marines, I found other similar things to do, over and over again. I made enough brilliant light to keep the shadows at bay and blind myself in the process.

This dream soldier is slashing my wrists with a razor blade, an image of suicide. The more I try to kill him, the more my own blood drains out of me. When I returned from Vietnam I lost some old and dear friends and one woman I loved. I lost them because they said I had become cold. When asked how I was, I'd answer, "I'm cool." And I was. I was holding down a full colonel's billet at Headquarters Marine Corps* and had enough medals to excuse any wayward behavior, and I took full advantage of the situation. Everything looked fine. But I'd died inside.

So to feel more alive and simultaneously avoid the pain of confronting the darkness and dark deeds I now carried with me, I came up with a creative and individual solution. I got into drugs, drinking, and sex. It never got too heavy. I could still hold down my job, and on occasion I did this literally. After a night of doing drugs I would sometimes have to hang on to my desk chair at work the next day while I watched the Key Bridge undulate like a sine wave over the Potomac or used my eyes like zoom lenses, alternating from close-up to distance, close-up to distance. Sometimes the walls would change colors. But Lieutenant Marlantes was "cool."†

I made friends with a Marine chopper pilot who, ever since his Vietnam tour, was such a serious alcoholic that often I'd have to go over to his apartment to get him into his uniform for work in the morning. We'd go to parties where everyone was too numb to talk and too high to care. I woke up one Sunday morning after one of these parties to answer the telephone. It was the airline-pilot husband of the woman lying next to me. He was calling to see if she was going to church with the kids. I tried to pretend I was the cool lover as I watched her get dressed to go. But I felt so sad and

---

*Just days before I reported for duty at Mobilization Planning, the colonel I was supposed to work for had a heart attack. I was the only one around who knew FORTRAN and PERT networks (Program Evaluation Review Technique), so I temporarily replaced him until I was discharged.

†I later learned to call it being "numb," the first sign of PTSD.

wrong inside. I felt her humiliation. I noticed her skin starting to go loose and dry on her face, and she noticed that I noticed. That was the last time I made love to someone I didn't know.

You don't need to go to war to find people fleeing from or fighting their shadows and getting their wrists slashed. I got my act together, got married, stopped the drugs, managed to climb to the top of a smallish heap—large income, first-class hotels, jets to Europe and the Far East. On the surface it was like an ad for Rolex watches—but something was missing.

One evening after dinner at a party in Singapore I joined the men, all corporate leaders of varying nationalities, men whom I still respect for the many corporate hills they've charged and taken. We were talking about issues that were important to us at the time. Maggie Thatcher was doing this. Lee Kuan Yew was doing that. The deutsche mark was doing such and such. We were responding this way and that way, all of us intelligent, responsible, powerful in our spheres.

Laughter from across the room pulled my attention away from the conversation. I turned and saw that a group of the wives had gathered around one end of the hostess's large dining table. Color jumped at me, the mauve and fuchsia of two Indian women in their saris and a Chinese woman in a green silk dress, her face animated as she listened to a French woman whose hands flashed light as she talked. I looked back at my group, powerful and successful but bloodless.

The first messages are gentle. Ignore them and the volume gets turned up, sometimes painfully high, sometimes to the point where it destroys your sense of hearing. I traveled constantly for about a year after this party. One night I came home from Indonesia around two o'clock one morning and found my ten-year-old son curled up asleep with a photograph of me held against his stomach. The picture was one of me laughing and holding him up over my head when he was about nine months old. He'd taken a ballpoint pen and stabbed out my face.

If you don't recognize your shadow sides, you'll be likely to cause a lot of damage trying to do your heroic deeds. How often we see the do-gooder politicians, the community boosters, the heads of charities with ruinous family lives. My own grandmother was an idealistic communist, IWW member, and labor organizer. The longest she ever lived with my mother was something like four months. My mother has carried the consequences of that neglect all her life. I used to condemn my grandmother for this. Then one day I found that my grandmother's mother was a famous midwife in her part of Finland. She was constantly away as well. When briefly at home, she was constantly irritable, yelling at and slapping her kids in her tiredness and frustration. Yet no matter how tired or how desperately needy were her own children, if there was any difficult case within several days' journey, she went. So my grandmother, and every one of her siblings, went too, to America. Great-Grandma never saw her children again.

Was Great-Grandma a heroine or merely transcending tedium at the cost of her children? She was both. And her daughter, who did almost precisely the same thing to my mother, was both. Luckily for my brother and me, my mother tried consciously to break that pattern. Still, even I, three generations on, will every so often succumb to some leftover reverberation of that original pattern of neglecting what's close to me in order to run off and prove my importance under the guise of doing good for the world.

Unrecognized shadow can also haunt the person who stays at home to raise his or her kids. One couple I knew, horrified by the Vietnam War and active throughout in the peace movement, had firmly decided to raise their two children, a boy and a girl, without guns or violence of any kind. They saw no violent TV or movies; nor did they read any books of a violent nature. Even pointing a finger and saying *bang* was quickly put down. Friends who played that way were no longer invited over.

One afternoon a mutual friend found the two children torturing insects in the backyard. Not one insect, not even one each, but a whole line of them, each one neatly pinned to a board waiting its turn.

The more you deny the shadow warrior, the more vulnerable you become to it. We in America did a pretty good job of denial in the Vietnam War era and the decades following. During World War II, the warrior or soldier had a place of high regard in American society. Our boys in uniform were seen as heroes, the good guys, just a wholesome bunch of gum-chewing, Coke-drinking, jitterbugging amateurs who destroyed Japanese militarism and Nazi brutality. We idolized MacArthur. We liked Ike. We let the shadow warrior do the stuff we never wanted to consciously think about, such as firebombing Japanese civilians living in paper houses and destroying Dresden when we didn't need to. Still in the grip of this white knight attitude, we spent most of the 1950s and '60s pulling off dirty little capers justified because we were fighting the "evils of communism." All this eventually led to, along with a host of other spurious reasons, President Lyndon Johnson telling us we were teaching that "little piss ant" Ho Chi Minh a lesson. Then we started seeing some hard-to-stomach reality on television. Rather than accept that this terrible reality was the result of our inflated ideas of being the good-guy soldiers we thought we were, and accept as well that we'd buried deeply our own despised Nazis and Tojos, it was easier to throw that darkness onto the people we asked to do the fighting. So the Vietnam veterans came home catching everyone's shadow, portrayed as dope-shooting, coke-snuffing, baby-killing mercenaries. They were far from that. They fought their war, held jobs, and raised families no more and no less capably than did their veteran fathers. Rudyard Kipling's "Tommy" isn't a poem about gratitude; it's a poem about attitude.

So where's the shadow now after the Iraq War? Try Abu Ghraib prison. However, it is always going to go underground, just as it did in Gulf I and World War II, unless we start getting conscious. We move from protecting food convoys in Somalia to "saving" Somalia from the evil warlords and the mission ends in bloody humiliation. We assume we'll be cheered as white knights by the people of Iraq when we arrive with no plan for the occupation and self-righteously eliminate all agencies of law and order because their personnel were labeled Baathists, but we and the Iraqi people instead get years of bloody chaos. It's not the activity itself that's in question so much as the self-righteous attitude that one brings to the activity. This is where the danger lies. This nation should be less worried about putting the Vietnam syndrome behind us than restarting the World War II victory syndrome that resulted in the Vietnam syndrome in the first place. If you go to war singing "Onward Christian Soldiers" you're going to raise the devil.

Shadow issues come around and around. There is no defeating the shadow. We have to live with it. It is part of us. But having this shadow is neither bad nor good, although it *is* very troublesome. If I have lazy Sarge in there, smoking marijuana every day, lying on a couch, this hurts nobody. It's when I start screaming at my kid because he is loafing on the couch, just the way I'd like to loaf myself, that someone gets hurt. Then what I'm doing, because of shadow, is bad. I'll never get rid of Sarge. Calling Sarge bad and trying to stuff him even further down in my psychic baggage will only mean it's more likely I'll scream at my kid or anyone else, people on welfare, for example, who "catch" my Sarge when he pops out.

We all have shit on our shoes. We've just got to realize it so we don't track it into the house. This realization is one of the things we must work on in training society's professional fighters: our soldiers, police, and bodyguards. We must take time to make these people aware of their particular shadows and have them clearly understand that they carry this shadow with them—always. This is so crucial to those involved in professions of violence because their job at times does indeed involve hurting or killing people. People holding these jobs cannot project their shadow sides onto "the enemy" or "the criminals" and hope to avoid excesses. Yet no one attempts to help soldiers or the police by dealing with this in their training. We prefer the easier route of casting our own darkness on them, braying "police brutality" whenever the excesses occur. This must change.

It must change because we lose control when we project our shadows onto others, and losing control in war is far more serious than losing control next to the living room couch. We then kill unnecessarily and for no greater good, and a greater good is presumably the reason we went to war in the first place.

How do we change? We should at least introduce all military people to the concepts of the shadow, to rage and repression, from the very start of their training. In addition, more individual time (here therapy and education become much the same) should be spent with NCOs and officers in combat units that operate directly with the enemy (infantry, armor, and Special Forces) or with prisoners (military police and shore patrol, intelligence interrogators). Even just a few sessions could save lives by reducing violent excesses. Almost by definition, atrocities result because people in authority let them happen. It would be exceedingly rare to see trained soldiers, even as we train them now, committing an atrocity if the commander on the scene, aware of his own shadow, said stop.

I have come to understand that there are three basic categories or types of atrocity, and almost all atrocities will be one or a combination of these three. There is what I call the "white heat" atrocity, where logic reigns supreme with no feeling or empathy. There is the "red heat" atrocity, where just the opposite happens and emotion, usually rage, rules to the exclusion of all logic and rationality. Finally, there is the atrocity of the fallen standard, where there is a large gap between what is spoken of as a behavioral standard by society back home and what the immediate society in-country actually expects. I have come to this understanding because of direct experience with all three. I'm no monster. I didn't participate in My Lai or anything close to it. But in combat we do dreadful things that are excused too easily. Had I been just a little more conscious at the time, I would not have done some of the things I did. More people would have lived and without any change to the outcome of the battle or the war.

Evil floats all around us like a ghost or an unseen, poisonous mist. It arises as the result of many rather ordinary things such as history, culture, attitudes, and child-rearing practices. And it's also manifest in the spiritual realm, a real but nonempirical potential. Good floats all around us too. It's all intermingled in this potential state. What we humans do is turn this potential into reality. Like television sets, we tune in to one frequency or the other and bring that unseen, unmanifested, floating mist into full-spectrum stereophonic reality. We humans make evil and good concrete. In Vietnam I did both. I don't know anyone who hasn't done so, in war or in civilian life. It's just that in war the results are terribly magnified.

I participated in a white heat atrocity so common that it's not even thought of as an atrocity by most veterans, but an atrocity it was. We were on Mutter's Ridge, a long chain of hills running east-west just south of the demilitarized zone. The Third Marine Division and the North Vietnamese 320th and 312th A "Steel" Divisions fought over that ridge constantly throughout the war. More worthy opponents would be difficult to find.

We'd assaulted and taken one hill,* suffering fifteen dead and about thirty wounded, whom we couldn't medevac because of the monsoon clouds. The next day we were ordered to take the adjacent hill down the ridge. By this time in my tour I'd been moved up to company XO† and was left behind with a small group to guard our dead and wounded from the first assault while the rest of the company took on the second hill. It was on this second assault that a significant death occurred.

"Canada" was a big, good-looking kid from British Columbia.‡ He was six-four and his jungle weight was over 200 pounds. He carried a stripped-down, sawed-off M-60 machine gun that was further modified by welding a wooden handle to

---

*The same hill I described in chapter 2.

†Executive officer, the second in command in an infantry company. In most tactical situations the commanding officer (CO) and the XO are separated physically to ensure that both won't be killed at the same time.

‡Canadians in the Marines were not unusual. I've often wondered how Canadian veterans have handled their return to a nation that already projects so much of its own darker side onto the United States.

the top of the barrel so he could control it without burning his hands. In addition he had an oddball arrangement of two metal machine-gun belt containers, called cans, that hung from straps he'd rigged around his neck and shoulders. He would feed the gun with a belt from either can. This was an incredible amount of weight. An M-60 machine gun is normally considered a crew-fired weapon, meaning two to three men are required to carry it and serve it with ammunition.

One day, some months before the incident I am about to describe, we'd come in from the bush to guard an artillery battery. Some of the cannon cockers started making fun of Canada, not to his face but to some of the kids in our company, saying it was John Wayne bullshit. No one could be accurate with a handheld M-60, particularly firing it standing.* The word reached Canada, as was probably intended, and Canada was not the type to let a challenge go unanswered. He slung the two extremely heavy ammo cans containing the carefully coiled machine-gun belts over his shoulders, securing them to his chest with the special straps he'd constructed. He then picked up the machine gun and walked up to where the artillerymen were sitting around their howitzers. People started gathering around to watch the fun. He stood by the group of artillerymen who'd issued the challenge and slid the cocking mechanism on the gun's receiver back and forth. No one said anything about John Wayne.

"I hear you think I can't shoot this thing."

One of the cockier cannon cockers retorted, "Anyone can shoot it. We were wondering if you could hit anything."

"Let's go see," Canada said.

---

*One of our guys retorted, "Who the fuck *needs* to be accurate with an M-60 machine gun?"

He walked off the top of the hill down toward our perimeter, a small crowd now following him. When he reached the lines he slapped a belt from one of the cans that hung from his neck into the receiver. He nodded to the nearest artilleryman and said, "Point at something." People started scrambling for holes yelling, "Test fire! Test fire!"* The artilleryman pointed at an empty box of C-rations about 30 meters off. Canada tore it apart on the first burst. Canada then himself pointed at a blasted tree even farther away. He again hit it on the first burst, then proceeded to chew it into splinters, standing firmly against the recoil of the gun, until he ran through the entire belt. When he stopped he cleared the gun and walked back to his own position without saying a word. He was as good at drama as he was at machine-gunning.

Canada liked walking point,† or at least he told us he did. In any case, he always took far more than his fair share of the point assignments. If he was ever out of the bush in the rear, you could always count on him to steal a case of long-rats‡ and then give most of it away. Whenever we'd get back from an operation

---

*Unannounced machine-gun fire would have made the whole hill come unglued. Etiquette and common sense demanded announcing any intentional fire where no attack was under way.

†"Walking point" means taking the lead position at the front of the unit. This is probably the most frightening of all patrolling experiences, particularly in dense jungle where you can't see more than two or three feet into the foliage. The point man is responsible for detecting any danger and is the one most likely to be sacrificed should that danger not be detected in time. I was excused from this role because I was an officer, but the few times I took it on just to prove something I was a nervous wreck and frightened out of my mind.

‡Long-range rations. Freeze-dried food that was not only light but a very welcome departure from the heavy cans of C-rations we usually ate. Long-rats were very new then and were supposed to be used only by special groups such as reconnaissance teams.

he'd occasionally disappear. Rumor was he had a wife in a Buru village. Whether he did or not, he inspired rumors like this. His occasional mysterious absences notwithstanding, he never missed a combat operation. He was always out in front with that incredible weapon few had the strength to use. Canada was the one you wanted on your side.

In the early part of the assault on the second hill he was badly wounded trying to break through a series of bunkers and fighting holes. The corpsmen had him in a shell hole with IV tubes* taped into his arm to keep him from going into shock when the word got passed back that a key machine-gun emplacement had pinned down his platoon. The assault had stalled and a real mess was developing. He ripped the IV tubes from the plasma bottle, grabbed an M-16 from another of the wounded, and ran up the hill. He charged the machine gun, rubber tubes dangling from where they were still taped to his arm, and killed the crew. This one-man charge provided the critical breakthrough. The company took the hill.

In giving us that victory, though, Canada was hit several times more. Although he was not killed instantly, this was too much damage even for his remarkable body. The corpsmen couldn't save him. His heart stopped about ten minutes after the hill was cleared. The corpsman radioed news of the death to the skipper. On the first hill, my own radio operator turned to me with anguish on his face and repeated the message he'd just heard. "The big C is dead." I was told later that the same message, "The big C is dead," was relayed back through the entire regiment.

---

*Intravenous fluid, plasma that ran by gravity from a bottle down a plastic tube and through a needle into a vein on the arm or leg. Loss of blood causes shock, which is a principal cause of combat deaths.

We still have champions. As with the death of Hector, this death of a champion asked for revenge. Hector, the Trojan champion in the *Iliad,* killed the best friend of Achilles, the Greek champion. Achilles later killed Hector and took revenge by dragging his body around the walls of Troy behind a chariot, defacing and mutilating it in full view of Hector's family and friends. The Trojans, in turn, thirsted for revenge against the Greeks because of this dishonorable revenge. But no dishonor had been done to Canada. He had not been dragged by the heels around the walls of Troy. He had died honorably, as fine a war death as one can imagine.* We survivors, however, let his death be one more reason to get even for what turned out to be a particularly bad time for us.

The North Vietnamese counterattacked with 82mm mortars located in four different positions. The company was getting pasted in two places now, with me and my little group protecting the wounded on the first hill and the rest of the company up on the second hill. After we got shellacked, I didn't have enough healthy people to carry our dead and wounded to the new hill and the rest of the company no longer had enough healthy people to man the second hill's larger perimeter. The skipper chose to abandon the second hill and consolidate forces with my group.

In one of the bravest medevac operations I ever saw we managed to fly out the dead and severely wounded from the second hill before we retreated. Twin-rotor CH-46s from Marine Air Group 29 came straining up the hillsides just above the trees because the cloud cover was so low they couldn't find the hilltop otherwise. Not only did they brave the usual dangers of crashing on the mountainsides,

---

*He was posthumously awarded the Navy Cross and four men wear silver bracelets engraved with his name because he saved their lives..

but they took considerable fire from small arms and automatic weapons all the way up, knowing that when they did arrive on top of the hill it was being plastered with mortar shells. From my hilltop position, taking quick looks between explosions from the mortar shells, I watched the first platoon radio operator, a kid who had been a fire-team leader when I had the platoon, standing fully exposed on top of that hill guiding the birds in while the shells exploded all around him. He had taken over from his lieutenant, who had gone down with an earlier shell. I could see Marines carrying the dead and wounded from their holes through that fire into each waiting chopper. My most vivid memory is seeing the dark body of some Marine who I learned later was one of my old squad leaders fall through the sky from the closing tailgate of one of the already airborne choppers. He'd been hauling his severely wounded platoon leader aboard when the pilot gunned the CH-46 out of the zone. He chose to jump to rejoin his squad back on the ground.

As soon as the last body was out, the company retreated back to my position with anyone who could still walk. There, we were shelled for three days, unable to move our wounded and dead out by air because the weather had closed in completely, and unable to move them out by carrying them to lower ground because the enemy was all around us. We had no food, had no sleep, and ended up sharing the IV fluid for water. Luckily, the clouds lifted on day four just enough to let us see the peaks of the ridge beneath the heavy gray ceiling. Reinforcements, which had been waiting for three days in the rain at a landing zone down in the lowlands for just such a brief opportunity, were rushed in with all the ammunition and water they could carry. We were ordered to retake the hill to "get our pride back." The hill was considered our company's. We'd lost it; it was up to us to get it back. The Marine Corps is funny this way.

On this second assault we were in a different state of mind than we had been on the first.

There are many different states of mind. Contrary to the popular conception, when one is in the fury of battle I don't think one is very often in an irrational frenzy. The "heat of battle" is used to somehow conjure up a moment of irrationality, a moment overwhelmed by passions. This, of course, is a possible state to find oneself in, as I'll relate, but I was more apt to experience "irrational frenzy" when the pressure was off and I was in the rear. For example, one day while I was waiting to go back out to the bush some bureaucratic tangle set me off and I unsheathed my kabar and attacked a large bush. I slashed it to splinters, screaming with rage at it. I ended up on my knees, stabbing the splintered pieces of wood in a frenzy, while people gathered around watching me. *This* is a moment of irrationality and overwhelming passion.

When I was fighting, though, I was usually in a white heat of total rationality, completely devoid of passion. I had a single overwhelming concern, to get the job done with minimal casualties to my side and stay alive doing it. Once I got up my nerve to cross the final line of departure before an assault, it was as if I'd turned into a computer that was going so fast you would be afraid it'd burn itself up.

To get our pride back we again went up against those same bunkers and machine guns. Now we had the advantage of having destroyed the barbed wire on the first assault and knew the hill's layout. As we'd lost all our platoon commanders but one, and he had been wounded, I had reorganized the remnants of two old platoons and some reinforcements into one platoon and taken charge of it. We emerged from the jungle, my large combined platoon on line with the second platoon under the remaining wounded platoon commander coming from another angle around the other side of a finger, onto the blasted open side of the steep hill, a muddy tangle of blown trees and torn-up ground.

Our former company executive officer, who had been transferred back to a safe job in the rear to await orders home, had heard about our situation. He left his job without asking permission and joined the newly arrived reinforcements waiting nervously on that rainy LZ. He stayed with these frightened Marines three days in the rain, encouraging them, joking with them. When he reached us on the hill that night he took command of an ad hoc group, and while we assembled in the dark for the attack the next morning they cleared a nearby ridge of NVA infantry that would have taken our assault under fire from the rear. Semper fi.*

Our assault bogged down as we came under machine-gun fire from the bunkers. People jumped behind blown logs and into shell and bomb craters. It was very clear to me that if we didn't get around the bunkers with the machine guns, we'd never take the hill. We'd suffer terrible casualties trying to withdraw and terrible casualties trying to go forward. That is, of course, precisely why everyone was hunkered down on the ground. The entire platoon was rational too.

I saw that one of my machine gunners, one of the brand-new replacements who just days earlier had been in America, had been hit. His right trouser leg was black with blood and clinging wetly to his calf. But I needed a machine gun. I had to have a

---

*Semper fidelis, "always faithful," is the motto of the U.S. Marine Corps. When originally coined it probably meant always faithful to the call of the nation. It still does, but it has taken on an additional, more personal meaning for Marines: always faithful to one another, in a variety of contexts ranging from risking your life for a fellow Marine in battle to getting a fellow Marine a date. In my darkest moments in Vietnam I never doubted that my fellow Marines would risk killing themselves trying to help me and it never occurred to me that I wouldn't do the same for them.

way to keep one of the enemy machine guns under fire so I could maneuver a couple of fire teams up around the bunker to get at it from behind. I shouted at the gunner, motioning him up toward me. He started crawling, dragging his wounded leg behind him. I saw that blood was running down over his boot and flecks of it spattered on the ground as he crawled and crabbed his way toward me. I remember screaming at him because *he wasn't crawling fast enough.* I didn't care for a moment about how he felt, his pain, his fear, or anything except his function. I *had* to have that enemy machine gun taken under fire or I wouldn't get the job done with the lowest casualties to my side and still stay alive.

The machine gunner was a tall skinny black kid, all elbows, knees, and cool grace. He would have been in total control hot-dogging a basketball between his legs in front of a crowd. It was his first fight. For several seconds after I got him on target I watched him pump out bullets in short disciplined bursts, just as he'd been taught. As he did this, the blood from his leg wound was pumping out in short bursts onto the ground.

Now I think all sorts of things and feel all sorts of emotions. Then, I remember thinking with satisfaction that he was a competent gunner and thank God someone at Camp Pendleton had done a decent training job on fire control. We were always short of machine-gun ammo to defend against the counterattack after a fight and firing too long bursts would burn out the barrel.

I left him there, alone, with the enemy machine-gun bullets coming right back at him. The two opposing machine gunners locked on to each other, ours pumping blood and bullets, giving me time to figure out how to scream around trying to organize the taking of the bunker immediately in front of us, at the same time already trying to figure out what to do after we got that bunker, and . . .

Thirty years later, while trying to write about this incident, I kept compulsively writing *then these three NVA stood up in their hole. I was in a different frame of mind. I gunned them down.* But this was a lie. I did no such thing. Yet through several drafts of the manuscript I kept writing this fictional ending of my story as if it were true. Something made me want to leave it in. It was only on the third or fourth draft that I finally threw it out and wrote the truth. What in the world was going on?

What actually happened, and what I wanted to leave out, was that the whole platoon was engaged in a no-quarter fight, one I had set up and planned. A no-quarter fight is a fight to the death where no one is allowed to surrender or run. Everyone on the losing side is killed. I didn't kill three soldiers all by myself. Would that it had happened that way. Not only would I gain a little warrior glory for a hat trick but, more important, I wouldn't have to own that the killing that followed Canada's death was far more of a personal moral failing than I wanted to admit. Many more than those three were killed, most of whom, in retrospect, probably could have been allowed to surrender or allowed to retreat. We'd decided to kill them. They deserved it. It was "justice for Canada." After that decision, it was just mechanics carrying out the sentence. Somebody had to do it.

You can imagine, given how I was treating my own machine gunner, my state of mind when I saw any enemy stand up to surrender. It's the prime example of how total rationality is an unbalanced and unhealthy state. Logic, devoid of empathy. If there was one tenth of 1 percent of a chance that one of those NVA was fooling, or maybe standing up to take a better shot, then a totally rational computer with my objective would ask, "What do I risk and what will it cost to make the odds of this particular situation 100 percent in my favor instead of 99.9 percent? No risk? The cost of the energy to pull the trigger and a few bullets? That's easy. Do it." It's done. Furthermore, if I can kill them before they have a chance to demonstrate beyond any doubt that they do want to surrender, by waving a white cloth or something, then I won't have to make a difficult moral decision that might endanger my life. Here is the rational mind of the individual doing *absolutely everything* to win the fight and throwing out any emotion that could get in the way.

By compulsively writing the fabrication that all by myself I'd killed three men who were trying to surrender I, in a way, wanted to take on the whole of the responsibility, absolving my fellow platoon members from their own responsibility. I, after all, had sanctioned it. I felt bad about what happened. But part of taking on all responsibility in writing appears also to be from a need for self-aggrandizement. Self-aggrandizement? In not allowing them to surrender and killing them? How can I explain this?

First of all, the criteria for being good are switched in combat. In the world of Vietnam, gunning down three gooks who stood up in their holes wouldn't have been considered bad at all, and while I am writing narratives of my experiences I'm back in Vietnam. In fact, the *badder* you were as an individual, the more esteem you had in that community, as long as the badness didn't spill over to those who were on your own side. There was an expression commonly seen scrawled on flak jackets saying, "Yea, though I walk through the valley of the shadow of death, I shall fear no evil. Because I'm the meanest motherfucker in the valley."

However, soldiers and Marines are also subtly prepared by our society from early childhood to accept this switch in what is considered good and bad. Healthy children eventually rebel against dependency. However, boys, when I was growing up, seemed more often than girls to do so by being bad. Girls weren't encouraged to do this. Girls were good. Therefore, if you were to prove you weren't a girl, then . . . you had to be bad. And so many of us grew up with a mixed message.

Add to this preconditioning the fact that in combat all-out total aggression will help save your life. When you're truly in the valley of the shadow of death, then, if you *can* become the meanest motherfucker in the valley, you will indeed try. This is, appropriately, encouraged. So being bad helps give many males identity as men; it fills a need for esteem. Add to this that in war it helps us survive and you've got a very potent motivation system for doing the so-called bad thing. Evil is very ordinary. We don't have to look far to see its causes. It's the little things, such as being tired and not inspecting the mortar tripod closely enough, or not recycling the plastic, or letting kids eat junk food that abuses their health because the parents' working or social life is more important than preparing a decent meal at home. It is not expressing horror at television violence. Cruelty in warfare is as mundane and common as cruelty in child rearing.

When I first finished writing "I was in a different frame of mind. I gunned them down," a long anguished cry broke through after all those years. Looking at the winter fields outside my window, I kept crying, "Oh, God. Oh God." Asking for forgiveness, perhaps? The snot was dripping from my nose onto the keyboard. It was some time before I could continue writing. When I was able to focus again, I realized that something significant had been going on when I kept compulsively writing down a bad deed that was a fabrication, something I didn't in fact do single-handedly. These three NVA soldiers were made-up images, icons for the sorrows of war. The true situation was Marines killing NVA without quarter wherever we could find them, with me doing no more or less than any of the others. That there were some NVA in groups of three I don't doubt, but this particular group in my mind was invented.

I realize now that what I did was make up a story in order to get back into my feelings, feelings I'd suppressed and ignored all that long day, and many long days and years before and following. I was too defended against regaining feeling from a factual account. Through the story I could take myself by surprise because I didn't have my defenses up. It's one reason why storytelling is so important. In gradually regaining those lost and suppressed feelings I began to heal myself, and I have come to accept the tragedy I participated in.

I can now tell the story truthfully. We all shot anybody we saw, never offering a chance for surrender. Finally the NVA started pulling back from their positions, firing at us, covering their retreat. I knew that we had them on the run and that now was the time to pour it on.*

I'd carefully studied the map and thought about the assault the whole night before. I'd anticipated this break. I knew, if we succeeded in pushing them off the hill, they'd be forced down a small ridge because of the way the terrain and our own forces would funnel them once they started withdrawing. I had ordered one squad with a machine gun through the jungle to set up there to wipe them out as they came hurrying off the hill.

The squad leader, Isle, was my former radio operator. He and I had already shared an entire lifetime, shivering together to avoid hypothermia under the same poncho liner; sharing our last meals, our last package of freeze-dried coffee; sharing our

---

*I never saw the NVA run. At most I saw them hurry from their positions to reach their main units, but their units always withdrew in good order and very dangerously to any pursuers. They were a disciplined and effective fighting force.

letters, the sad ones and the glad ones. Sharing the decisions and the anguish. More than once we had shared what could have been our last moments alive.

Isle was smart. Even though he was only a lance corporal and nineteen, because we'd lost so many squad leaders during the previous fighting, I had put him in charge of a squad and taken on a new radio operator.

I remember screaming at Isle over the radio. "Move it! I want you there and I want you there *now!*" The enemy was doing just as I'd planned, but Isle wasn't in position yet. "They're starting to break! Get that gun set up! They're going to get away, goddammit! Move!"

I'd gone over some edge. This was blood lust. I was moving from white heat to red heat. My assigned objective, winning the hill, was ensured. I was no longer thinking how to accomplish my objective with the lowest loss of life to my side. I just wanted to keep killing gooks.

I loved Isle like a younger brother, and Isle, like any younger brother perhaps, wanted to do well by his older brother. In any case, he'd do virtually anything to please me. He broke from the cover and safety of the jungle, the reason for the slow progress, and sprinted with the squad across exposed ground to set up the gun. Two rockets flashed out from the hill we were assaulting. Isle's close friend Tennessee, a kid I'd often talked with as he was visiting Isle, was packing Isle's radio. Both were killed. P-Dog, the machine gunner, took over the squad. He pulled the squad and the two bodies back to the safety of the jungle.

The squad rejoined us after it was all over. I was so exhausted, and there was so little light because of smoke from burning napalm and thick clouds, that I always remember the scene as being near evening. It was, however, only eight or nine in the morning. I watched P-Dog climb wearily past all the smashed holes and bunkers, past the bodies. Isle was slung over his shoulders. When he reached me he just looked at me with a sad, sad look. Then he dumped Isle's body to the ground at my feet.

I didn't know what to say.

Another kid arrived with Tennessee slung over his shoulders and dumped him next to Isle.

I asked P-Dog how it happened. P-Dog told me.

When P-Dog left I went through Isle's and Tennessee's pockets. Isle had a letter from his mother saying, "Don't you worry, Chip, you'll be home in just seventeen more days." I never knew, until that moment, that his nickname back home had been Chip.

A week before he was due to go home my friend Mike committed a real read-about-it-with-horror-in-the-papers red heat atrocity. Mike was a good steady combat-experienced lance corporal in my company who was transferred to a CAG* squad toward the end of his tour. After more than a year in Vietnam he'd seen a lot of combat and lost friends. Mike's squad had been assigned to protect a small village. One day he captured a Viet Cong guerrilla near a village where just a week earlier Mike had lost several friends to land mines. The prisoner, like Mike, was around eighteen or twenty. He had been captured loaded with land mines. There was no doubt about his, or his unit's, intentions. When you step directly on a land mine the explosion often kills you by going up

---

*Combined Action Group. Marines who could operate very independently were chosen to work in small groups that were assigned to villages too far from main cities to be covered by more conventional forces. They usually operated in combination with local Vietnamese militia units.

between your legs. The survivors have to look around for missing pieces and make sure they get thrown into the poncho with the body so you get all of your pieces buried in the same place.

Mike decided not to turn the prisoner over to the usual authorities, the South Vietnamese military, no paragons of human rights. He kept the prisoner to interrogate himself. The rational purpose for this so-called interrogation was to find out where the prisoner's unit was and where they were setting booby traps or perhaps ambushes in order to avoid any more casualties to Mike's squad. But, as Mike told me later, he "simply lost it." He was "filled with rage."

Mike kept the kid for a day, beating him until he grew too tired to beat him further. He would then rest up, fly into another rage, and beat him some more. In Mike's own words, "I beat him to a pulp." He then hung the kid upside down from a flagpole, hoisting him in view of the entire village, to "let the village know what Marines did to VC who killed Marines."

The prisoner was seen hanging from the flagpole by an American Army unit who got him out of Mike's hands. Fortunately, for both of them, the prisoner lived. Mike was tried, busted back to private, and discharged without honor. He has had to live with the fact that after months of honorable and difficult service he certainly had lost it, and this was his sad return to America.

Mike now has a wife, kids, and a steady job in the upper management levels of a large corporation. When he told the story to me and a small group of veterans his eyes flickered from our faces to the floor and back again. I could see how desperately he wanted us to understand about the brutal and ugly way his friends had died, about his state of mind at the time. I could see his nervousness, even fear, that in admitting such an act he'd lose our respect. That he told this story is witness to his basic integrity.

We didn't condemn Mike, but many of us, thinking we'd seen and heard it all, were still shocked.

This act haunts Mike still. He did it. It happened.

I search my soul for whether or not I could have done what Mike did—or worse. I say no, but where is that "I" after months of killing, no sleep, and sheer horror? What, indeed, is the last straw when that "I," facing the longest, most terrible storm of its life and fearing the loss of all hands, finally abandons ship, leaving only the primal split-off core, a core in too many of us that is a primitive enraged child?

What pushes the few over the edge into perpetrating something like My Lai, or what Mike did, I don't know. But with my war experiences behind me, and five kids, I can only say I no longer make hard and fast judgments. What amount of pressure is reasonable before one checks out and lets the rage take over? How do you judge another human on this level?

In the My Lai massacre Calley, Medina, and a bunch of others all lost it one day, just like Mike, just like me. The degree to which we each lost it varied. Suppose we all sat in a nice comfortable living room and watched a videotape of me shooting people who probably could have been taken prisoner and screaming at Isle to kill the fleeing enemy or, even harder, watched Mike hanging a body beaten to a pulp upside down from a flagpole. It will be close to impossible for people who have never experienced anything like these circumstances to reconcile the person on the video with this seemingly normal individual sitting next to them. Even I have a lot of difficulty. We veterans know this. We may wish it weren't true, we may resent it, but deny it we cannot. This is yet another factor that drives us into silence.

Suppose Mike had killed that kid? Mike would have been no different, his motives no different, his "red heat" no different. Should he have been sent to prison for life because he happened to be placed in that particular circumstance and the cumulative effects of months of warfare finally caused his particular ego to crack, to lose it? I become very uncomfortable when I'm around people with a superior and self-righteous attitude—a conviction that they could never have done such a thing as Mike did. True enough, perhaps, but if they had been in Mike's skin from day zero, with Mike's genetic makeup, specific childhood culture, and experiences of evil and of Vietnam, could they have acted any differently? Could they have had the "power and the freedom to do otherwise"? When we meet the next test, we can meet it only with the character we have at the time, and in this way we aren't free. Our freedom lies in the fact that we can continually work to improve our character.

Still, we can't let the Mikes of the world off the hook because of this lack of freedom at the time. This is because the threat of punishment for committing atrocities probably saves lots of prisoners' lives. It provides just that much societal structure to help keep a wobbling ego from collapsing. And egos get pretty wobbly in warfare. But when we punish, the correct attitude should be not self-righteousness but sorrow. There, but for the grace of God, go I.

The third kind of atrocity is the atrocity of the fallen standard. This doesn't happen instantly, nor does it happen only under the stress of actual fighting. Remember, in my story about the no-quarter fight, we'd actually decided ahead of time not to take prisoners and not to let any of the enemy get away. I had even devised a plan for it. It was clearly premeditated.

We didn't decide this by vote. We didn't talk about it. We just knew what we were going to do—shoot anything that moved that day until it stopped moving—and we did.

Marines have traditionally engaged in fierce no-quarter combat. The very nature of their traditional mission, as shock troops against tough objectives, puts them in situations where the taking of prisoners is not even close to convenient and is usually downright dangerous.* The Marines were the ones who primarily fought the so-called Banana Wars of the 1920s and '30s. These "wars" were some of the first the United States conducted against guerrillas, excepting the American Indian wars. Guerrillas faced very probable death if captured, because they would be tried as traitors or criminals, not prisoners of war. Men in these circumstances are much less likely to surrender. The fighting, necessarily, gets more brutal for both sides. The war in the Pacific against the Japanese was an order of magnitude worse in this regard. The Japanese soldiers considered surrender to be shameful, while dying for the emperor was believed a great honor for them and their families. Not only did the Japanese not surrender; they would often commit suicide trying to take some of the enemy with them.† Trusting the surrender signal, only to have the hidden hand grenade go off, soon led to not trusting surrender signals. It was also well known that surrender *to* the

---

*Trained as elite shock troops, with a specific history of acting that way, and with logistical support designed for short tough fights, the Marines were misused in Vietnam. The generals in the first Gulf war, almost all of them veterans of Vietnam, used the Marines correctly: first, as a quick reaction force to help defend Saudi Arabia; then, as an offensive threat to the beaches behind Iraqi lines; and, finally, as shock troops to drive through the heavy Iraqi fortifications near the coast.

†We consider this to be fanatical. If an American did this we would consider it heroic.

Japanese entailed a very high chance of death through starvation and brutality. This too was a far different circumstance from surrender to the Germans, no picnic but a situation with much higher survival rates.

The Pacific theater fighting grew more brutal. New recruits had to be prepared for all of this. The wisdom of past mistakes got incorporated in the training and the culture, even though you'd be hard pressed ever to find a Marine, during World War II or in Vietnam, who would have said Marines don't believe in taking prisoners. Don't get me wrong. Marines do take prisoners. But, back then, in Vietnam, closer to World War II than it is to us today, with most of the very senior officers and noncommissioned officers having fought against the Japanese, the code of conduct concerning the taking of prisoners, at least in my unit, was "not very goddamn often."

When I arrived in-country I heard stories about previous operations where it was clear that no one took prisoners. The remarks seem callous now. Obviously many of the enemy soldiers were conscripted, as were ours. Surely, most of them must have wished they were back home, just as I did. I had nothing personal against these people. I actually admired them for their fighting abilities. It now seems obviously senseless and unnecessarily cruel to have continued to shoot at them when they wanted to quit or retreat.

Yet our *job* was to kill as many as possible, retreating or not. Taking the hill was only secondary to the strategy of attrition and its measurement, the body count. No-quarter fighting fit perfectly with that disastrous and stupid notion of body count upon which all professional soldiers in Vietnam were judged. I remember the crisply starched major giving our bunch of brand-new lieutenants our first briefing on the division's current operation, which we were about to join. "It's a war of attrition, gentlemen. We're here to kill the enemy, and kill him in far greater numbers than he kills us. Don't ever forget that."

I didn't forget.

During the war we were constantly faced with the stark fact that taking prisoners entails risk to your own side. You are slowed down and divided in order to guard them. You risk your own helicopters and helicopter crews to fly them out. They can turn on you if you fall asleep.

And I wanted to live too. I wanted to be the meanest motherfucker in the valley, and if I couldn't be, then I wanted him on my side.

No-quarter was floating around. I tuned in.

Racism and pseudospeciation were also floating around. If you were a soldier during World War II and your own grandparents were German or Italian, or if people in your unit spoke German or Italian as a mother tongue, it was far more difficult to fall into thinking of the enemy as animals deserving of slaughter. If they stood up to surrender, you were a little more likely to see them as humans wanting to quit, just as you would want to quit under similar circumstances. But if someone is of a different color and a vastly different culture, as was the case with the Japanese, it gets a lot easier to pseudospeciate. And both sides did. On the Japanese side this was exacerbated by a government policy of isolation from foreign influences for years. On the American side this was furthered by government policy that directed second- or third-generation Japanese Americans away from fighting in the Pacific, making it even easier to dehumanize the Japanese, since no one on our side looked like them.* Worse, the U.S. government officially condoned racism by sending innocent Japanese Americans to concentration camps, making the "Jap" scapegoat USDA approved.

Pseudospeciation happened in Vietnam, as in all wars. Most Americans were big and black or big and white compared with most Vietnamese, who were small and sort of brownish. The Americans had very few small brownish people on their side to remind them that small brownish people are people too. We had no Asian Americans in my particular unit, and they were rare in the Marine Corps in general. I don't know why. Perhaps a lingering suspicion of racism in the Marine Corps steered them toward other services. Perhaps their culture didn't send young men into volunteer military organizations during the Vietnam War as blindly as did other cultures.†

Fallen-standard atrocities don't occur just around taking prisoners. Another example of an atrocity of the fallen standard was the time several of the kids in my platoon cut off ears from the bodies of the NVA that they'd killed. They did this as a way of gathering a sort of trophy. I don't believe they actually thought for a moment in any conscious way about desecrating or dishonoring the dead soldiers—no more than a hunter would think about taking the antlers from an elk to hang over the barn door. The ears went into rubber bands on their helmets or were hung by string around their necks. "I killed this many. Look at me. Seven with

---

*Most Japanese Americans fought in Europe with the justly famous Nisei Division, although some acted as interpreters in the Pacific.

†I'll always remember a Chinese businessman in Malaysia being astounded when I told him I had volunteered for the Marines and fought in Vietnam. He said, "We Chinese see our sons as fine steel, not nails to be thrown away."

one blow." It's similar to the psychology that lies behind letter jackets. It's just that these eighteen-year-olds weren't playing high school basketball.

After all the horror I'd seen already, this particular act actually didn't bother me at all. I could easily have let it go. I pretended to be angry, but they probably saw through it. It goes back to Lawrence's comment: "What now looks wanton or sadic seemed in the field inevitable, or just unimportant routine." The ordinary dead body in Vietnam was usually a mess. Whether it had an ear or not was nothing. One might just as well have taken belt buckles, as we often did. We could trade them for socks and beer with the guys in the rear areas. Ears could also be traded. One pair was worth about a case of beer.

The ear cutters were surprised when I disciplined them by making them throw away the ears and then go outside our lines and bury the bodies, hard hot work in an environment definitely lacking OSHA approval. I should have had them bury the ears with the bodies, but it didn't occur to me then.

We have an idea of what is right or wrong. And we can debate moral issues as ideas. But moral *standards* are not ideas; they exist in the form of observable measurable behavior. What one sees, hears, and feels every day, by observing how people around one behave, inculcates such standards of behavior. Take standards of excellence in companies. Everyone knows what perfect quality is. That's an idea. But if every day a worker trashes some 3 percent of the production through carelessness, and no one says anything, pretty soon the standard is a 3 percent error rate, even though the ideal is perfect. Three percent was pretty well accepted as an American standard in the manufacture of memory devices in the early 1980s. Then along came Japanese memory-component manufacturers. These people would get very exercised about even one mistake—one—not 1 percent. They would fly a vice president over to apologize if it happened. You can imagine what got said to the employees involved.

Both sides of the ocean had the same ideal. They both knew what "meets specifications" was. But the Japanese *behaved* differently. Behavior sets standards, not ideals. So the Japanese ate American market share like park bears going through picnic baskets.

We talk about moral ideas. We operate on standards. It's the same in war, where cruelty not only is allowable but often is encouraged.

The answer to fallen-standard kinds of atrocities is quite simply to never allow behavior to differ from what is stated publicly. We do this by very quickly punishing even small lapses. We punish with compassion and understanding. War is cruel. People crack under its pressure. But we punish—and we try to help the one who failed to unravel the complex feelings afterward. The instant any excess in cruelty occurs it must be noted and screamed about. Not only did few scream about taking ears; many commanders actually encouraged it "to confirm the body count." It was as if we were back in the days of my childhood in Oregon shooting crows for bounty, cutting the feet off and turning them in to the Department of Fish and Wildlife for fifteen cents a pair.

6

LYING

One of the greatest tests of character is telling the truth when it hurts the teller. The Vietnam War will be infamous for the way those who perpetrated it lied to those who fought and paid for it. Lies in the Vietnam War were more prevalent because that war was fought without meaning. Death, destruction, and sorrow need to be constantly justified in the absence of some overarching meaning for the suffering. Lack of this overarching meaning encourages making things up, lying, to fill the gap in meaning.

People lie. They lie in business, they lie in universities, they lie in marriages, and they lie in the military. Lying, however, is usually considered not normal, an exception. In Vietnam lying became the norm and I did my part. In Vietnam, lying became so much part of the system that sometimes *not lying* seemed immoral.

Kill ratios and body counts were the prime example of how "normal" became abnormal in Vietnam. Or was it vice versa? Take a typical squad-level firefight on a routine security patrol, Lance Corporal Smithers in charge. All sorts of shit breaks loose. Teenagers get killed and maimed. The radio nets go crazy with artillery missions, sit-reps, mortar missions, anxious platoon commander, anxious company commander, anxious battalion commander, S-3, S-2—all wanting to know what's happening. Good communication is definitely a two-edged sword. When the shooting stops, the pressure begins for the most important piece of information, the sole justification in the Vietnam War for all this sorrow: the body count. Smithers, what's the score?

The teenage adrenaline-drained patrol leader has to call in the score so analysts, newspaper reporters, and politicians back in Washington have something to do. Never mind that Smithers and his squad may have stopped a developing attack planned to hit the company that night, saving scores of lives and maintaining control over a piece of ground. All they'll be judged on, and all their superiors have to be judged on, is the kill ratio.

Smithers's best friend has just been killed. Two other friends are missing pieces of their bodies and are going into shock. No one in the squad knows if the enemy is 15 meters away waiting to open up again or running. Smithers is tired and has a lot of other things on his mind. With scorekeepers often 25 kilometers away, no one is going to check on the score. In short, Smithers has a great incentive to lie.

He also has a great *need* to lie. His best friend is dead. "Why?" he asks himself. This is where the lying in Vietnam all began. It had to fill the long silence following Smithers's anguished "Why?"

So it starts. "Nelson, how many did you get?" Smithers asks.

PFC Nelson looks up from crying over the body of his friend Katz and says, "How the fuck do I know?"

His friend Smithers says, "Well, did you get that bastard that came around the dogleg after Katz threw the Mike-26?"

Nelson looks down at Katz's face, hardening and turning yellow like tallow. "You're goddamn right I got him," he almost whispers. It's all he can offer his dead friend.

"There's no body."

"They drug the fucker away. I tell you I got him!" Nelson is no longer whispering.

"We can call it a probable," says Smithers.

"Do what you fucking like, but I tell you I got him. I saw him jump. Half a fucking magazine. He's dead. He's greased. Now fuck off."

The patrol leader doesn't have a body, but what are the odds that he's going to call his friend a liar or, even more difficult, make Katz's death meaningless, given that the only meaning now lies in this one statistic? No one is congratulating him for exposing the enemy, keeping them screened from the main body, which is the purpose of security patrols.

He calls in one confirmed kill.

Just then PFC Schroeder comes crawling over with Kool-Aid stains all around his mouth and says, "I think I got one, right by the dogleg of the trail after Katz threw the grenade."

"Yeah, we called that one in."

"No, it ain't the one Nelson got. I tell you I got another one."

Smithers thinks it was the same one but he's not about to have PFC Schroeder feeling bad, particularly after they've all seen their squadmate die. Then there's still the problem of getting them all out alive, and who the fuck cares if it was the same one, and he's on the radio about the medevac anyway, so. "Wait one, Delta. I got another probable here. Now, I copy, the bird can pick up our Coors and Pabst* at Pall Mall plus two point two, Winston minus . . ." The last thing on Smithers's mind is the integrity of meaningless numbers.

The message gets relayed to the battalion commander. He's just taken two wounded and one dead. All he has to report is one confirmed, one probable. This won't look good. Bad ratio. He knows all sorts of bullets were flying all over the place. It was a

---

*Dead and wounded.

point-to-point contact, so no ambush, so the stinkin' thinkin' goes round and round, so the probable had to be a kill. But *really* if we got two confirmed kills, there was probably a probable. I mean, what's the definition of probable if it isn't probable to get one? What the hell, two kills, two probables.

Our side is now ahead. Victory is just around the corner.

Then the artillery commander calls in. "How many kills did we get in support of that firefight?" The infantry commander knows how important the kill ratio is to the artillery commander's career, and here he has only two kills and two probables to share out. But you don't want the artillery to feel demotivated, and maybe you played football together at West Point or Quantico. There's only one decent thing to do. Give the artillery credit for a kill. (But really, the infantry did do the killing, so why change the infantry numbers?)

So a kill goes up from the artillery battery, through the artillery regiment. One kill, and ... What's this? One probable. It only makes sense. After all, we were dropping in 105mm high explosives with timed air bursts and that new cluster round with the flechettes, and, man, that combination is some kind of lethal and, besides, you know how the sneaky bastards haul their dead away to fuck up our damage assessments. We, of course, do it to properly bury our dead.

By the time all this shit piles up at the briefing in Saigon, we've won the war.

Imagine the scene in ancient Greece if the Greeks had the same attitude. Word has just reached Greek headquarters that Leonidas and the three hundred Spartans have all died defending the pass at Thermopylae.

"Good Zeus! They're all dead? What was the body count? What do you mean you didn't think it was important? If you think

I'm going to take this news to Themistocles with nothing to show for it but a bunch of dead Spartans, you'd better think again. Now either I want this goddamn thing hushed up quick or you get your ass back up to that pass and get me a body count we can take to Athens. I don't care if you have to include Persian chickens . . ."

Why don't decent people stand up and scream? It's because there's nothing in it for them. They're in a system in which they wish to survive. Assume you're a decent soldier, like me. You and I are decent, aren't we? You know there's a bunch of lying bastards, the other guys, who will do anything to get ahead and who aren't decent at all. If you naively turn in only one probable, when you *know* that under similar circumstances the other sobs are going to turn in at least five of one kind or the other, well, who's going to end up running the place? A bunch of lying bastards. It's actually your moral duty to keep up.*

When Norman Schwarzkopf told reporters during Desert Storm that estimates of how many Iraqi soldiers had been killed were meaningless, I raised my fist in the air and shouted for joy. The pressure for numbers and statistics comes from people who don't have anything to do, don't know what it's all about or how it happens, and are frustrated because they're left out of what looks to be, at a safe distance, something exciting. The press people are constantly pushing briefers with inane questions like "What percentage of the Republican Guards is destroyed?" Suppose I just told you that half of my platoon had been destroyed but didn't tell you the remaining half is so goddamned mad we're going to fight twice as hard. What meaning will be conveyed by statistics like

---

*It's no different from grade inflation or putting all excellents on fitness reports for average work. If others are doing it, why would you ruin some student's chance for Yale or a guy's career just to be a one-person crusade for rigor and honesty?

"50 percent destroyed"? The only meaningful statistic in warfare is when the other side quits.

This nonsense went on in Vietnam for several reasons. Probably the most important was that the president and a group of advisers insisted on running things from Washington with no clear military objectives to pursue. So they had to have something upon which to make decisions, because, after all, if they didn't make decisions, what the hell were they doing in charge? The second factor was military careerism, in both competing with statistics and not blowing the whistle on their stupidity. This happened all the way up the line. And finally the lying took place because the kill ratio statistics were so totally out of line with the ordinary grunt's psychology that lying about it was a trivial and meaningless act for him.

When the system starts seeking goals that are out of line with individual values, the individual, who is usually trapped in the system, can either get hurt or survive by lying. We all like to survive and people lie all the time because of this. People in oppressive state systems learn to lie as a normal part of their lives, simply to get along. People raised in alcoholic or other kinds of dysfunctional families learn to lie as a normal part of their lives, simply to get along. People in fear of losing their jobs learn to lie, simply to get along. It should come as no surprise that in Vietnam people learned to lie, too. It should also come as no surprise to find out that lies or partial truths were told in the current wars in Iraq and Afghanistan. We kid ourselves when we think lying is abnormal behavior. Lying may be bad, and we can even believe it is bad, but it is quite often the norm.

Although I blame the top military and political leaders for not squaring this system up from the top, a massive moral failure, it's just too comforting to think that it was a bunch of brass trying to get ahead who did all the lying in Vietnam. I also blame all of us who participated in it for falling into cynicism rather than trying to stop it. Cynicism is simply the flip side of naïveté. You're no more mature, just more burned.

Even so, it isn't so easy to just say lying is wrong and shouldn't be done. Sometimes lying was good. It takes a very mature person to know when one or the other is appropriate.

Sophocles writes about this in his play *Philoctetes*. A warrior, Philoctetes, carries the magical bow of Heracles, the great immortal now departed from the earth to live with the gods. It has been foretold that only with the magic bow will the Achaeans defeat the Trojans. On his way to fight the Trojans, however, Philoctetes is severely wounded by a snake. The wound festers and rots. It stinks. It drives everyone on his ship mad. Finally his shipmates can't stand it any longer and they maroon him on a deserted island, hoping he will die quickly. In Greek and Roman mythology the snakebite is a metaphor for consciousness. Most people can't stand having someone with a new and different consciousness in the same boat. Society does often isolate people like this.

After nine years of getting nowhere the Achaeans remember the prophecy and decide to send two men to get the bow back, however they can. The only person who can use the magic bow is Neoptolemus, the young son of Heracles. But he is inexperienced and naive. They send Odysseus, who is neither, with him.

The story revolves around the enormous unfair suffering that Philoctetes has endured, his anger against his fellow Achaeans, and how very unfair it would be to take the bow from him, since it is his only source for getting food. Neoptolemus befriends him, according to Odysseus's scheme, which is basically to lie about everything in order to trick the bow away from Philoctetes. But at the last minute

Neoptolemus wavers, feeling sorry for Philoctetes. Then, Odysseus steps in and deceives Philoctetes with a bold lie and gains the bow for the ultimate victory against Troy.

I lied in Vietnam but, unlike Odysseus, I was never consistently in control of my lying. My lying fell into two very distinct categories: the lie as a weapon and the lie of two minds.

Prairie Dog, or, more often, P-Dog, was an eighteen-year-old black machine gunner from one of our eastern seaboard ghettos. He and I had been in the same platoon. P-Dog got his name saving a squad that was pinned down in the DMZ. He took off on his own at a rapid crawl, cradling the heavy and cumbersome M-60 machine gun in his arms. Elbows and knees flying, he outflanked the enemy and blasted them with his machine gun, freeing the pinned squad. Such a maneuver, under heavy fire, takes more than just raw courage. The name came when a friend of his, talking about how low and fast he'd been crawling, said, "Like a prairie dog with his ass on fire." It stuck.

P-Dog had about ten days to go before he was due to rotate back to the States. He'd managed to wangle his way out of the bush back to Quang Tri to sit out his last week at the same time I was there awaiting reassignment to the air-observer squadron.

About eleven o'clock one night we got a call from another battalion up the road. Three of our guys had been picked up smoking marijuana. Could the duty officer come over and take them into custody? That was me.

Smoking dope in those days meant a mandatory court-martial and dishonorable discharge. Any kid with a dishonorable discharge would lose his GI Bill benefits, and typically this meant also losing any chances for further education. In addition he would never be able to join a union and would therefore never be able to get a decent job. Color that kid black and you've just shut him out of normal society for life. In short, these three kids were had. So much for serving their nation.

I sighed and said I'd come over. I left the duty NCO, a career gunnery sergeant, in charge and took the sergeant E-5 who was in charge of the battalion office and a driver along with me.

I walked into the other battalion's headquarters hooch and there I saw P-Dog and the two other kids under armed guard, squatting on the floor, their hands stretched out on a bench. When P-Dog saw me he turned his head away. He would look only at the floor. I began shaking inside, knowing the consequences that were going to have to follow. Applying military justice to strangers is a lot easier than applying it to a friend. We'd been through a lot of shit together, and now this was the way we'd say good-bye, with me sending him to jail and then a lifetime's purgatory.

The other battalion's duty officer, an old mustang, said he hadn't searched these guys yet, because they weren't in his battalion, but they hadn't had their hands anywhere near their pockets. He'd already searched his own guys and they'd been put away. He was giving me an out. I took it.

I ordered the three of them into the jeep and took off. I turned to the driver and the sergeant when we were well down the dark road and said in a very loud voice that I had to piss, didn't anyone else? We all three walked away from the jeep and stood in the dark with our backs to it. After about a minute or two of muffled scrambling and whispers from the three in the jeep, we all turned around and climbed back in.

We arrived at battalion headquarters, which like most head-quarters never shuts down. In full view of the entire staff I ordered the three of them searched. All three were grinning. They started turning their pockets inside out on their own. P-Dog, ever the showman, flipped open his last pocket with great gusto—and a joint fell out onto the floor.

In the hush that followed, the duty NCO quietly reached down to the floor, picked up the joint, looked at it, and held it under P-Dog's nose. He handed it to me. No one said a word. Everyone just looked at me.

I was representing the commanding officer, conducting an investigation of what was considered a serious criminal offense that had been recorded in the logs of two battalions. In front of at least a dozen witnesses P-Dog had popped a joint out of his pocket. All I could think of was mandatory court-martial and dishonorable discharge.

I told the other two kids to get out. They looked at P-Dog, frightened for him, really saying good-bye, and then scrambled out the door.

I looked at P-Dog, then at the silent group of clerks and radio operators, and then at the duty NCO. He was a lifer. These men are the core of the system. They love it, and they maintain it with pride, often savagely. He was also a man I respected immensely.

I looked him in the eye as square as a young lieutenant can look at a man with twenty more years in the Corps than he. I said, "I know this man. He was with me in the bush. He's a good Marine." I paused and held up the joint. I wished my hand weren't shaking. "This looks like tobacco to me, Gunny."

The duty NCO looked at P-Dog. P-Dog was as white as a black kid can get.

"May I have that, sir," he asked quietly. I handed him the joint. He said to P-Dog, "Lieutenant Marlantes says you're a good Marine. He must know something I don't." He took the joint over to the sergeant. He held the joint up in front of him. "This looks like tobacco to me. You agree, don't you, Sergeant?"

"Yes, Gunny. It's definitely tobacco." The gunny then walked the joint around the room, with that wonderful career NCO and former drill instructor's flair for drama, and asked everyone in the room whether it was tobacco. No one disagreed. He handed it back to me. "We all agree with you, sir, it's tobacco."

When I saw P-Dog later that night I expected some thanks. I didn't get any. He was too angry over the fact that he could have gone to a naval prison and had a dishonorable discharge after, as he put it, "leaving a couple pint a my own blood in this shithole place." This was one of the reasons he was a particularly good fighter: he didn't let the target get obscured by sentiment.

That deliberate "lie as weapon" is one I'm still proud of, and I'm proud of all those that night who lied with me. Lying, in rare cases, can actually exhibit good character.

I used the lie as a weapon on other occasions. Shortly after the incident with P-Dog I was flying as an air observer, forward air controller, and naval gunfire spotter. We did a lot of low flying in hazardous conditions. As long as we felt this was justified, such as when troops were in trouble or there were big targets, we risked our necks. There were occasions, however, when we just felt abused.

One day we caught a glimpse of something that indicated a bunker complex. We didn't have any Marine or Air Force aircraft on station, nor were we sure how big the target might be, because of the NVA's normally excellent camouflaging, so we didn't want to scramble a flight up from Da Nang. We also knew there was a lovely Navy cruiser off shore. We asked if it'd like to take on the target.

If you lob a shell from a bobbing ship, through a lot of air currents, in a long trajectory several miles high, and you are good, you will hit somewhere in the area of where you're aiming. By *somewhere* I mean to within tolerances of a few meters over distances of miles. This is, by any count, highly accurate. It is not, however, a smart bomb going through a ventilator shaft. It is virtually impossible to destroy a bunker set into the earth with a shell coming in at a low trajectory. Even land-based artillery, which has a much steeper angle, has to hit directly on the roof to have any effect. In short, if you hit the bunker, you're lucky. If you land all around the bunker and don't hit it you're as accurate as you can be, and you're unlucky. This ship was unlucky.

The cruiser plastered the bunker complex. Shell after shell piled in there; dirt, smoke, tree limbs, the whole place was plowed up. We were delighted with the accuracy and told the crew so. Then, naturally enough, when all the shooting was over with, they wanted to know how they did.

This is not a trivial request. To go in low over a bunker complex in an unarmed kite like an O1-Charlie, after you've just brought the whole world down on the inhabitants' heads, is like the dog sticking his shiny black nose into the hole of the hornets' nest after master just stirred it up with his walking stick. We obliged, however. It was our job.

We took a considerable amount of automatic weapons fire going in to assess the damage. We pulled up out of the danger zone and I radioed back to the cruiser. "You were right on target. Great shooting. Unfortunately, you didn't get any bunkers. They're all uncovered though and we'll get some aircraft in and blow hell out of them. Thanks much."

There was a quick "Roger that." We turned for home, as we were low on fuel. The bunkers were dead ducks because we had them totally exposed. The pilot was already radioing in the target to the next air observer coming on station from Quang Tri. He would have enough fuel time, and a fat enough target, to scramble and direct some Marine A-4s or Air Force Phantoms from down south.

Then a new voice comes up on the radio. "Uh, Winchester, this is Round Robin, uh, are you sure about that no-hits damage assessment?"

"Roger that, Round Robin. Good shooting. Bad luck. We're out of here. I'm bingo fuel."

There was another pause. I figured we must have the fire control officer on the hook instead of the radio operator. "Look, uh, we fired off a whole lot of rounds at this target. You sure you didn't see anything? You know . . . Would you mind going in for another check?"

Now this guy is asking us to risk our necks for a second look. But we're good campers. We don't want to upset anyone. So without either of us even talking on the intercom the pilot sighs and heads the plane back toward the bunkers and I tell the guy we're heading back in.

We came in low from the west, trying to take the NVA by surprise. It's hard to sneak up on someone in an airplane with no mufflers on the engine. We got plastered, taking several bullets through the wing. I'm glad to say the NVA were as unlucky as the Navy that day. We climbed for altitude and I radioed back in—great job, blasted the entire area—no bunkers destroyed. Sorry. Now we're heading home for sure.

Two minutes later there's a third voice. "Winchester, this is Round Robin Six Actual. This damage assessment is totally unacceptable." Now "Six Actual" means the skipper of the ship, which, since it happens to be a cruiser, means this is no small potatoes. Even sarcastic, arrogant Marine lieutenants get nervous when senior Navy captains get upset. "I'm making a formal request for a serious damage assessment, and I expect it to be complied with. Do you copy?"

I said I copied. Given the kind of guy I was dealing with, that was probably put on record. This captain had just shot up a whole raftload of ammunition with nothing to show for it. Never mind that he'd just exposed the target for an easy creaming by the Air Force; the stats looked bad. And that's no way to make admiral. Especially when cost effectiveness was a primary way up in a war where black-shoe Navy didn't get much action.

I now had some choices to contemplate. I could go in again and hope three wasn't the charm as far as ground fire was concerned. This would also risk not making it home before running out of gas. Or I could refuse the request and face the chickenshit that would almost certainly come down the chain of command. This would cause the pilot and me considerable pain as well as embarrass our own commanding officer, who would be honor bound to go to bat and defend my decision, but at the risk of his own career and an unbelievable amount of paperwork. Or I could lie.

I lied. For the same reason Smithers did. The request was stupid, and it risked two lives and an airplane for an unworthy objective. We continued to head toward home while, after a suitable dramatic pause, I radioed in hundreds of meters of trench line destroyed, five bunkers destroyed, two secondary explosions, and a major road intersection completely put out of commission. (A road intersection?)

Everyone involved had to know it was a total fabrication. But I was the only *official* liar. The captain got what he wanted. So did the statistician in Washington. In fact Washington got double pleasure because, of course, it got added to the Air Force's report of the actual destruction, which occurred later that morning.

(*Two* road intersections! Call the *Washington Post.*) If the public had only known the irony in these kinds of statistics. A "bunker" can mean anything from the Guns of Navarone to a rectangular hole in the ground covered by logs and dirt. These happened to be the latter, like almost all bunkers in that war.

Had there been some strategic objective being pursued by the ground forces in the immediate vicinity, which happened to be an Army armored infantry division, this bunker complex would have caused a lot of damage and death. The fact that a Marine naval gunfire spotter got lucky and saw something suspicious in an Army tactical area of responsibility, that the Navy shot away all the camouflage, and that the Air Force came in and pasted it when it was totally exposed could have been seen as a great example of interservice cooperation, professional coordination, and military savvy. But because all the Army was doing there was replacing the Marines, who by this time didn't know why they had been sent there in the first place, because everyone was being judged on numbers of enemy killed and lineal feet of trench line destroyed, objectives no decent fighting individual would care to pursue, everything had turned into competition, lying for promotion, cynicism, and a total misrepresentation of what was actually going on. And I deliberately added to the confusion.

I would still not expect anyone, especially myself, to put his life on the line for a corrupted measurement system. I probably should have spent more effort trying to change the corruption than bitching about it, but I was young and very jaded.

Then there are the "lies of two minds." An example of this, of which I'm still ashamed, had to do with a very common battlefield myth, the enemy tying wire around themselves so they wouldn't bleed so fast. It's plausible. It is told of the battles against the Moros in the Philippines at the turn of the twentieth century and was probably true there, although vines were used instead of wire. The Persians probably said that the Greeks used grapevines. It's usually an indication of how desperately the enemy was defending the position, which enhances one's own esteem if one happens to have taken the position away from the enemy. I, like most people, could always use some more self-esteem. The more you have, the less you lie.

The action in which I lost Isle was the tail end of days of the worst fighting I experienced. We took a heavy licking in casualties and deaths. When I returned from the hospital ship to the company I recognized only about one in five people. Since I seemed to be the talker in the group, the company commander asked me to write something in order to begin the process of putting the company in for some sort of unit commendation.

Unfortunately, we had a very large problem to overcome. The numbers looked bad and instead of thinking of putting us up for a unit citation some officers on the battalion staff were thinking of relieving the skipper because he'd lost so many men without enough enemy dead to show for it. Taking the hill meant nothing in the overall scheme of things. Here was the morale effect of the overriding strategy of the war in a nutshell. We who had done the fighting all felt immensely proud of what we'd done. We were proud we held the hill. The staff, however, was stuck explaining a poor kill ratio, the only number that supported the overall strategy of the war. The staff members didn't know the facts about the actual fighting; they didn't witness any of the actions—understandably, given that they weren't there. What they needed to look good, and to make the company look good, was body counts way in excess of KIAs. Unfortunately, we timid types, who were there, never particularly wanted to leave the perimeter—under fire from an enemy who'd dug in all around us—to count bodies so the staff could get their numbers. So we had bad numbers. Somebody had to be responsible. (But we held the hill. We won, didn't we?) It so happened that our company commander was a first lieutenant of twenty-three. He was cocky and more than a bit brash and had managed to get his picture in the papers several times already for previous actions. Many of the older career officers would have given a left nut to have a company in combat on their records and here was one being wasted on a hotshot ex–fraternity president who was probably going to go back to America and develop real estate. He was the easy choice for scapegoat. I, of course, was firmly with my company commander and very much wanted to give my version of the facts, so I was doubly motivated in this report to strike a blow for justice and truth. The skipper said we should write up the entire company for a unit commendation, so by God I was going to do a good job of it. I'd overcome those bad numbers.

I had been told by some of the kids that they'd seen wire wrapped around the NVA bodies. I never saw any. I wrote it in the commendation as if it were a fact. I was going to get my guys that commendation no matter what.

This may seem pretty trivial to a civilian reader, decades after the war, but the reader must realize how much the ideal of professionalism and honor means to the military. Believe me, it is not trivial to lie in a report. I still feel ashamed of doing it. In one of those terrible ironies of war, the battalion commander was killed and the report must have gotten lost or thrown away by some wiser officer. The point I want to make, however, is not just that I felt I had done wrong. What amazes me to this day is that at the time I wrote it I actually believed what I wrote to be true, fervently. I'd have fought anyone who called my troops liars or me a liar and thrown my honor right on the line. I had convinced myself that NVA soldiers had wrapped barbed wire around themselves to slow their bleeding while making a fight to the death of it. This made our struggle for the hill that much more heroic. "In the face of a fanatical enemy . . . etc." Yet, when I wrote it, I also knew it wasn't true. I call this the lie of two minds.

"I" convinced "myself." The I that did the convincing was the one who needed desperately to justify the entire experience, to make it sane and right and okay and approved. Myself was convinced as the moral self, the part of me I would want to be a judge in a legal system. This moral part of us, however, in these extreme situations, is vulnerable to the overwhelming force of that part of us that needs to justify our actions.

I am ashamed of this lie because it was done for nothing more than self-aggrandizement. There was no greater cause, such as saving lives. Also, in both of the previous examples of lying, I wasn't of two minds. I didn't believe what I was saying for a moment. I was in control. With this lie I'd lost myself. Perhaps this too adds to the shame.

It is the lie of two minds that is the most dangerous. I'm sure William Westmoreland believed Khe Sanh was important militarily in order to justify the importance it gained politically back in the United States.* Oliver North probably got into the lie of two minds when Congress told him he'd have to abandon people he'd promised to help. This was a Marine officer and Naval Academy graduate, absolutely steeped in the tradition of never abandoning fellow fighters, and it conflicted mightily with his promise to uphold the Constitution of the United States and probably a naive view that American leaders would never welsh on a deal in the first place.

---

*After an epic defense and one week after Westmoreland left Vietnam the Marines abandoned it with Creighton Abrams's full blessings. The decision to make a stand at Khe Sanh is still controversial.

The deliberate lie is an intentionally launched piece of misinformation, which, like any other missile, can be launched for good or for evil. Its morality is dependent upon the intent of the launcher. Its effectiveness, as with all missiles, depends upon the launcher's skill and judgment. The lie of two minds is like a wild card thrown into the system. There's no control once it happens. It's like the gods coming in and messing with our heads: "Let's see what they do with this information, yuck, yuck." The shame of the lie of two minds exists not only because it often ends up hurting a system you believe is a good one, but because it's like abdicating the control of your weapon. No warrior could ever do this with pride.

We lie because we find ourselves in positions where it appears the truth will hurt us. But a truth isn't a thing like a flying rock. So by "hurt us" we must mean it will hurt some goal toward which we strive. And we've managed to confuse that goal with a definition of ourselves. "Hurt our ability to achieve our ends" equates to "hurt us." Worse, we have such a large number of goals to use to define ourselves that we rarely know which to apply at any particular time. I want to be a hero. I want to stay alive. I want to be a good officer. I want my troops to like me. I want to defend my commanding officer. I want his job. I want to tell the whole world how incredibly difficult a time I have just had. I don't want to look like a crybaby. I want to uphold the honor of my service. I want to get even.

It's quite clear I can't give a straight report and achieve all of the above. It is also clear that I can't consciously give an intentional lie, as that makes several of the above impossible to achieve as well. I therefore give a report that fits, and I *believe* it. Never mind that I shove the lie well down into my unconscious, where it lies buried for years. Lie as in "falsehood" also means "lie in wait."

To avoid the lie of two minds the warrior must do two things: first, consciously rank personal goals so their order of importance is clearly differentiated and, second, see which subpersonalities of his psyche will most benefit from each of those goals. Then, that part which is always there standing back and able to watch all the subpersonalities has to step in and choose which one gets satisfied and which ones don't. When there are conflicting aspirations, one or more must be put aside. This takes a lot of difficult soul-searching and time and is extremely difficult to accomplish in the heat of war when you are young. Yet it must be done.

7

LOYALTY

Warriors have always had to deal with loyalty. Concepts of loyalty change, however, and warriors have to cope with that as well. Through much of history loyalty pretty much meant being faithful to the leader of your group. In many parts of the world today loyalty is given to some concept of the nation or the state and leaders are simply viewed as temporary managers of these larger entities. No matter the course of the future the warrior will need to constantly reevaluate to whom or to what he is loyal and why. There will be situations when loyalty to the side of the fight or even some higher value is in direct conflict with loyalty to one's own moral code. The warrior must live with these tensions and consciously choose among them. Sometimes the conflict will be unbearable. The warrior will fail and will have to learn to live with that.

In 1964 I stood with a bunch of other kids, raised my right hand, and joined the United States Marine Corps. I swore an oath to follow the orders of the commander in chief and defend the Constitution of the United States of America. I don't remember the precise words. I do remember the solemnity and seriousness with which I swore that oath. I believed in God. I believed in the Constitution. Most important, I believed that a president of the United States would never give me an order that would cause me any moral conflict.

Three years later I was in my room at University College, Oxford, England, struggling with my friend John about just such a moral conflict. We were both trying to decide whether to give up our Rhodes scholarships: in my case, to join my fellow Marines who were already fighting in Vietnam or to desert to Sweden or Algeria; in his case, to turn in his draft card, an act which entailed permanent exile in Canada.

Earlier, in September, my commander in chief, President Lyndon Johnson, had given a speech in El Paso, Texas. I had listened to it in a 1954 Buick driving across South Dakota with a friend from college. We were on our way to New York from Seattle, he to the Columbia University business school and eventually the Peace Corps and I to Oxford and eventually Vietnam. I was by then a Marine second lieutenant with a temporary duty assignment to Oxford so I could take up my scholarship.* In his speech, Johnson had made a remark about "cocktail critics," people who bitch about things at cocktail parties but never have to face any of the hard choices. That remark hung with me all across the brown plains and all across the gray early-winter Atlantic on the S.S. *United States* with my fellow scholars. And it hung with me every day of what should have been the time of my life at Oxford.

By the fall of 1967 I couldn't defend the war politically. Nor did I. John and I basically agreed it was a mistake. But I would get news of friends getting killed or wounded. I think I kept hoping, probably like the mystified battered wife who keeps hoping her husband will change, that there really was some sort of reason

---

*I was well aware that I had received this assignment when the Corps was desperately short of infantry officers. I felt grateful then and still do.

behind the tragedy, that it would all turn out okay and understandable in the end.

John was from a small town in Minnesota, the son of a truck driver. Although a similar social background made it easier for us to be friends, John was quite unlike the other Rhodes scholars and me. Most of us exuded the look of earnest young men on the way to power. John had a beard that touched the top button of his work shirt. His hair hung over his collar. When I first met him on the *United States,* I worried that he'd find me too conventional, too square. After we were at Oxford a few weeks, I found we shared the same passions. John taught me my first talking blues.

Above all, we shared a fierce passion not to be cocktail critics. For some reason, neither John nor I could sit it out with student deferments like others. The war kept at us. We both felt we were just hiding behind privilege. The discussions got more heated; the stakes were raised. Stay and be a coward, go to Sweden or Algeria and be a deserter and never go home again, or sign up and kill other people for no apparent good reason or be killed yourself. I kept thinking of my friends, both from the Marine Corps and from my high school, already fighting and dying in Vietnam. Then there was Meg: beautiful, deep, warm Meg. I was in love for the first time in my life.

I lived racked at two levels. I could stay with friends, parties, studies, and, most important, Meg or choose between exile for life and war. Worse, the wrong war. For me the penalty of refusing to fight wasn't draft dodging but desertion, a far more serious crime, involving a military trial instead of a civilian one.

Studies lost all value. Who cared what Locke, Berkeley, or Hume thought about reality? I couldn't go to a party without thinking of my Marine friends, terrified in the jungle while I was hanging on to Meg's very beautiful warm body with one arm and holding a pint of bitter in the other. Oxford, a place I'd happily be buried in should I happily die there someday, became a cold gray limbo between black choices. And the one choice my conscience would not allow was to sit it out in college, a cocktail critic.

John and I decided what to do around three o'clock in the morning. The narrow Oxford streets were cold, wetly reflecting yellow sodium vapor lamps. The pubs had closed hours before. I feel now as if there were a candle lit in my room, but I can't imagine there was. Still, that is the image I carry, this sputtering little light, this bit of warmth, that cold North Atlantic drizzle outside, and John and I alone.

I had to force back tears when the decision came. Neither of us could sit it out in college while those with less education bore the burden. I could not desert and go with him to Canada and he could not go with me to war, but we would both leave Oxford together. I walked with him to where he had to climb over the back wall, as the college gates had long been closed. I shoved on the cold gritty sole of his shoe to boost him over. That was the last memory I had of him, a cold gritty boot in my hands launching him into darkness.

John had to get to Canada before the State Department pulled his passport. I had no intention of waiting around Oxford for the Marine Corps to decide what to do with me. I pulled all of my scholarship money from the bank and went to Africa, harboring some vague idea that maybe Algeria and exile wouldn't be all that bad and I'd desert after all. But after weeks in North Africa, smoking all the hash and kif I could get my hands on, I decided to face the music I'd started. I can still see the amused look on the face of the young Navy lieutenant at an American base north of Casablanca when a desert-darkened hippie in a camel hair djellaba and heelless yellow leather slippers announced he was Second Lieutenant Karl Marlantes, USMCR,* reporting for active duty.

He advised me to go back to where the bureaucracy thought I was. So I returned to England, received my orders, and had a hell of a farewell party. The last I saw of Oxford was two friends waving good-bye to me from the train platform and my pockets full of hash slabs. I clearly remember thinking I would not be likely to see them again.

I had a terrible aching parting from Meg. She hadn't come to the party, nor did she come to the train. We'd said farewell alone in a drizzly dawn in Christ Church Meadow after being up all night. Her face was wet with the fog from the Thames and tears. We walked along the river's edge, occasionally throwing a small stick into the water, disturbing the quietly feeding ducks. We kept making a foolish joke through the sadness about some crazy notion of taking the first duck to London. I was terribly frightened that I would be killed and had already started withdrawing from her. She felt betrayed and hurt by my actions. Not only did I not consult with her about my decision, I didn't even *think* about consulting her. This hurt her—and it was true. In those days it would simply never occur to me that my business was anyone's but my own, particularly decisions of conscience. Meg's hurt translated into anger and eventually a Dear John while I was in Vietnam. I wrote to her for several years but she never wrote back. I eventually gave up. I've never gotten over it. Yet,

---

*United States Marine Corps Reserve. In the Marines in those days there was a very clear distinction between those who elected to make the Corps their career by "going regular" and those who didn't. Those who hadn't gone regular, by signing a formal agreement with the Corps, were designated USMCR.

given who I was then, I don't think I could have done differently, nor could she. Even given who I am today, I still would not choose any differently. But I wouldn't leave Meg out.*

What I was experiencing was my first moral dilemma about where my loyalties lay. On a psychological level I was facing a hard choice between duty and heart, loyalty to an abstraction such as a unit or even ideals and loyalty to a person. In the months to come I would often face this conflict between loyalty to some abstraction such as "unit" or "country" and loyalty to those immediately around me—loyalty to duty or loyalty to those who were going to get killed and maimed doing the duty. Many times, someone I considered to be a complete ass would order me to do something I thought stupid or even stupidly dangerous and I, cursing out loud at my superior's stupidity, would go off and do what he'd ordered, knowing that a terrible price would be paid. In those cases I remained loyal to the larger unit, to the abstraction of structure of command.

I must also add that it wasn't purely a choice of loyalty upward versus loyalty downward. Loyalty downward included not only the unit immediately around me, my platoon, but also the smallest unit of all, myself. There was always the pervasive fear of the consequences of disobeying a direct order while in combat, none pleasant and some, like a long prison term, very unpleasant. This fear provided a very easy rationalization for following stupid orders, a common defense used by many of those on trial at Nuremberg, though to little avail. No professional warrior should be ignorant of Nuremberg. What one

---

*Meg and I had a poignant reunion and emotional reconciliation some three decades later. She told her story and I told mine. We both sadly accepted that we were dumb kids in love who hurt each other. I am blessed to have her as a friend.

thinks about Nuremberg will have a great deal of influence on what one thinks about following orders.*

It is easier to disobey orders in some systems than in others. This doesn't change the morality, but it changes the anguish and the cost. Anguish and cost are significant factors in making moral decisions. We agree that to kill is wrong. Yet most would agree that to kill someone who is torturing you is right. The difference is the anguish of the person being tortured.

In nations such as Baathist Iraq or Nazi Germany, the consequences of disobeying orders were extreme, like death by torture and strangulation from meat hooks—not only for the individual but for his family. I reiterate: identical moral choices can require far more personal courage in some instances than in others and those who do the right thing under such circumstances are very brave indeed. An individual in the military service of a Western democracy has considerable freedom to disobey orders. This is certainly true in the American military. Nonmilitary people will be surprised at how often, particularly in combat, you can work things around. For example, you can make a mistake. You can not understand. You can lose communication. You can even tell the idiot that you think he's an ass, you won't obey his stupid order, and you want a transfer. There are very few officers who want to have the question of whether or not they are stupid asses debated in a court-martial.

---

*I think the smugness and ease with which this line of defense was dismissed had less to do with fairness than with the self-righteous morality of people on the winning side. Japanese and German military people committed terrible crimes and deserved punishment. However, the large number of death penalties handed out to so many should have been tempered with some recognition of the awful choice of disobeying an order in a frightening dictatorship as opposed to the relative ease of disobeying an order in a democracy with rule of law.

Even in circumstances where I could have very likely escaped punishment, however, I followed the "stupid" order. I even did it in circumstances where any possible punishment later compared with what I was being asked to do now looked trivial. Surely, the risk of death through a court-martial in 1968 was nearly nonexistent as compared with the extremely high risk of death through assaulting a hill. Why did I follow patently stupid orders to my own detriment and the detriment of my men? To whom or what did I give my loyalty? Obviously it wasn't to my own men. They would pay as dearly as I would. Nor was it to myself, because good lieutenants in battle have even higher casualty rates than their men.

For me, my loyalty was to the mythic/historic/psychological projection called "the unit." It has a thousand specific names. It's the Marine Corps, the Legion, the 82nd Airborne, the Gordon Highlanders, and the Oxfordshire and Buckinghamshire Light Infantry. It's all those flags, all that history, all that dying. We'd like to make it something simple, like an internalized parent whom we are used to obeying. Certainly this is part of it, but it is far more than that. Ignoring this mythic/historic/psychological projection ignores reality. You know that tens of thousands of people before you have listened to thousands of similar asses and still gotten the job done. You would be letting down all those bighearted ghosts who waded in and did the job in spite of the idiots. Because of them we alter our actions. Those ghosts are as real as the hill.

A warrior must learn to recognize that this intense feeling of loyalty to the unit comes from the warrior's own psyche and nowhere else. What actually physically exists is mud, fire, mangled corpses, and anxious, frightened people. He must also learn that individuality must not be suppressed even though individual action is subordinated. One is very vulnerable when joining the unit, whether military, corporate, charitable, or governmental, voluntarily surrendering individuality to a greater ideal and feeling wonderful for it.

Eric Hoffer, in *The True Believer,* had this pegged decades ago. This surrender is intoxicating. The more history, glory, and psychological resonance the unit has, the bigger you feel. The more glorious the mission, the more glorious you feel. You don't need to join the Foreign Legion to understand what I mean. Think of it as playing for the Yankees. "The Yankees" isn't just a group of overpaid athletes on the field today. It's Babe Ruth, Joe DiMaggio, Micky Mantle, and titanic struggles with the Brooklyn Dodgers. All long gone—but yet so real.

There's a dark side to this surrender, however. You impair, and in some cases lose altogether, your ability to make sound judgments as an individual, whether in the mud of war with all these frightened kids around you or in the battle for corporate survival.* You are far more likely to engage in groupthink. You are far more likely to go along with the bad assumptions, the wrong perceptions of reality. The primary reason for this abandonment of the individual viewpoint is simply that with so much pain and grief going on, who would want to make individual judgments? This would entail taking responsibility for the pain. I certainly never wanted to feel responsible for all the death, misery, and destruction I was

---

*The primary reason you don't make sound judgments in combat is that you too often are exhausted and numbed. There is little that can be done about this except training under extreme duress to learn how to function at such times—one very strong reason why I deplore ignorant attempts by civilians and noncombat veterans to make boot camp more "humane." There is nothing humane about dead kids because someone cracked under pressure.

in fact responsible for in Vietnam. That would entail coming to terms with just exactly why I was doing what I was doing, and in my case, in Vietnam, this presented some very ugly facts.

We are generally *delighted* to be cogs.

Nor is this entirely bad. I doubt the great cathedrals of Europe would have been built if individuals hadn't given up their individuality and made the enormous sacrifices those buildings required. I also doubt that Europeans, and certainly doubt that Americans, could today do the equivalent. And this isn't all bad either.

Choosing when to surrender and when to stand alone is an art. There is no science about it and unfortunately the military isn't the greatest place to gain this sort of now-a-cog, now-not-a-cog wisdom. In fact, the military idealizes and strives to inculcate the surrender of individuality. It is equally tragic that too many of our national leaders are also the least experienced in living as individuals. The very essence of being a winning politician is to behave so that one's actions are in accord with public opinion, the unit chosen by most politicians and precisely defined by their pollsters. There is an argument that by following the polls, politicians are only doing what the people want. It is after all a democracy. Where this breaks down is when the people want something stupid.

It is precisely because we have a choice about which unit to identify with that issues of loyalty and following orders cause such difficulties. This choice was at the heart of Nuremberg. Was your unit humanity, the German state, Aryans, the Gestapo? The more narrowly defined the unit, the more often one will get into situations of conflicting loyalties and murky ethical water. The smallest unit is the individual, and we've seen the consequences of this loyalty all too often, in business, politics, and war.

To be effective and moral fighters, we must not lose our
individuality, our ability to stand alone, and yet, at the same time,
we must owe our allegiance not to ourselves alone but to an entity
so large as to be incomprehensible, namely humanity or God.
As mere mortals who can't grasp the incomprehensible, we limp
along with allegiances to various stepped-down versions of the
incomprehensible that seem to suit us, such as the Marine Corps,
the family, France, the Baptist Church, or the Order of the Eastern
Star. We must strive, however, always to see these smaller entities
as only pieces of the larger one we'll never comprehend. That
is because when the moment comes for a tough decision, we *can*
make it in light of the larger ghosts, even if we are scared to death
in the mud with all those frightened kids around us.

It was monsoon time and we patrolled in perpetual twilight. Heavy
gray clouds commingled with the trees. The jungle floor was wet
from the constant dripping, and by the time the first ten Marines
had passed it was changed into slippery and sucking mud. The
company had been operating in these conditions alone in the
mountains for weeks, constantly crossing or wading up roaring
torrents in steep canyons. We often had to rope up to negotiate cliffs. Now, because of a screwup at battalion regarding our
last possible resupply in a valley below the clouds, we had been
several days without food and, this high in the clouds, resupply
was impossible. Even more worrisome, so were medevacs and air
support. No one could find us beneath that perpetual cloudy floor.
It was as if the company had turned into a submarine, moving
dark, deep, and silent beneath the monsoon clouds.

Battalion was constantly on the radio, pushing the skipper,
who just one year earlier was president of his fraternity house at

USC, to make certain checkpoints selected from the maps that covered the bunker walls at headquarters. We weren't told what the hurry was. One checkpoint was at the top of a mountain that we battled a full day to climb. After radioing in proudly that we'd done it, we were given another checkpoint down the other side and told we were falling behind schedule. This got old.

We were already moving very slowly because of the terrain and torrential rains, but we were now getting slower because of hunger. By the third day without food I had five very sick kids on my hands, dry-heaving and vomiting bile as we pulled them up behind us, because they'd eaten bark from the wrong kind of tree. In our weakened condition we all started worrying about accidents. The normal good-humored bitching turned to serious questions. "Is someone in trouble? Why the fucking rush?" Marines, like good troops of any service, will literally die trying if it's for someone in trouble. But none of us could answer the question. It looked suspiciously like an exercise in making checkpoints on time.

Then what we had feared happened. An exhausted kid carrying a heavy mortar base plate lost his grip and fell off the ledge of a cliff. He took two others with him as he fell, never uttering a sound, the hundred-plus pounds of gear he was packing acting like some terrible silent bowling ball tearing through a line of pins strung out directly beneath him on precarious perches.

Standing with my back to the cliff on a small ledge myself, looking out across what I assumed to be a deep gorge but seeing nothing but constantly shifting fog and slashing rain, I still remember the feeling of helpless dread as I heard the corpsman's report. One kid in great pain, not responding to questions and confused and disoriented from concussion, maybe with a broken back. One with a broken ankle. A third, woozy from having his head beat around inside his helmet, was mostly just spitting mad. I remember thinking it would have been better if the kid with the broken back had died.

It turned out that his back wasn't broken. He could be moved supported by two others, but in great pain. The corpsman splinted the other one's ankle and loaded up both the injured with as much Darvon as they could take and remain conscious, and we hauled them up the cliff by rope, distributed their gear, and continued. Even if a chopper could have found us, it could not have set down without smashing its blades against the cliff. We had to find flat ground.

That night we sat in a wet steaming circle on a small hilltop covered with jungle. We were waiting for the skipper to start the daily meeting with his platoon commanders. I was shivering constantly from cold and lack of calories. I remember the steam rising from our wet clothes, and another platoon commander and the executive officer bargaining over a can of peaches, the only food left in the company, because the wiser and more experienced executive officer had refused to eat it. He still wouldn't sell it at $35, around $120 in today's money.

The skipper said quietly, "I'm thinking of disobeying the last order."

This was, well, mutiny. The bantering stopped.

We'd been ordered to another checkpoint, which, if we were to reach it when we were ordered to, meant we'd have to move at night at an impossible speed and still with the two injured Marines. The risks were tenfold we'd kill somebody falling off a cliff in the dark. We still had been given no reasons for the haste. We'd asked several times what the hurry was, only to get rude and exasperated comments, but no answers. It made sense that no one wanted to broadcast what we were about, but this could have been gotten around by encoding the message. Instead, we got uncoded messages like "Do I have to fly out there and kick your butts for you?" Leadership at its best.

Much later, I was able to piece together some idea of what was going on. Like most situations, it was part circumstance and part human failure, in this case arrogance, ignorance, and very likely alcoholism. We launched on this particular nightmare to follow up on a fight between another company and an unknown-sized force of NVA. That company had uncovered an ammunition dump but had run short of ammunition in the firefight to capture it and, more important, had also run out of explosives with which to blow the dump.* They had to be pulled out, since they were out of food and exhausted and too high in the monsoon-shrouded mountains for resupply. Our company had to be dropped at a low enough altitude to get under the cloud cover and then climb up to them. They were to walk out to the same place we inserted to get lifted out.

We met them just outside the landing zone. They were pasty with waterlogged skin, gray with exhaustion, carrying their dead slung on bamboo poles, hanging from tied wrists and ankles like slain animals. Their wounded they carried on their backs. We offered them some of our own food supply. Semper fi. They took some for the wounded and some cigarettes to fight the cold and gloom, but no more, knowing we'd need the food more than they and that they would soon be getting out. Semper fi back. The ghosts of acts of kindness like these haunt all fighting units.

---

*People have this idea that you just touch a match to an ammo dump and it goes off. Actually, very little powder is exposed. It's all encased in metal. Shells, bullets, and rockets all take a lot of explosives to get cooking. Once they do, *then* you have the popular image of an ammo dump going off, which is, indeed, spectacular.

A second company had been lifted from a fire support base to follow in our trace in such a hurry that they did so with insufficient rations for an operation. We were ordered to leave half of our rations for them in a cache.

After two days of slogging we had run short of food. But no one was worried; in fact, our spirits were pretty good. We had had only one small skirmish with nobody injured, we had reached the ammo dump and blown it sky high to the great amusement of everyone, and we knew that we'd be down and lifted out by the next day or so. We had actually started back down toward the landing zone when an order came asking us to stop and wait for further orders. We waited half a day, the bitching starting to mount. Being hungry just naturally increases irritability. Unknown to us, someone in Da Nang or Saigon was putting the final touches on a plan that called for the opening of a new firebase on top of a certain mountain located in the area.

Now, "in the area" is relative. To someone in Da Nang or Saigon, with large-scale maps, one fingerwidth covers a lot of ground, and our company was only a few fingerwidths from the objective, practically next door. For us in the jungle with smaller-scale maps we were *sixteen* fingerwidths, as the crow flies. And we weren't crows. In one day, humping from dawn to dark, we made about two and a half fingerwidths. It is impossible to convey to a staff officer who has never had to watch his hands blister away from having to hack his way through thick jungle with a machete just how slowly you move. Most North Americans have seen wild blackberry patches that stand well above head height. They would consider it madness to try to enter one of these. This is the kind of thick I mean by thick jungle. Add to this the fact that every chop sends a precise signal of where you are and, by the way, you're working uphill at about a forty-five-degree angle. Oh, and you haven't eaten for two days.

The radios burned with questions about our progress. Artillery batteries, helicopters, supply depots, and all sorts of other units were all being held up because our company didn't take that designated hill and open up a landing zone as promised. Careers get hurt over things like this.

We tried for a long time to assume that there was a good reason for this mad rush. But after a few days we became convinced that it had nothing to do with Marines' lives. This is a crucial element. Other lives are worth risking your own life for. Generals' timetables that don't have lives at stake are not. They were certainly not worth it in that environment where no hill was important and no battle critical other than for a body count. The unit with which we identified began to change. Loyalty started to wobble.

George Patton once said, "There has been a great deal of talk about loyalty from bottom to top. Loyalty from the top to the bottom is much more important, and also much less prevalent. It is this loyalty from the top to the bottom which binds juniors to their seniors with the strength of steel."* This reverse loyalty was clearly absent.

In the bush we rarely saw officers over the age of twenty-five. If we did see older officers, it was when *we* went to a rear area. Even then, we didn't talk with any of them. This was in part a result of the particular kind of widely dispersed company-sized warfare that was being conducted. It was also because there were too many career officers, with no combat experience, who knew

*Charles M. Province, *The Unknown Patton*, 1984.

that their bread was buttered by those above them and not below them, and who simply didn't give a shit.

In addition to the breakdown in downward loyalty there had been another change. It had become clear to us that the mission was no longer a matter of life and death for someone else. This went a long way toward making it no longer a matter of life and death for us. In the absence of incredible coercion, Clausewitz's often misunderstood dictum that war is diplomacy by other means simply won't work. Troops won't fight for oil. Troops will fight to stop murder and torture of other human beings and to stop terror-ism and threats of mass destruction to their people. "Diplomacy by other means" is going to have to line up with nineteen-year-old psychology or it will fail. This is not at all bad.

When the basic psychology of the warrior—to feel oneself to be the protector of lives in one's relevant unit—has been violated, as it was in our particular case that winter in the mountains along the Laotian border, the only way to get it right again, to get feeling lined up with one's gut instincts, is for unit loyalty to shift. In this case it shifted downward. This seems to be the easiest solution. It sort of works with gravity.

The skipper presented us with three options. He could do what he was told and risk losing lives stumbling off a cliff in the dark; he could directly oppose the orders as stupid and endanger-ing his troops; or he could "lose comm," blaming low radio bat-teries, and simply not respond to any more orders. He would be suspected of doing this on purpose, but it could never be proved, so he would probably face only losing the esteem of the battalion commander, an eventual transfer, and a career-damaging fitness report.

We all decided to lose communications. The skipper did, indeed, pay the price, just as described. For the skipper it was a sacrifice of the self for the unit. I bless him to this day. For the rest of us, there wasn't much sacrifice.

Another interesting aspect of loyalty, perhaps an atavistic one, had become clear: loyalty to the leader. We had all decided to throw in our lot with the skipper. I, for one, would have supported him no matter which option he decided on. If the unit's integrity or safety is at stake, then you will do what the unit needs to do to save itself. My unit had become the company, not any greater entity like the Marine Corps or the nation, because my basic psychology had been violated. There were no lives of others at stake, and no downward loyalty toward us was being exhibited. The skipper had now taken on, in some deeply symbolic way, the representation of this entity to which I was now loyal.

This shifting of loyalties between different groups is a psychological phenomenon that warriors need to recognize, not because it is inevitable and explains behavior under stress but to help them choose consciously when placed in circumstances where loyalty is tested. I have no trouble defending my choice to go along with losing communications instead of either obeying the orders or refusing openly and accepting the personal consequences. I point out, however, that this decision was at variance with that extreme formalization of loyalty inculcated in Bushido, the samurai code of conduct that values honor and loyalty above life. Bushido is loyalty's most severe philosophical exposition and elements of it exist in all military traditions. No military person can come to terms with loyalty until he or she comes to terms with Bushido, both its light side and its dark side.

Inazo Nitobe relates a classic illustration of the code of Bushido in his retelling of the story of Michizane's retainer.*

---

*Inazo Nitobe, *Bushido: The Soul of Japan*, 1969.

Michizane, a samurai lord, loses power through various machinations of his enemies and is exiled from the capital. These same enemies then seek to wipe out Michizane's entire family. They learn through their spies that Michizane's young son has been secretly hidden in a village school run by a teacher named Genzo, a former vassal of Michizane.

The game is up. Genzo, on pain of death, is ordered to present the head of the son. Genzo seeks desperately for a substitute, but none of the village children have the young son's features. He is in despair. Just before the execution is to take place, however, a woman arrives with her son to place him in the school. Her son is just the same age and of remarkable resemblance to the young son of Michizane. Genzo suggests the idea of a substitution. The mother and son never give a hint that both had already, in the words of Nitobe, "laid themselves upon the altar; the one his life—the other her heart." The mother leaves the boy to his fate. Genzo kills the child and nervously presents the head to the samurai inspector at the appointed time, his own hand on his sword, ready to fight or kill himself if the inspector isn't fooled.

The inspector, himself the son of a former retainer of Michizane but now through circumstances a retainer of the new lord, looks carefully and long at the head and then announces in a businesslike tone that it is indeed Michizane's son and leaves with it, to present to his new master.

That evening the mother waits for her husband to return. When the door opens the husband announces, "Rejoice, my wife, our darling son has proved of service to his lord!" The inspector was the dead boy's father.

One can grasp this tale only if one understands the basic philosophy of Bushido. The inspector's own father had long been in the service of Michizane and had received much from this lord. The inspector himself, because of Bushido, would never be untrue to his own cruel master, but the inspector's son could still be true to the cause of the inspector's father's lord, Michizane. Mother, father, and son, together, had all agreed upon the plan.

The heart of Bushido is that loyalty is more important than life, yours or your child's. A follower of Bushido would immediately sacrifice his life to avoid betraying his master or his own conscience. This looks crazy to most Americans, but that is because we value individuals above the group or society. The Japanese, certainly back then, did not. The fundamental essence of Bushido does, however, remain true. Loyalty should always be to the higher cause.

Again Nitobe, in *Bushido*, writes, "Bushido did not require us to make our conscience the slave of any lord or king ... When a subject differed from his master, the loyal path for him to pursue was to use every available means to persuade him of his error, as Kent did to King Lear. Failing in this, let the master deal with him as he wills. In cases of this kind, it was quite a usual course for the samurai to make the last appeal to the intelligence and conscience of his lord by demonstrating the sincerity of his words with the shedding of his own blood."

The Japanese don't have a monopoly on this positive aspect of Bushido. Erwin Rommel and his fellow conspirators in the attempted assassination of Hitler and those Iraqi officers who were executed for opposing Saddam Hussein's plan to invade Kuwait all understood well the value of and the price of placing conscience first when it was in conflict with loyalty. But men like these are rare. Back there in the jungle I didn't have the wisdom or maturity to make such a choice consciously, and I was able to do so without personal sacrifice because the skipper took it all upon himself.

Upon reflection, I would have made the same choice, but I also would have had to choose to hang with the skipper should he be court-martialed. I simply didn't think about that. In combat, one should be very suspicious of painless moral choices. When you are confronted with a seemingly painless moral choice, the odds are that you haven't looked deeply enough.

8

HEROISM

The heroic journey can be taken consciously or unconsciously. There's a time in one's life when the unconscious heroic journey is understandable, when one is young and in positions of little authority. The young warriors of the future will still largely perform their heroic tasks unconsciously. It is a part of development, eventually to be outgrown. As warriors grow older, however, and move into positions of power and authority, far more is at stake because their actions affect a far wider field. Because there is more to lose, they will have to perform their heroic acts with full consciousness of the often painful consequences for everyone, including themselves. Many heroic acts of this kind will go unnoticed by society—if not actively denigrated. There will be no medals. This makes such acts far more difficult to do, and therefore even more heroic.

A wise man once said to be careful of what you wish for, because you may get it. I wanted to be a hero.

Our company had been pulled out of the bush to act as a reaction force. On the one hand it meant a rest. We got to be in tents set up next to a small airfield in the center of a narrow valley about 20 kilometers east of Khe Sanh. There were showers heated by diesel fuel, hot food, and a portable electricity generator so that in the evenings we could sit outside, rain or mist, and see a movie. Then there was the other hand. We were in combat readiness at all times, waiting. We sat there, most of the lower ranks unfairly having to fill sandbags, all of us whittling, writing letters, bullshitting, but always listening in on the battalion and regimental nets, trying to determine which firefight was going to turn into the mess that would send in the Marines.

So whether in the outdoor shower or at the movie watching Clint Eastwood, we were constantly aware that within minutes we could be running for our rifles and packs, the skipper shouting for the platoon commanders, maps out, hearts racing, while the thumping of rotor blades echoed off the green walls of the valley as the choppers peeled off one by one to take us to where some of us surely were going to die.

I remember that particular dying day. The soft gray of the sky was slowly going dull as the sun began its afternoon slide into Laos. I watched two squads, who'd been filling sandbags for some one-star general at a place called Task Force Hotel, run full bore the long half mile to their gear, which waited neatly stacked by the runway. Marines were in trouble. Semper fi.

I remember the stomach-turning lurch of the chopper as it came out of a deep spiral just north of the Rock Pile, about 10 kilometers south of the DMZ. I was trying to get my bearings on the revolving hilltops and rivers, my map out, my hands trembling. My neck snapped backward, whipping my helmet against the bulkhead, as the chopper jolted into the ground. I remember the crew chief screaming at us to get out of the chopper because we were taking fire standing in the landing zone. Several kids on the helo team had to jump for it because the pilot lost his nerve and gunned the chopper out of the zone too soon. The last one dropped around ten feet with ninety pounds on his back. He broke his leg. We temporarily lost his squad because they had to stay on the LZ to protect him, weakening the company, and then another chopper crew had to risk their lives to get him out. Combat magnifies small acts terribly.

The shooting was all over before I knew what was going on.

A company from another battalion had been in a fight somewhere to our east with an NVA unit of unknown size but big enough to cause some heartburn when they started chewing on each other. We were launched to take the NVA unit from behind, simultaneously blocking their exit in this narrow valley. They'd taken us under fire as we came in, but, seeing they would soon be between the hammer and the anvil, they had quickly disengaged. Now they were moving toward an ominous-looking ridgeline that stretched across our northern horizon, dark and gray-green in the somber light, sheathed in clouds and fog.

Through our field glasses, whenever the swirling fog would thin a little, we could see movement and fresh diggings of a sizable unit already on top. And now reinforcements were climbing to join them. The order came to exploit the situation. The other company and our company would assault at first light. To do this meant we had to sneak up on them that night. We stripped down to essentials, leaving our gear in a neat pile on the jungle floor, and started climbing at around 0130 that night.

In war you need to be lucky. Be at war long enough and you'll have some bad days. Just before dawn, about 500 meters from the NVA position, we started running into booby traps, trip wires leading to mines lashed in the trees at chest level. Our point men were terrified. We rotated them every five minutes, pushed ahead. Then we stumbled into a listening post and a brief firefight erupted. So much for surprise.

The other company, working up another finger to our right, took a couple of nasty hits. I heard someone screaming after the dull crump of an explosion. The screaming went on for a full minute, a lone voice, piercing through the fog and jungle from a couple of kilometers away from us until abruptly cut off. I found out later it was a friend of mine from the Basic School. I was told that his lower jaw, his entire face, and a leg had been blown off by a DH-10 directional mine, normally used against tanks. His platoon sergeant had run up to see what the screaming was all about and had cut it off by placing his hand against the hole where the voice box was still intact. Eventually, I understand, he pinched off the carotid artery and my friend died, still fully aware.

The other company commander lost his nerve and stopped. It happens, even in the Marine Corps. Our company made the assault alone.

The next day we took a second hill just to our west but couldn't hold both for lack of Marines. We regrouped on the first hill and were assaulted that night by NVA sappers and ground troops. Another friend who'd gone with me through PLC* was in the company that stopped. He took his platoon, on his own authority, and worked his way up to join us. He reached us when we were much in need defending the hill against counterattacks. The greater part of our ammunition had been spent in the assault and we were now two full nights without sleep. I remember him and his platoon sergeant making the rounds of the holes under fire just after they'd arrived, eager to make amends for not joining the assault, eager to prove themselves always faithful—which they did.

Instead of going with them to help familiarize them with the perimeter, I just watched, telling myself that I'd already risked my neck enough. I'm still ashamed of it.

*Platoon Leaders Class, a U.S. Marines officer candidate school.

In the midst of all this chaos and carnage, cowardice and honor, I won my first medal, a Bronze Star. It was during the initial assault. The platoon commander who replaced me when I was moved up to XO was green. He had been in only one real fight, not counting the hot landing. I couldn't stand to have my old platoon make the assault without me. My actual post, as number two, was with the command group on a small knoll just down the ridgeline from the hill we were assaulting. My job was to help the skipper direct the artillery and the supporting fire from the weapons platoon and be there to take over if he got killed or wounded. I couldn't stand it. I told the skipper I was joining the assault and didn't wait to hear an answer.

The small knoll and the larger hill where the NVA were dug in were connected by a blasted barren neck, the top of the ridge. I ran alone down this neck between the command post and the assaulting Marines. The assault group was already at the FLD* draped across the ridgeline, one end of the string hanging down the south slope and the other end hanging down the north slope. I knew that one very critical tactical task would be to keep the assault together, as the tendency is for the squads to slide down their respective sides of the ridge, opening a gap in the assault and weakening the force to be applied against the NVA bunkers. In any assault the defenders are usually considered to have at least a three-to-one advantage, mainly because they are dug in and have prepared defensive fires on all the easy ways up. *Up* is the other operative word. Assaulting a hill slows and exhausts the attackers enormously, making them very vulnerable to fire.

---

*The final line of departure, the preplanned line on the ground that is the last stop before committing everything to the assault and the control point for managing artillery, naval gunfire, and air support just prior to the assault.

To succeed, an assault depends on all-out fury focused at the smallest possible point.

Artillery shells were piling into the hill above us. Pieces of nearly spent shrapnel were falling beside me as I ran toward the FLD. While I was running toward my old platoon and the coming assault, I felt an overwhelming sense of excitement, almost joy. I was rejoining *my* unit. I was nearly crazy with adrenaline. The screaming and earth-shattering artillery rounds filled the air around me with vibrant shaking noise that I felt pounding right up through the soles of my jungle boots and smashing into my face and ears from the shivering air. I've jumped out of airplanes, climbed up cliff sides, raced cars, done drugs. I've never found anything comparable. Combat is the crack cocaine of all excitement highs—with crack cocaine costs.

The artillery stopped, smoke grenades were popped, and we stood up and walked up the hill in an eerie silence, waiting for the first bullets. Then, all across our front, unseen machine guns and small arms opened up. Bullets cracked past our ears, kicked dirt, and killed. We surged forward. Everything was blood in the throat, shouting, running, furious thinking, noise, and chaos.

I kept screaming at the troops to try to keep the gap from opening. They responded admirably. We hit the slope of the hill as one. Then began the extremely hard job of climbing it under fire. The new platoon commander immediately had his hands full trying to force through, or around, a concentration of bunkers and holes on our right flank, about midway up the hillside. I went tearing around a small bump of dirt to the left of where the ridgeline joined the steeper hill, working my way sideways on the hillside, trying to link two squads that had drifted apart while at the same time spreading people to our left trying to keep them from bunching up.* There I saw Utter, a tall awkward kid of eighteen, leaning with his back against the steep hill, frantically trying to clear his M-16. I remember his Adam's apple pumping up and down. He was near panic.

I threw myself against the hillside, so steep here that both of us were actually standing, leaning our backs against it, looking out over the valley below us. Bullets, exceeding the sound barrier, made loud sonic snaps over our heads, but we were safe in this little cup that protected us. Utter's magazine hadn't been properly seated, causing the bolt to hang up on its forward edge, a common problem with the M-16. I cleared it for him, fired a short burst, and handed the rifle back to him. I asked him where his squad leader was. He didn't know exactly. Over there someplace.

I looked up over the lip of the cup and could see that the brush had been carefully cleared away from the ground up to about knee level. By this time I'd been around long enough to know this meant a machine-gun emplacement. They'd shoot the legs first. When the attacker fell, the bullets would finish him off as the body fell through the kill zone.

I grabbed Utter by the shirt and forced his head above the lip to show him the trap, shouting at him not to go up that way, to try to find some way around. He stared at the cut brush. I yanked him down and then told him to stay put. I'd find his squad leader and we'd get a team together and get the gun by flanking it from the left side. Don't go up there. He nodded, still dazed with fear. I made him shoot a couple of rounds. He nodded; he was all right.

---

*Controlling an assault—and the word *control* is used loosely—treads a fine line between not having any gaps, which weakens the attack, and not bunching up, which makes it too easy for the defense to kill you.

I took off to organize an attack on the machine gun. As I left the protection of the cup I saw Utter take off, straight up the hill. I'll never know why. Perhaps he too wanted to be a hero. Maybe he just wanted to show me he was a good Marine.

My former platoon sergeant, Staff Sergeant Bell, came running around from the opposite side. His radioman, Lance Corporal Putnam, piled into the hillside right after him. Bell, a terrific platoon sergeant, was doing the same thing I was, trying to get the two squads back together, but from the other direction. So the gap was getting closed.

I shouted at him, "Utter's just gone up the hill toward that machine gun. Where in hell's Second Squad?"

He just pointed over his shoulder and leaned his back against the side of the hill, his chest heaving. I saw movement in the brush and heard the sound of an M-16, so knew that Bell and the second squad leader had closed the gap.

Then we all heard the enemy machine gun open up. You can definitely tell this machine gun by its heavy popping sound, methodical and hammerlike, unlike the heavy slapping sound of the AK-47 or the tense, high-pitched scream of our own M-16s.

I heard Utter cry out, "I'm hit."

The machine gun kept firing.

I looked at Bell and he looked at me. He shook his head, lips pressed tight. I finally said, "I don't have anything else to do. I'll go get him."

Bell looked directly at me and said, "Don't go up there, Lieutenant."

I was split three ways. I'd known Utter for months. He was my guy, even though I'd just been replaced. He was hit. I simply wanted to get him before he bled to death. Another part of me was screaming to listen to Bell and stay safe. Then there was the third part. I wanted a medal.

I'd always wanted a medal, ever since I looked at my father's medals from World War II, ever since I'd seen Audie Murphy in *To Hell and Back*, ever since I was never chosen first when we chose up sides. All that. It wasn't enough to do heroic things. I had to be recognized for it. That meant putting the ribbon on my chest so that when I went home other Marines would know not only that I'd been there but that I'd done something extraordinary. I would be extra ordinary. I'd be special among a special group.

I have heard Napoleon quoted to the effect that an army runs on its stomach and ribbons. This man understood the desire to feel special and how it motivates. This man, who could have been the savior of the French revolution and all its ideals, as much revered as George Washington, also blew it by making himself emperor. He too wanted to be special.

When I first got back from Vietnam I hadn't yet received any medals except my two Purple Hearts and Combat Action Ribbon,* paperwork being paperwork. I felt proud. They showed that I'd been there, that I was one of the group. But while I was at the Pentagon the paperwork started catching up with me and it seemed as if every few weeks I was in front of some general getting another medal. It became a sort of office joke. And I, Mr. Hotshot, got more and more special.

Wanting to be a society-certified hero is a specialness issue. I see people killing themselves at work and at home to pay for

---

*The Purple Heart is a medal given for wounds received in combat. The Combat Action Ribbon is awarded to people who have experienced combat, although this is a tougher one to judge on the surface. A person could be at an air base, where one rocket hit the base half a mile from the person, and still be awarded a CAR the same as an infantryman who spent months fighting in the jungle.

mortgages that are too much for them, or taking vacations they can't afford in the right spots, all to be special. Wanting a medal in war is just killing yourself at a faster pace, for all the same wrong reasons.

With every ribbon that I added to my chest I could be more special than someone who didn't have it. Even better, I quickly learned that most people who outranked me, who couldn't top my rows of ribbons, didn't feel right chewing me out for minor infractions.* I pushed this to the limit. I read the regulations on hair. I grew mine to the absolute limit allowed, getting it cut weekly to keep it there on the margin of acceptability. I found out mustaches were permitted. I grew a scraggly little thing that made me look like a corn-fed Ho Chi Minh.

It all came to an abrupt halt when a major from another department with whom I occasionally had to work asked me into his office. He had nowhere near my rows of medals, but he had been in Vietnam. I remember him sitting on his desk, looking out of the window while I stood there, quite at ease. Then he turned to me and said, "Marlantes, I don't give a fuck how many medals you've got on your chest. You look like shit. You're a fucking disgrace to your uniform and it's a uniform I'm proud of. Now get out of here and clean up your goddamned act."

I can't remember the man's name. If I could, I'd thank him personally. He called my shit.

I walked away feeling terrible. Too many of my friends had died wearing a Marine uniform. I cleaned up my act. It also started me thinking about why I was behaving so badly.

---

*Medals have a hierarchy. In the Marine Corps the order of medals for valor in combat, from top to bottom, is Congressional Medal of Honor, Navy Cross, Distinguished Flying Cross, Silver Star, Bronze Star, Single Mission Air Medal, Navy Commendation Medal. Once you're in the service, you can read a person's ribbons and quickly know where you fall in the hierarchy.

We all want to be special, to stand out; there's nothing wrong with this. The irony is that every human being is special to start with, because we're unique to start with. But we then go through some sort of boot camp from the age of zero to about eighteen where we learn everything we can about how not to be unique. This spawns an unconscious desire to prove yourself special, but now it's special in the eyes of your peers and it comes out in the form of being better than or having power over someone else. In the military I could exercise the power of being automatically respected because of the medals on my chest, not because I had done anything right at the moment to earn that respect. This is pretty nice. It's also a psychological trap that can stop one's growth and allow one to get away with just plain bad behavior.

To a large extent my behavior could be explained as a result of experiencing the dreadful time of return that so many Vietnam veterans experienced. I desperately wanted to be accepted by my other peer group, college-age kids in civilian society. So to prove my loyalty to the college kid crowd and try to gain their respect and admiration by being the "war-protesting rebel Marine" I started to put down military values such as pride in one's uniform. Some protest.

Looking even deeper, I realize now that I also had very mixed feelings about some of the medals on my chest. I knew many Marines had done brave deeds that no one saw and for which they got no medals at all. I was having a very hard time carrying those medals and didn't have the insight or maturity to know what to do with my combination of guilt and pride. So I attacked my image. Some solution.

The truth is there were important aspects about the medals that weren't in the write-ups. That day on the assault I felt like someone in a movie. I remember thinking, "This is like a movie. I'm the hero, and the dumb kid has just gotten in trouble with the enemy machine gun, and now the hero will go rescue him." The movies are America's mythological matrix. I also remember thinking, "This is your chance. You throw this one away and you'll never get your medal."

I turned to Bell and made a wise-guy sort of joke out of it. I was aware that I was talking as if I were reading a script. I had become a character, come out of myself somehow. "Is it worth a medal if I go get him? You write me up for one?" I laughed to make sure he knew I was joking.

"Don't go. You'll get killed," was all he said. Bell, around age twenty-seven, with a couple of kids at home, was far more mature than me.

"He's going to die if someone doesn't go get him," I said. I actually think I was bargaining with Bell. I'll go get him *if* I can get a medal.

If Bell hadn't said what he did say I'd probably still have gone because I'd already been taken over by this inner (or maybe outer) force. But he said, "I'll write you up, but you'll be fucking dead."

That was all the hero needed. You see, heroes don't die. They're immortal. They return from the land of the dead and bring back the boon.

The land of the dead was that thin zone of cleared brush, just over a foot high, through which the bullets were tearing with a methodical deadly intensity. The boon to bring back was Utter. I was going. There was no stopping me.

I told Bell to pass the word for Doc Southern and seated a fresh magazine in my rifle. "I'll be firing as I go up. You and Putnam try and keep the gunners' heads down."

Bell shouted at the fire team to our immediate left, telling them I was going after Utter and not to shoot my ass and help try to force the gunners down with rifle fire. Putnam was shouting, "Corpsman! Corpsman!"

I threw myself up over the protecting lip of the hillside, rolled quickly sideways, and opened up on full automatic, straight up the cleared zone. I crawled on my elbows and knees as fast as I could, firing my rifle with one hand, trying desperately to keep the heads of the NVA machine gunners down while I moved up toward Utter, not knowing where he was, just going by the fix I'd gotten when he'd cried out.

I found him staring up at the sky, feet uphill toward the machine gun, head toward me, rifle flung back downhill.

I tried to tug him back down, actually sheltering behind his body. The machine gun had opened up and the bullets were impacting all around me. I couldn't drag him: too much friction.

I turned him sideways to the hill and flung myself forward on top of him. I wrapped my arms and legs around him and our rifles and started rolling with him, embracing him as the machine-gun bullets went slamming into the dirt all around us. Me on top. Utter on top. Over and over, down the hill together, me on top, Utter on top, bullets thudding into the wet clay around us, sounding like someone clapping his hands next to my ears as they passed overhead.

I remember desperately hoping that if the bullets hit us Utter would be on top when they did. This was the same part of me that had wanted to stay with Bell in the first place. Now that the deed was nearly over, the hero in me was departing, and the other parts of me were coming back to the fore.

We reached the steep lip and thudded to the ground. Doc Southern was just arriving. Bell and Putnam took off. They had other jobs to do. I covered for Doc Southern as he bent over Utter, giving him mouth-to-mouth resuscitation. Utter was spitting up vomit and blood and Southern kept spitting it out of his mouth and onto the ground next to Utter, sometimes right on Utter's shirt. He kept pushing and pounding Utter's chest, now sticky with vomit and blood, trying to keep his heart going. He'd suck in a lungful of air while doing this and press his mouth to Utter's over and over again.

Suddenly he looked up at me and sighed, slowly shaking his head back and forth. He cradled Utter's head in one hand and pulling back bloody matted hair exposed a neat hole in the top of Utter's skull. "I just saw this, sir. He ain't going to make it." He laid Utter's head on the wet red clay and scrambled off to attend the constant chorus of "Corpsman! Corpsman!"

One night, alone on watch, I began to think. How could Utter have cried out "I'm hit" with a bullet in his brain? The bullet must have gone in after he'd cried out. He had been lying head down toward me. The bullet went into the top of his head. I could have put it there myself when I was trying to keep the machine-gun fire down as I crawled up to get him. I'll never know.

The best words I've ever heard on the subject of medals come from a fellow lieutenant who'd been my company XO when I first arrived in Vietnam. The company came under mortar attack. Tom, then a platoon commander, had found a relatively safe defensive position for himself, but he stood up, exposed to the exploding shells, in order to get a compass bearing on where the shells were being fired from. He then called in and adjusted counterbattery fire, which got the company out of the shit. He was awarded the Bronze Star. When I heard the news and congratulated him, he said, "A lot of people have done a lot more and gotten a lot less, and a lot of people have done a lot less and gotten a lot more."

Medals are all mixed up with hierarchy, politics, and even job descriptions. What is considered normal activity for a grunt, and therefore not worthy of a medal, is likely to be viewed as extraordinary for someone who does the same thing but isn't a grunt, so he gets a medal and maybe an article in *Stars and Stripes.* Your common garden-variety grunt is only doing his job, and is usually someplace too dangerous to be interviewed by a reporter anyway. Rank counts for the same reasons. Major Smith grabs a grenade and overruns a bunker and it's at least good for a Bronze Star. If Lance Corporal Smithers does it, it's likely to go unnoticed, because Smithers did it yesterday and two weeks earlier as well. If the colonel and his favorite haven't gotten quite enough stuff on their record to ensure their next promotion, well, remember that night when they had to leave the Combat Operations Center to piss because they'd had too much beer and the north end of the perimeter had a rocket come in? Well, that certainly showed bravery under fire . . . It was ever thus.

I got my medals, in part, because I did brave acts, but also, in part, because the kids liked me and they spent time writing better eyewitness accounts than they would have written if they hadn't liked me. Had I been an unpopular officer and done exactly the same thing, few would have bothered, if any. The accounts would have been laconic, at best, and the medals probably of a lower order. The only people who will ever know the value of the ribbons on their chests are the people wearing them—and even they can fool themselves, in both directions.

After the experience with Utter I was no longer so anxious to get a medal of any kind. But the same phenomenon of being taken over by something, or someone, still seemed to operate. What is extraordinarily hard for me to comprehend is that I won my next medal during the same assault where I lost myself to the bloodlust and lost my radioman Isle.

We had moved up in the dark and waited in the jungle, strung out on line as the jets roared in to bomb the enemy defenses at first light. But because of a screwup the jets dropped their bombs on the wrong hill. I screamed bloody murder over the battalion FAC* net but was told I was out of line and to get off because I couldn't possibly see what was going on.

Going up against bunkers is hard enough, but doing it without any air prep was decidedly unnerving. A huge value of the air prep is the boost to the morale of the attacking infantry. We came out of the jungle onto the exposed earth below the bunkers and were instantly under fire from the untouched machine-gun positions. Everyone dived for logs and holes. The whole assault ground to a halt, except for one kid named Niemi, who had sprinted forward when we came under the intense fire and disappeared up in front of us somewhere. We figured he was down and dead.

I actually don't know how long we all lay there getting pulverized out in the open like that. I knew it would be only a few minutes before the NVA rockets and mortars found us.

Again, I seemed to step aside. I remember surveying the whole scene from someplace in the air above it. I saw the napalm smoke burning uselessly on the wrong hill. The machine guns had us pinned down with well-planned interlocking fire. The NVA were pros. Everyone was strung out in a ragged line hiding behind downed trees and in shell holes, even me, tiny and small, huddled down there below me with the rest. I distinctly remember recalling the words of an instructor at the Basic School, a particularly colorful and popular redheaded major who taught tactics, talking to a group of us about when it was a platoon leader earned his pay.

*Forward Air Control.

I knew, floating above that mess, that now that time had come. If I didn't get up and lead, we'd get wiped.

I reentered my body as the hero platoon leader, leaving the rest of everyday me up there in the clouds. It was at this point I started screaming at the wounded machine gunner to crawl up to my log and start that machine-gun duel, which would keep the crew of one of the interlocking machine guns busy. I then got an M-79 man to move up next to me and had him start lobbing shells at the observation slit of an adjacent bunker that was also giving us fits, directly up the hill from us. Then I stood up.

I did a lot of things that day, many of which got written into the commendation, but the one I'm most proud of is that I simply stood up, in the middle of all that flying metal, and started up the hill all by myself.

I'm proud of that act because I did it for the right reasons. I once watched a televised exchange on the hero's journey between Bill Moyers and Joseph Campbell. The camera had cut to a boot camp scene with Campbell saying, "There are some heroic journeys into which you are thrown and pitched." The camera then cut to scenes from Vietnam, helicopters, a young black man limping forward in agony. Then, it cut to war protesters, and Moyers then asked Campbell, "Doesn't heroism have a moral objective?"

Campbell replied, "The moral objective is that of saving a people, or person, or idea. He is sacrificing himself for something. That is the morality of it. Now, you, from another position, might say that 'something' wasn't worth it, or was downright wrong. That's a judgment from another side. But it doesn't destroy the heroism of what was done. Absolutely not."

I was no more heroic this time than when I went after Utter. Both times I faced a lot of fire. In fact, both times my actions were an effort to save a person, Utter, or a people, my little tribe exposed and dying on that scourged hillside. But my motives had changed. And because my motives had changed, I feel a lot better about what I did.

I made no heroic gestures or wisecracks this time. I simply ran forward up the steep hill, zigzagging for the bunker, all by myself, hoping the M-79 man wouldn't hit me in the back. It's hard to zigzag while running uphill loaded down with ammunition and grenades. Every bit of my consciousness was focused on just two things, the bunker above me and whether I could keep running and zigzagging with everything I had. Another 400-meter sprint with Death. A long desperate weekend. A time out of time.

I was running in a long arc to get between the machine-gun bunker and the one I was heading for, and to avoid the M-79 shells now exploding against the observation slit, which I hoped were blinding the occupants. As I made that arc I was turned sideways to the hill and I caught movement in my peripheral vision. I hit the deck turning and rolling, coming up in a position to fire. It was a Marine! He was about 15 meters below me, zigzagging, falling, up and running again. Immediately behind him a long ragged line of Marines came moving and weaving up the hill behind me. Behind the line were spots of crumpled bodies, lying where they'd been hit.

They'd all come with me. I was actually alone only for a matter of seconds.*

We took the bunker, and the next, and together with Second Platoon joining up with us on our right flank broke through the first line of bunkers, only to come under fire from a second,

---

*The official commendation makes it sound as if I took a bunch of bunkers all alone. I did lead the charge, but I often remind people that none of those kids who wrote the eyewitness accounts could have done so if they hadn't been right there with me.

interior line of fighting holes higher on the hill. At this point I
saw the missing kid, Niemi, pop his head up. He sprinted across
the open top of the hill, all alone. The NVA turned in their positions to fire on him. I watched him climb on top of a bunker and
chuck two grenades inside. When they went off I saw him fall
to the ground. I assumed that this time he'd been killed for sure.

Being hit from behind by Niemi both unnerved the NVA and
encouraged us to hurry to reach him. All semblance of platoon
and squad order were gone by now. Everyone was intermingled,
weaving, rushing and covering, taking on each hole and bunker
one at a time in individual groups.

It was just about that time I got knocked out and blinded by
a hand grenade. I came to, groggy. I could hear my radioman, who
seemed very far away, telling the skipper I was down and that he
didn't know if I was dead or not. I grunted something to let him
know I wasn't dead and tried to sit up, but then went back down. I
felt as though I couldn't get my breath. Then I panicked, because I
knew I'd been hit in the eyes. I started rubbing them, desperate to
get them open, but they seemed glued shut. My radioman poured
Kool-Aid from his canteen onto my face and into my eyes, and
I managed to get one eye to clear. The other eye was a bloody
dirt-clogged mess and I thought I'd lost it.*

We kept scrambling for the top, trying to reach Niemi, trying
to win, trying to get it all over with. I got held up by two enemy
soldiers in a hole and was attempting to get a shot or two off at
them and quickly ducking back down when a kid I knew from
Second Platoon, mainly because of his bad reputation, threw

---

*I stayed with the company until we were relieved, I must say feeling very sorry for
myself. Luckily, the blindness was temporary. The surgeon on the hospital ship, the
Repose, later told me that several metal slivers were just microns from the optic nerve.

himself down beside me, half his clothes blown away. He was begging people for a rifle. His had been blown out of his hands.

He was a black kid, all tangled up in black power politics, almost always angry and sullen. A troublemaker. Yet here he was, most of his body naked with only flapping rags left of his jungle utilities, begging for a rifle when he had a perfect excuse to just bury his head in the clay and quit. I gave him mine. I still had a pistol. He grabbed the rifle, stood up to his full height, fully exposing himself to all the fire, and simply blasted an entire magazine at the two soldiers in front of us, killing both of them. He then went charging into the fight, leaving me stunned for a moment.

Why? Who was he doing this for? What is this thing in young men? We were beyond ourselves, beyond politics, beyond good and evil. This was transcendence.

Many of us had by now worked our way almost to the top of the hill. Fighting was no longer them above and us below. Marines and NVA intermingled. Crashing out of the clouds into this confusion came a flaming, smoking twin-rotor CH-46 helicopter. It was making a much needed ammunition run to the company waiting in reserve and firing support for us from the hill we'd taken several days before. We think that the bird got hit by a mortar round as it was coming in and, in the confusion and scudding cloud cover, the pilot picked the wrong hill or he did it because he had no choice. The result was the same. Down it came, right where we were assaulting, and the NVA just tore that bird to pieces. Spinning out of control, it smashed right on the very top of the hill, breaking its rotor blades.

I saw Niemi pop into sight again. He sprinted to the downed chopper. Later we found out he'd spent his time crawling behind holes and bunkers, shooting people from behind. He'd watched aghast as the chopper came screaming out of the sky nearly hitting him. Later he told me that it looked as if the thing simply started sprouting holes as the NVA turned their weapons on it. When he saw the crew bail out and crawl for cover underneath the chopper,* the only thing he could think to do was sprint across the open hilltop to see if he could find a place from which he could lay down fire to protect them. He didn't debate this. He just did it. It was an unconscious, generous, and potentially sacrificial act.

Many of us coming up the hill saw Niemi sprint into the open. Knowing now that he was still alive and that he and the chopper crew were dead for sure if we didn't break through to them, we all simply rushed forward to reach them before the NVA killed them. No one gave an order. *We,* the group, just rushed forward all at once. *We* couldn't be stopped. Just individuals among us were stopped. Many forever. But *we* couldn't be. This too is a form of transcendence. I was we, no longer me.

Lance Corporal Steel, nineteen, who'd been acting platoon commander until I reorganized things and was now acting platoon sergeant, got there first. The crewmen were so grateful and happy they gave their pistols away. I got the pilot's .38 Smith and Wesson.

Niemi got a Navy Cross.

I got a Navy Cross.

The helicopter pilot got a front-page story in *Stars and Stripes* with the headline, "Copter 'Crashes' Enemy Party, Takes Hill."†

The kid who borrowed my rifle didn't get anything.

---

*Aircrews are armed only with pistols, virtually useless in a fight like this. They may as well have been unarmed.

†To be clear, I know the stupid headline was completely out of the control of the pilot and crew, who, like all aircrews, were risking their lives to help us.

9

HOME

Returning from the initiatory space of the battlefield to the normal world is every bit as mysterious a journey as entering the Temple of Mars. The world you left behind has changed and you have changed. You know parts of yourself that you, and those you've lived with all your life, never knew before. You've been evil, and you've been good, and you've been beyond evil and good. You've split your mind from your heart, and you've split your heart with grief and your mind with fear. Ultimately, you've been in touch with the infinite, and now you are trying to reconcile yourself to the mundane. The warrior of the future will need to know how to enter and exit both worlds, if not with ease, then at least without permanently disintegrating his or her personality.

I was walking in uniform down M Street in our nation's capital. I had been back perhaps a month. A group of young people, my age, began to follow me down the street on the opposite side, jeering, calling me names, chanting in unison. They were flying the flags of North Vietnam and the Viet Cong.

I stood and looked at them across the chasm of that street, not knowing what to say or do. I tried to think of something that would allow me to make friends with them. I didn't want to fight them too. I was sick of fighting. I wanted to come back home, to be understood, to be welcomed.

I still see those flags, waving back and forth, insults in the cold wind, well-dressed people hurrying by, their heads down, eyes avoiding me, as the group continued to taunt and jeer me.

I couldn't get a date with any girl born north of the Mason-Dixon Line. There were signs at restaurants and bars saying "No military!" Two of my fellow lieutenants were murdered, gunned down from a passing car in their dress whites outside a hamburger joint on M Street. All this in our nation's capital.

Two months before I was discharged I boarded a train for New York at Union Station. Again I was in uniform, even though we'd had explicit instructions to avoid problems by not wearing our uniforms when around civilians. This put us in a bit of a bind. You could get half price on train and air fares, going standby, but only if you were in uniform, and we weren't exactly paid like junior executives.

I passed a nice-looking woman who looked up at me and quickly looked away. I sighed inwardly as I continued down the narrow aisle, too shy to sit in the empty seat next to her. I found a seat at the far end of the car and settled down to read but wished I were talking with her instead.

About five minutes later I saw her get up and come down the aisle. She was looking right at me, lips pressed tight. She stood in front of me and spit on me.

She walked back to her seat. I was trembling with shame and embarrassment. People hid behind newspapers. Some looked intently out dark windows that could only reflect their faces and the lighted interior of the car.

I wiped the spit off as best I could and pretended to go back to reading, trying to control the shaking. The woman moved to another car. Small victory. I eventually moved to a different car in the opposite direction, embarrassed to stay where people had seen what had happened.

The frequency of spitting incidents is a raging controversy. I think the number was very small. None of my friends experienced it. The image of being spit on, however, became a metaphor for what happened to returning Vietnam veterans. I think that this is what fuels the belief that spitting was a more common occurence than it was, in reality.

My first day back home my mother and father were at the airport, and so was, to my surprise, Maree Ann, a girl I'd dated when I was in high school. With Maree Ann were her four-year-old daughter, Lizzy, and Maree Ann's aunt, a friend of my mother's. My small hometown is only a hundred miles from the city and my close relatives still live in the area. Many had followed jobs to the city itself. My mother had called all of them to tell them I was coming home and when I'd arrive. Could they please come to the airport to welcome me back? There was only this little anxious group: Mom, trying unsuccessfully to hold back tears; Dad, more successful than she but close to losing it; Maree Ann; little Lizzy; and Maree Ann's aunt.

It would have been nice if some of my extended family had come to the airport. But I told Mom I didn't much mind. I'm not a public person. We'd see them later.

There was nothing later. To me, and to my parents, I'd been gone an eternity; to everyone else, a flash. This is no one's fault. Life is busy and full.

Still, I wish it were otherwise. Maybe if there had been some sort of hokey family potluck dinner. A toast by Uncle George, who was wounded in Italy (funny how we say wounded in Italy instead

of wounded in the leg); or my dad, who hauled gasoline to Patton's
tanks in France and was at the Battle of the Bulge; or Uncle Kim,
who fought the Japanese in the Pacific. Maybe some teary speech
by one of my aunts saying how glad she was that I'd come back safe,
or even my old communist grandmother could have gotten up and
said how it was all because of those Wall Street millionaires but
now that her lumpen proletariat grandson was back home she was
happy again. And maybe, well, was it too much to at least expect a
thank you from the people who voted to send us over there?

This was mistake number one—lack of extended family
involvement. The psychology of the young warrior is, I think,
almost entirely related to hearth and kin. You can subvert that
into patriotism and nationalism if you're clever and work at it
long enough, but I'd been detoxified.* A homecoming of yellow
ribbons and throwing out the first ball at the local game would
have made me feel like puking.

So we stood around, nervous, happy, after stiff public hugs,
waiting for my seabag to come through the baggage hole. I hadn't
seen Maree Ann since I left high school, but one day on a blasted
hilltop in Vietnam a package arrived from her and her aunt. The
first of many. In the diary I kept throughout my tour I copied a
scrawled "L" and some indistinguishable following marks from
where Lizzy had carefully written her name on Maree Ann's
Christmas package.

Maree Ann was a fourteen-year-old freshman when I last
knew her, the age when girls spell their name with two *e*'s instead

---

*Upon being asked back then if I'd ever fight again, I remember saying yes, I would,
when the enemy crossed the local river. I've since extended my geographic con-
straints. Metaphorically, it is better for my family if the fighting is on the other
side of the river.

of *y* and dot their *i*'s with little round circles. She was smart and funny, a great rider and rodeo princess who loved animals and belonged to 4-H. I was the big senior class president and probable valedictorian and an all-league football player. She asked me to the Sadie Hawkins Day dance. Well, I was surprised. I went.

Back then I was always looking to get out of town, looking to the future, and not seeing her in it. She, just starting high school, was bound in the present, too smart with a too finely tuned mind and sense of humor to be content with remaining where fate had landed her, a high school girl from an alcoholic and broken home in a cultural vacuum.

Shortly after I was graduated she got pregnant by some guy from out of town. He left her, or she left him, or each had left the other. How it is, outsiders never know. I think her aunt in the city took her in while she had Lizzy. She somehow managed to finish high school there.

I told them about my flight all the way across the Pacific Ocean, about seeing my older brother at Stanford, what it was like in California. They told me about old friends of mine and the garden. Then my sea- bag came out on the baggage conveyer. I shouldered it and we started for the door. Then Maree Ann asked me if I wanted to come home with her.

Well, I was surprised.

I could see that some things about Maree Ann hadn't changed. I looked at my mother and father. I looked at Maree Ann. Maree Ann is a good-looking woman. I went home with Maree Ann. This was mistake number two and entirely my own. I started feeling bad about leaving my folks, and a few other things, just after I reached Maree Ann's single room and kitchenette, which she rented in an old house in one of the city's poorer, but still respectable, neighborhoods.

The homecoming soldier may want to make love to any woman who moves, but any young man who hasn't seen a woman for even a few days wants to do the same. I was no exception, but I now know this was a part of me that needed some help and guidance. Other things having to do with returning warriors, not lonely young men with sex on their minds, needed to be put in place first. They weren't. No one knew any better. This was mistake number three, which had already been committed two weeks earlier on Okinawa.

We talked, we drank some tea, and I watched and listened while Maree Ann put Lizzy to bed, reading her a story. It felt so warm and comfortable there, the old lighting soft on the fir tongue-and-groove walls with their patina of years. I was so grateful she'd come to the airport to see me. We talked some more. We were tender with each other in many ways. But when she put on her nightgown and got into bed I couldn't go through with it.

I'd contracted NSU* from one of the prostitutes who lined Gate Number Two Street outside Kadena Air Base on Okinawa. This was the result of a lot of alcohol to satisfy the shy one and a seventy-two-hour nonstop answer to the needs of that other part of me I just mentioned. This piece of information I never passed on to my parents to explain why my arrival home was delayed ten days. I claimed military inefficiency. The fact was that the Navy doctor wouldn't endorse my orders until the NSU had cleared up.

Although I wasn't dripping anymore, I still wasn't completely sure the penicillin had totally wiped out the problem. I couldn't imagine transmitting NSU to Maree Ann. But there was more to it than just that.

*Nonspecific urethritis.

The fact was I felt unclean, insecure, strange, and awkward. I didn't feel right—with anyone. This feeling of being "wrong" somehow had dogged me since the minute I boarded the chartered 707 for California. The NSU was my own doing, or at least my own bad luck and my lack of someone to take me aside and say, "Look, what you think you need isn't what you need. All that's egging you on is the misplaced idea that being masturbated by a paid pair of labia is somehow manlier or more satisfying than doing it yourself. They're exploiting your loneliness. You're exploiting their poverty. You're both just using each other and it is going to make everyone feel bad. And, oh, by the way, you can catch a venereal disease."

Perhaps the awkward wrong feeling started with the stewardesses on the airplane treating us as if we were tourists. The thing no one recognized, including the stewardesses and even most of us, was that just two or three days earlier many of us had been in combat, scared to death we were going to die and watching the deaths of others just like us. Now we were being served peanuts and Cokes by stewardesses, most of them unaware except on a vague subconscious level of what was happening to us. It was the same jolting juxtaposition of the infinite and the mundane that hit me on my R&R to Australia. It wasn't the stewardesses' fault. They were just doing their job, handing out smiles and Cokes. We loved it. But we should have come home by sea. We should have had time to talk with our buddies about what we all had shared. We joined our units alone, and we came home alone, and this was a key difference between us and veterans of other wars, including today's.

Perhaps the awkward wrong feeling started when my brother mumbled something to try to make me feel better as we drove past the war protesters at Travis Air Force Base just outside San Francisco, where he picked me up. They were pounding his car with their signs and snarling at us through the closed car window. Or maybe it got started when he showed me around the Stanford campus—being looked at by girls in long clean hair and boys in long not-so-clean hair, all dressed somewhere between Newport Beach and Haight Ashbury, me in no hair, with jungle-rot scars on my face and hands, dressed in clothes that smelled like mothballs and looked like something handed down from the Kingston Trio.

No one shouted obscenities, or even said anything, maybe out of deference to my brother. No one needed to. You know the feeling, as if you've made a mistake coming to the party but no one is going to tell you to your face.

At one point I waited at the Stanford bookstore for my brother to get out of class. I had to squeeze by a girl in one of the aisles. I said excuse me, politely. She looked at me with contempt and wouldn't move aside. I tried to slip past her and accidentally knocked a book from the shelf. I hated my clumsiness and flushed face as she watched me stoop to pick it up. I remember wishing she knew I'd won a Navy Cross and was trying to reach the poetry section. She was joined by two long-haired boys who further barred the aisle. Trembling with anger and humiliation, this Marine chose to advance in the other direction.

No matter where I went, I felt something was not right about me. I still felt it at Maree Ann's. I knew that to make love to her would be wrong for me and, if wrong for me, then wrong for her. I was again bound away, this time with orders to Headquarters Marine Corps in Washington, D.C. I simply wasn't interested in a relationship with a woman with a four-year-old daughter, no matter how good-looking or how tender the woman was. She must have known that, and it added a terrible poignancy. I think I told her about the NSU but don't know for sure. I'm quite sure I was incapable in those days of explaining how I felt to anyone.

I didn't want to reject her—far from it. But I didn't want to mislead. There was too much past between us, too much linkage, and perhaps yearning and loneliness. To be sixteen with a baby and no husband, on your own, then seventeen, and then eighteen, must be one of the loneliest situations life can hand us. And here comes the hero back from the war and he doesn't want to make love and maybe tells her he's got NSU, even though he's also afraid of telling her that he's afraid of the emotional consequences. My God, how we waste our lives hurting each other.

Maree Ann didn't know what to do any more than I did, but she showed up. She was the only other person, besides my parents, who'd kept the linkage with my past, with my little town, my tribe, as it were.

It was clear that the others of the tribe, "my fellow Americans," as the politicians say, had worse than abandoned me. Imagine the damage to young Aborigine boys returning from their frightening and mind-altering initiation only to have the villagers pelt them with garbage.

I needed desperately to be accepted back in. I think I ended up assuming unconsciously that I must have done something wrong to have received all this rejection. To be sure, I had been engaged in dirty business. Somebody, usually the man, empties the garbage and turns the compost. But when he's done, he comes back in the house, he washes his hands, and someone says thank you. War is society's dirty work, usually done by kids cleaning up failures perpetrated by adults. What I needed upon returning, but didn't know it, was a bath.

What I needed was for Maree Ann to sit down with me in a tub of water and run her hands over my body and squeeze out the wrong feelings and confusion, soothe the pain, inside and out, and rub the skin back to life. I needed her to Dutch-rub my skull with soap until the tears came, and I needed her to dry the tears, and laugh with me, and cry with me, and bring my body back from the dead.

That body had suffered. It was covered with scars from jungle rot. It had had dysentery, diarrhea, and possibly a mild case of malaria. It had gone without fresh food for months at a time. It had lived on the knife edge of fear, constantly jerked from an aching need for sleep with all the cruel refinement of the best secret police torturer. It had pumped adrenaline until it had become addicted to it. There were scars where hot metal had gone in, searing and surprising in its pain, and scars where a corpsman had dug most of it out. There were bits of metal still in it, some pushing against the skin, itching to get out. The eyeballs were scarred where tiny bits of hand grenade had embedded themselves. The inner ears rang with a constant high-pitched whine that ceased only in sleep, when the nightmares started.

That body was shut down against pain as far as I could get it shut. Shut down to where it would not feel a thing, while my mind was still seven thousand miles away, unattached, floating, watching.

I needed a woman to get me back on the earth, get me down in the water, get me down *under* the water, get my body to feel again, to slough off old skin, old scars, old scabs, to come again into her world, the world that I'd left, and which sometimes I think I've never returned to. But I kissed her and went home.

When my mother shook me awake late the next morning, she tells me I reached out and tried to choke her. I don't remember this. At least I didn't try and choke Maree Ann.

I do remember the careful way my bedroom had been restored with my old letter jacket, pictures, trophies. This care I remember and this a mother can do to welcome someone home— make it feel like a home, not just a house.

We left the next day for Cortes Island, which lies between Vancouver Island and the British Columbia mainland, a favorite place of mine. On the Victoria–Port Angeles ferry I fell asleep. A woman tripped over my feet, startling me. Again I reared up, reaching out to choke her. There was great embarrassment all around, my mother trying to explain to this middle-aged Canadian who was trying to explain how she hadn't meant to step on me and me explaining how I hadn't meant to . . . and how she understood and . . . In any case, this kid was not ready to go on a public ferryboat ride. This kid was still in the jungle.

My body was trying to tell me I was choking the feminine, but I didn't get it. Twenty years later I had a dream in which I was going to a wedding. The bride was waiting. A friend asked where the groom was. I had to explain to him that the wedding wouldn't occur until the groom came home from Vietnam. I had been reading a lot of women writers. This time I got it. The hypermasculine warrior energy has to be balanced by feminine energy, but it must come home to do this.

I think the American people tried to reestablish balance by shaming the masculine principle and leaving a huge chunk of it in the jungle so it wouldn't bother us at home. This had profound influences on men's very identity, with profound influences on society. Trying to bring about balance by squelching the masculine won't work any more than squelching the feminine. Pushing Mars into the jungle of our unconscious results in the frightening energy that fuels gangs, drug wars, and increased violence in general. When the Jesse James gang rode into Northfield, Minnesota, to rob the bank, they thought that the town would fall prey to terror just as did all the other small towns they'd raided earlier. They were met by the men, all Civil War veterans, and the gang was destroyed. If drug dealers had shown up at the school in my 1950s logging town, the men would have been down there with rifles. I am not advocating vigilante justice. I'm talking about a basic attitude about a traditional male role: protecting the community. I'm worried that somewhere between the women's movement and the nation's reaction to the Vietnam War, this traditional role came to be viewed as obsolete, even déclassé. Too many men abandoned it. Today we expect the police to do everything. We've hired out community protection just as we've hired out military service. Unfortunately, there are never enough police, nor will there ever be.

* * *

Many of my compatriots are still not back from the war. Some are still in the bush, in places like Alaska or Montana. I am not. This is because some things were done right. Recall my recurring nightmare of slashing and being slashed in the muddy Ben Hai. There was always a corpsman who pulled me from the water and got an IV tube into my arm before I died. The corpsman is a combination of warrior and healer. Without my being aware of it, this corpsman was constantly at work when I came back and got into that self-destructive, and other-destructive, round of drugs, alcohol, and empty coupling.

My usual pattern when somebody hurts me—and I was hurt badly coming home to America—is to put out the antiaircraft guns, set up the land mines and claymores, string the barbed wire, and just let the sons of bitches try to hurt me again.

The first break in my defenses was made by an old friend from my secret society at Yale. Biggs was working for a senator at the time. He's now a lawyer in New England. He would call

me several times a week and just talk to me. He got me to rent a
little house at the beach with him. He'd pick me up, every weekend, no matter how messed up I was, and we'd drive over to the
Maryland shore, and the first thing he'd do upon arriving would
be to fix a truly sensuous hamburger—lovingly "moojied up,"
as he called the process, with unexpected ingredients, including
substantial amounts of hash. This didn't help my drug problem
any, but Biggs wasn't into therapy. He was into friendship. He
pumped blood back into me, weekend by weekend, by the simple
act of being with me.

Ben was an older friend, a political commentator and writer.
He'd have me over to his house in Maryland and just let me
spend time with his family. He'd explain Jewish holidays to me
and talk politics. One day I went with him to buy groceries and
I tried to buy some beer. The man wouldn't sell any to me because he thought my identification was faked. Ben lit into him.
"This guy's just come back from Vietnam. He's been old enough
to kill people for us and you don't think he's old enough to buy
a beer. Sell him the goddamned beer." The man did. It wasn't
the beer. It was the first public support. In fact it remained the
only public support I ever got until the current wars in Iraq and
Afghanistan and a very welcome change in the public's attitude
toward returning veterans.

We have grown, and to be fair, the majority of people in the
peace movement did not treat the returning veterans badly. Small
towns in the Midwest and South welcomed their veterans home.
I experienced kindness as well.

There was the sister of a Marine friend who was still in Vietnam when I was at Headquarters Marine Corps in Washington,
D.C. He had written to her saying I was probably finding it hard
to meet girls. This was true. The phrase "politically incorrect"

hadn't been invented yet, but I was a living prototype. She invited me to her house several times. There I could talk to her and her friends. One of them became my first wife, Gisèle.

There was a friend from another small town next to my hometown who was stationed in Washington with the Navy. He and his wife let me sleep in their living room while I searched for a hard-to-find apartment. I was there several months.

There was a group of girls who worked at the CIA who decorated my guitar case for me. I still keep it.

Salley was the sister of another Marine friend. He'd also asked her to call. One day, when she was in town for a peace rally, she did. She was a senior at Mary Washington College and lived in an isolated farmhouse near the Wilderness west of Fredericksburg with several other girls. I'd get off duty late at night and drive down, hoping someone was still up, anticipating and then receiving the joy of seeing their mellow light from the farmhouse window in the winter-bare forest. The girls were still awake. My welcome would be warm.

These simple contacts, even if I wouldn't allow them to go very deep, made it possible to avoid another self-inflicted wound. The CIA needed people to train hill tribesmen in Laos. I was approached—flattered. "Lieutenant Marlantes, we're very impressed with your war record. You might know So-and-So from Yale. We get some of our best men from Yale." It appealed to me. More bloody transcendence? No, just escape, from pain, from the feeling of being wrong. I had all the skills. They'd put my salary in a tax-free 10 percent savings account. Although this was not part of the official pitch, it was clear there would be all the dope and girls I'd ever want. It would be the parties without the telephone call from the angry and hurt husband the next day. And there would be the biggest drug of all, and one I still miss, the passionate intensity of life on the edge. It was perfect heroic self-destruction.

Had it not been for these few who showed me what I needed, and a timely letter from E. T. Williams, the warden of Rhodes House, inviting me to retake my scholarship at Oxford, which I thought I'd given up by going off to the war, I might have gone for the brass ring instead of the gold one. I might have taken the short-term jolt of adrenaline and power and probably never re-integrated into society.

The warden's offer took me out of the country, away from the anger, pain, and humiliation. It took me away from drugs, because Oxford was, and still is, for all its pretensions otherwise, a pretty middle-class sort of place. Most important, of all the right things about my homecoming it connected me with a group of women at Oxford whose ability to feel had not been politicized away.

They healed me simply by letting me sit in their rooms, drink their tea, and listen to them talk, which I did nearly every afternoon for two years. One of them took me home with her for Christmas. Another invited me to her home in Switzerland over spring break. Another asked me to her twenty-first birthday party, where she played the piano for us. One invited me to her wedding. They accepted me. I wasn't wrong. They brought me back to life, pouring tea and life back into me by the orange glow of their electric coil heaters. I'll never cease to love them for it.

It is primarily women who reintegrate the warrior back into society, the energy of the queen, not the king. Women carry this queen for most young men. Joking about men getting in touch with their inner woman aside, this is healthy, but it usually doesn't happen until they're quite mature, at least in their forties. When a young man comes home from war, he's all testosterone and he's scary.

When Cúchulainn, the warrior hero of the *Táin,* returned to the walls of Emain Macha from combat, the three heads of Nechta Scéne's sons with him, a swan flock he'd captured fluttering above him, a wild stag behind his chariot, he turned the left chariot board toward Emain in insult,* and he said: "I swear by the oath of Ulster's people that if a man isn't found to fight me, I'll spill the blood of everyone in this court."†

"Naked women to him!" Conchobar mac Nessa (the king) said.

The women of Emain went forth, with Mugain (the queen), the wife of Conchobar, at their head, and they stripped and showed their breasts to him.

"These are the warriors you must struggle with today," Mugain said.

Cúchulainn "hid his countenance" and immediately was thrown by the warriors into a cold bath, which began to boil from his heat and burst the vat. They threw him into another vat and that boiled with bubbles "the size of fists" and then they threw him into a third vat and he warmed it to the point where its heat and his own were equal. At this point Mugain clothed him in a blue cloak with a silver brooch. He at last has shed his warrior garments and is ready to be part of the community again. Then he "sat on Conchobar's knee" (the king's knee, not the throne, and certainly not on the floor) and "that was his seat ever after."

Can you imagine how much raw courage it must take for a woman to stand naked and defenseless in front of a raging boiling warrior like this? See yourself, on the empty plain, a cold damp

---

*I can take you "left-handed," with my disadvantaged side. Possibly, I can take you with the hand I wipe with.

†I am paraphrasing or quoting from Thomas Kinsella, trans., *The Táin,* 1982.

wind blowing in from the sea, chilling your naked legs, making goose bumps on your back, stirring the hair on your head and vulva, tightening your exposed nipples. There you stand, naked in front of rude wooden walls, the mud beneath your feet, your king powerless to resist this onrushing force, a man who can kill anyone who stands in his way, a man boiling with battle rage, the very air above him captive to him, vibrating with the spirit power of wings and the wild stag of all the hunts that ever were tied captive to his chariot. And you stand there, small and straight, or maybe fat and a little foolish looking, but you stand your ground, totally vulnerable. And you stun him like a bird from a slung stone.

We don't understand this feminine courage anymore; in fact, we denigrate it.

Can you imagine Cúchulainn raging before the gates of a modern American Emain Macha? The king is inside the walls, quivering with fear, and he shouts for the queen. She's a lawyer. "We'll get a court injunction against him," she cries. "He can't run around the walls slandering and threatening us like that."

The king, who's afraid to talk back to his wife because she'll accuse him of being insensitive or exploiting his position in the patriarchy, thinks to himself, "Good idea, Mugain. But isn't Cúchulainn the guy we send for to back up the court orders?"

The baring of women's breasts to the returning warrior could take many forms today. For me it was as simple as girls serving tea. Bared breasts symbolize nurturing milk, children, family, community, life. Finally, for all of us, the breast that we lie upon as newborn babies is as home as we ever get.

Too many veterans, from Vietnam but also from Afghanistan and Iraq, are still waiting to come home. Take Raymond, who'd been a Marine in Vietnam and now sells commercial real estate. Raymond is big. You could hug only half of him at a time. Yet his bulk contains a stereotype-defying sensitivity.

I went to a party at Raymond's over the holidays. Kids wrestling in the basement, running around the furniture upstairs throwing a football. A piñata. The adults lit candles for the new year in a quiet ceremony in the living room as the children drifted in and out, some participating, some not.

In the kitchen, the quiet eye of the storm, I talked with Raymond's wife, Dee. She and my first wife shared the not uncommon and deeply disturbing experience of living with a man with posttraumatic stress disorder without knowing where all the craziness was coming from. These women are veterans of a different war. For every veteran who goes through a divorce, a wife goes through one too. For every veteran alone in the basement, there is a wife upstairs, bewildered, isolated, and in despair from the dark cloud of war that hangs over daily family life. For too many years the public hasn't recognized or sympathized with families of veterans coping with PTSD and has left them in silence.

Dee and Raymond had just been to Washington, D.C., for the tenth anniversary of the Vietnam Veterans Memorial. I asked her how it went. She looked quickly at the kitchen door, checking her flanks. "Pretty well, until the parade."

"They had a *parade*?"

"Well, you know, everyone getting with their state contingents. They marched right through the middle of town."

I listened.

"Raymond kept expecting to see the people on the sidewalks. There'd been a lot of press about the anniversary. There'd been the big turnaround about veterans after the Gulf War. And there were lots of veterans there. It seemed like a big success." She turned the water tap on and turned it off again. *Shhhhht.* It was like the static burst from a lonely night listening post keying the handset. "But there wasn't anybody there. Raymond kept thinking they must be up ahead. Maybe when we get to Constitution Avenue. They're probably waiting there. It's right in the center of town. But when they swung around the corner into Constitution Avenue—uh-uh, no crowds."

I was thinking to myself, *They expected crowds?*

"Some of the men started to drop out."

The cynical voice whispered again, *They still expected a crowd?*

"Finally, they heard cheering up ahead. Clapping. They quickened their pace. Guys got back into formation. Of course, they thought, everyone is at the memorial where the parade ended."

"Were they?" I asked. Maybe there *was* a crowd, my whisper said. I felt my own dead hopes start to rise.

"No. It was the veterans at the front of the parade welcoming the ones at the back."

"Ah." *What did you expect?*

"Guys started packing and going home just after that."

Raymond came in the door just then to get something from the kitchen. Earlier in the evening he had told me several stories about the anniversary. He had crashed a party of the 101st Airborne, U.S. Marine written all over his jacket. A silence. Old rivalries. The clubs within clubs. He had grabbed a beer, raised it overhead, and shouted, "Airborne!" Laughter. Cheers.

Raymond had told stories like these. Solidarity stories.

"I just heard about the parade," I said.

"Yeah." He walked back into the living room, forgetting what he'd come in for.

"Was Raymond sad?" I asked.

"Yeah. Raymond was sad."

"And you?" I asked.

"Me? All those years? Raymond crying every Christmas because he lost his entire squad on Christmas day? Him sitting at dinner with his eyes darting all over? The rages? Going to bars in black neighborhoods and shouting 'Nigger' just to start a fight and coming home beat to hell? And no one ever told us what in hell was happening? What to do? No one. No help. Me, sad? I'm goddamned furious!"

There is a correct way to welcome your warriors back. Returning veterans don't need ticker-tape parades or yellow ribbons stretching clear across Texas. Cheering is inappropriate and immature. Combat veterans, more than anyone else, know how much pain and evil have been wrought. To cheer them for what they've just done would be like cheering the surgeon when he amputates a leg to save someone's life. It's childish, and it's demeaning to those who have fallen on both sides. A quiet grateful handshake is what you give the surgeon, while you mourn the lost leg. There should be parades, but they should be solemn processionals, rifles upside down, symbol of the sword sheathed once again. They should be conducted with all the dignity of a military funeral, mourning for those lost on both sides, giving thanks for those returned. Afterward, at home or in small groups, let the champagne flow and celebrate life and even victory if you were so lucky—afterward.

Veterans just need to be received back into their community, reintegrated with those they love, and thanked by the people who sent them. I wanted to be hugged by every girl I ever knew. Our more sane ancestors had ceremonies like sweat rituals to physically bring the bodies back into civilian mode. Mongolian warriors were taken into heated yurts and had every muscle that could be reached pressed and rolled with smooth staves, squeezing out toxins, signaling the psyche and the body that it was time to stop pumping adrenaline.

There is also a deeper side to coming home. The returning warrior needs to heal more than his mind and body. He needs to heal his soul.

It was two in the morning and dark. The dead had been summoned for several days before and were now gathering outside Old Mission Santa Inez. It was cold for southern California, and wet. Six months of drought had just been broken by the first Pacific storm and the surfers were reporting twenty-footers.

My friend Brother Mark, a Capuchin friar, had spent the evening before with a friend of his, a former nun, setting up candles and laying out the tools of ritual, and the large old mission was hushed in their glow. On the floor in front of the altar stood a large single paschal candle, the sign of the risen Christ, and deeper yet and beyond, into twenty thousand years of our common ancestry, it was the power of the phallus rising from the earth. I had spent the evening writing what I wanted, and never had the chance, to say to my dead friends killed in the Vietnam War.

Brother Mark was in full regalia. "If we're going to do this thing, Karl, we're going to do it full force, with two thousand years of tradition behind it."

It was the Mass for the Dead.

I handed Brother Mark my diary, the battered book that I had kept with me every day I was in Vietnam. It was with me on every godforsaken hilltop in the mountains of the north. It was with me in every firefight. It was with me when Isle died and when

Utter died. And it was with me when I died. It was with me on the
hospital ship *Repose*. It was with me when I was drunk on my butt at
Vandegrift Combat Base. Along with it was a small green notebook,
filled with medevac numbers, R&R dates for kids in the platoon,
notes about the last Red Cross message to talk to the three kids who
hadn't written home in the past two months and whose mothers
were wanting to know if they were okay, hastily scribbled defense
plans, hole arrangements, machine-gun fields of fire, possible lines
of approach by an attacking force. It had patrol checkpoints and
daily brevity codes for radioing in positions. "Cigarettes will be at
7530. NFL stars at 8131." I could radio in that we were located at
"from Pall Mall, up 11 and right 5" or "from Hornung down three
and right seven," and the skipper could figure out where we were,
so we could rain down fire and death on others than ourselves.

Brother Mark placed these books on the altar next to the
wine, water, and bread.

"You ready?"

I nodded.

He handed me a silver spoon and I spread frankincense on
the glowing charcoal in the censer. I carried it, tossing smoke,
while Brother Mark spread holy water, and together we walked
toward the huge oak doors at the far end of the aisle. Brother Mark
unlocked the doors. I pushed them open into the night.

"Welcome, friends of Karl. Welcome, former enemies. We
welcome you. Come in."

I felt them filing in. They had been waiting, patiently,
gathering outside beneath the dry grass hills dotted with dark
green oaks. Gathering to wait there in the dark. They had waited
for a quarter of a century.

And they filled the church. My dead friends. Kids who died
before I even learned their names. North Vietnamese soldiers

I had killed, and the ones my friends had killed, shadows and wraiths connected with us all, connecting us to each other. I had invited an officer I just hated. It hadn't been easy. Truly, there was a time when I wanted to kill him. A friend talked me back to normal insanity. But I knew there could be no forgiving of myself without the forgiving of him. And I also knew that he never thought too highly of me either.

Then my grandparents all filed in and sat down in the front pew.

We began the Mass. About halfway through I stopped Brother Mark.

"What's going on?" he asked.

"They've all gotten up and have crossed the aisles. They're hugging one another, shaking hands."

We waited about five minutes, until they got back into their seats again.

I read aloud to them what I'd written the night before. "Andersen, all the sergeants thought you were kind of a fuck-off. Maybe you did too. But on Helicopter Hill you did everything—gave your life, maybe to prove you weren't. You're not a fuck-off in my mind. Thank you." I told Clifton, "You took me on my first patrol. You took out the machine gun and died. Thank you, Teacher." All I'd learned from Clifton probably saved many others long after he died. I told Isle how sorry I was I'd rushed him that day to kill the retreating NVA. He piped back, "Hell, Lieutenant, I was a Marine. I wanted to kill them too." Others laughed, even the NVA. I told the officer I was sorry for hating him so. I thanked him for coming. "I know you thought I was just a fucking hippie. Neither of us was a perfect officer. I forgive you. Please forgive me." When I saw him seated below me in one of the pews, he was no longer an old man against whom I'd held bitter anger for all these years. He was a relatively young man, killed when he was around thirty-eight or forty. I saw him as a young man assigned a battalion in combat and in over his head. I no longer felt angry. I felt sad. He and I just looked at each other and understood where we both had fallen short.

The door had been left open. I would occasionally look at it, open to the night, afraid some unsuspecting parishioner would arrive early for quiet contemplation before the morning Mass and find us there with the dead. But the night held us in secret.

As the Mass was ending, the light built up around the Santa Ynez Mountains, outlining their barren ridgelines against the gray. The open door changed from a black hole leaking light and warmth to a gray portal, where light came in.

"This Mass is ended," Brother Mark said. "Go in peace to love and serve the Lord."

And they went, slowly, silently, with joy, with the feelings of a good class reunion, the feelings of a good wedding.

Brother Mark shut the doors and we put away the vessels and hung up his robes and we drove into town and had breakfast.

Two nights later a dark presence entered my bedroom, waking me from a sound sleep, a presence so malignant and evil it seemed to fill the room with dark oppressive liquid, squeezing the very air from my lungs. I felt the prickles running up and down my spine. My wife was sleeping in another room, unsuspecting; my kids were in their bedrooms. Whatever it was, it was angry, and it had to do with Brother Mark and me messing with the dead. I knew this was way beyond me, so I just started praying for help. I got the one-armed Viking who'd been with me in Vietnam. I got the Great Mother. I got the Archangel Michael. I grabbed the crucifix of the risen Christ that Brother Mark had given me at breakfast after the ceremony and I held tight and I whispered, "Jesus, if I've ever needed you, I need you now." I sat there, terrified, for over an hour while this presence beat against me and my helpers.

I'm not a person who is into pixie dust. I didn't know what to make of this. It returned two days later, and the same scene ensued, with me terrified and my spiritual helpers holding off that evil. A Jungian would say I'd encountered the archetypal shadow, not just my own shit this time but the shit of the entire world, the entire race of humans and beyond humans from time beyond reckoning. I knew in my head that evil existed, but this was the first time in my experience it was palpable. This time, instead of merely seeing the results of evil, bad enough to give me nightmares for thirty-five years, I had hooked in direct. I went for days feeling the house was under siege. I talked to Brother Mark. He and I decided it was beyond us but he'd ask around for help. He called an older priest who was familiar with the Mass for the Dead. This man was now at the Vatican. He told Brother Mark that when you try to break the hold of evil on a soul, evil will fight back—hard. Brother Mark came over to the house and we sprinkled holy water all through it and even around it. What I had come to call the Presence came back anyway.

The day after the latest encounter with the Presence was a Thursday, my day for group therapy at the Vet Center. After the meeting I met with my friend Bear. Bear, the nephew of a Chumash shaman, was an LRRP* in Vietnam.

"Oh yeah, evil spirits," Bear said, as if I were describing a termite problem. "Here's what you do." Some cultures are simply better able to handle this stuff than my own. We drove over to Bear's apartment and I waited there while he drove out to the valley to talk with his uncle. He came back with a tape of his uncle

*Army, Long Range Reconnaisance Patrol.

chanting, and he gave me his own clay bowl and some sage his uncle had personally picked and blessed. Two nights later when the family was away, I sat alone on the living room floor in my house, put on Bear's tape, and crumpled the sage into the bowl and set it on fire. I began to imitate the chants, letting the sage smoke seep all over the house, all over me, making the space uninhabitable for evil spirits. For good measure I tossed holy water from the mission all around the windows and doors of my children's bedrooms. I got only a few funny looks and brief comments on the smell when everyone came home.

The Presence never came back. On rare occasions I feel its whisper on the edge of my consciousness, but it has never returned as it had in those days after the Mass for the Dead. It wasn't defeated. It's never defeated. It just stopped bothering *me*. It left for other fields to plow. I know that, if I allow it, it will come back, but it will come back unseen and unfelt. It's the problem with evil. As I've said, it's usually ordinary stuff.

Civilization advances because we have the ability to pass on culture to the next generation. We don't have to start from scratch like other animals. But, unlike the Chumash, most Americans have stopped passing on the cultural gains of ritual and consciousness, while we continue to pass on the gains in technology. Grandma and Grandpa are in Sun City.

A special problem for warriors, however, is that Grandma and Grandpa can't come to war with you. There has to be another way of taking this wisdom with us to avoid being sent to war on a physical level only. You can't have a successful homecoming without preparing for it *before* sending people out to fight in the first place.

One of the best methods will be to employ the spiritual wisdom of the master martial artist. Most people think the martial arts are ancient. They are actually relatively new to the world, the very earliest records of martial monks appearing not much before the sixteenth century in China. Most martial arts practiced today originated in the twentieth century. Recently, the Marines have made more of a commitment to martial arts training. This is a welcome sign. The spiritual component, however, must never take second place to the physical—always a danger in a society dedicated to separating religion from government and a culture conditioned to favoring the practical over the impractical. Training must move beyond *here's how you kill*. It must include why you kill, and here's how killing fits in the great scheme of things, and here's how you are likely to feel afterward. Without this preparation, homecoming will be orders of magnitude more difficult.

In addition to training with an eye toward the eventual return to society, there are also many practical things that can be done outside training to improve reintegrating returning veterans. First of all, the military should never discharge people immediately from combat as it did during Vietnam, no matter how anxious the kids are to get the hell out of uniform. They should be taken in groups, preferably the group they fought with, through ritual ceremonies and counseling.

There should be a ceremony of handing over the weapons. I have a strong physical memory of the barrel guard of my M-16 resting in my left hand, sort of wide, rocker-shaped, cool, grainy plastic. I have just as strong a physical memory of holding my kids, feeling their puffy diapers through their clothes. What I'm saying is that I was very connected psychologically to my weapon.

Most important, we need ceremony and counseling to help returning veterans move from the infinite back to the finite. I'm reminded of the opening of a Tim O'Brien short story: "The war was over and there was no place in particular to go."* The story is about a veteran who wants to talk about what happened to him but can't. He ends up aimlessly and endlessly driving a car around a small lake in a small town in Iowa. At the end of the story there is a note, whether fictional or true I don't know, explaining that the story was about a friend of Tim's, Norm Bowker, who hanged himself without explanation in the locker room of his local YMCA after a pickup basketball game about eight years after he got back from Vietnam.

What returning veterans need is someplace to go that will fill a vast empty feeling, and it's not the YMCA or the video store or the tavern. The first emptiness is that caused by missing your friends, your unit. Some are dead. All are gone. To regain that same feeling would require going through a similar experience with another group. This very few veterans would ever want to do.

The great writer Norman Maclean writes about this feeling of longing in a story about a U.S. Forest Service crew in Montana just after the First World War. The crew had decided to go into town and take revenge on some local cardsharps who had cheated one of them. "And at the end we banded together to clean out the town—probably something also that had to be done for us to become a crew. For most of us, this momentary social unit the crew was the only association we had ever belonged to, although somehow it must have been for more time than a moment. Here I am over half a century later trying to tell you about it."†

---

*Tim O'Brien, "Speaking of Courage," in *The Things They Carried*, 1990.
†Norman Maclean, "USFS 1919: The Ranger, the Cook, and a Hole in the Sky," in *A River Runs Through It and Other Stories*, 1976.

The second emptiness is the hole of trivia. About five years after I'd returned from Vietnam, I was down in the basement of our new fixer-upper tearing out walls, redoing the wiring and the plumbing. I stopped for a sandwich break and idly started reading a section of the paper that happened to be lying on the floor next to me. The Federal Reserve was doing this. Business leaders were expecting the economy to do that. Somebody in New York was being honored for something. The usual. It was mildly entertaining. I was about to toss the paper aside when I noticed the date, 1926.

I sat there stunned. That news was fifty years old and I hadn't even noticed. It had apparently been stuffed in the wall I'd opened. Then I started laughing, at myself, at the whole situation. Suddenly everything seemed so trivial, me trying to fix up this old house, my job, the news, marriage, history. Everything. There I was, in the basement of my new fixer-upper with "no particular place to go." It seemed that nothing, absolutely nothing, could stack up against the intensity of war and war's friendships. I felt only intensely empty. I fantasized about flying to Chicago to find an old Marine friend of mine. We'd get involved in running drugs from South America. Something like that. What the hell. But I was married and we wanted kids and we needed a house. I picked up the crowbar and continued working on the house while just about that time Norm Bowker killed himself. So did too many others. We'd have saved lives if returning veterans had been better prepared for reentry.

We need to give returning veterans some sort of commitment to the future they are returning to. Most veterans can return to families or build them. All veterans can return to communities or build them. All veterans can return to a world where they can pursue their individual callings. To do this, however, eventually the war has to be integrated, the horror absorbed, the psyche stretched to accommodate the trauma. This requires tools. Most veterans come from the strata of society where counseling is something that happens to crazy people. Counseling should be required. This will eliminate the stigma. A further way to eliminate the stigma would be to train senior officers and NCOs in the techniques of helping men and women leave military service, honoring parting as much as entering, with equal emphasis on ritual. Counseling for the veteran and his or her family should be paid for or supplied by the Department of Veterans Affairs for as long as the veteran or his family may want it. There should be special religious services for each faith, specifically designed to get returning veterans back on home ground and reconnected to the infinite through something besides dealing and avoiding death. Ideally, these would be performed in the churches of those who have them. The chaplains, again, have missed their marks here, not contacting and not encouraging the religious leaders of the churches in the veterans' communities. For those without a church, or with no particular denomination, chaplains could conduct ceremonies on the military bases before final discharge. For those who don't feel connected with any particular religion, it could be something as simple as sharing poetry and stories.

I'm aware this would take lots of time and effort. But it would save the nation billions in wrecked lives and heartache. I'm also aware that young men of this age might find such ceremonies funny or a waste of time and they'd be cool. I once attended a church service just after a battle. It was meant to be a memorial for those we lost. Everyone was polite during the service, but there were jokes afterward. The service was meaningless because we were all still out in the bush, psychologically, and the people leading the service hadn't been out there with us. This wasn't their fault; it was just a problem. Also, we all just sat there. No one participated. This is why the Vietnam Veterans Memorial works so well. You can physically do something there, touch a name, leave a flower. You've got to engage the bodies of these young fighters before you can engage their spirits. They live and thrive in the physical world. Engaging the physical is the only way to break through. Include something as simple as a group recital of the names of their dead friends and they'll know that they're touching the transcendent. I will never forget a solemn group of three kids beating on a cardboard C-ration box down on the perimeter of a new hilltop position, chanting the names of their dead friends in the jungle twilight.

Before being discharged veterans should be gathered in small groups with career veterans who have had some training in group dynamics and be allowed to talk themselves down. Just talk, in a safe place, with other veterans. It gets the talk started, breaks the damaging code of silence that stops the integration process. This process could then go on in civilian life, because now it's legitimized and the young veterans know how to do it. Some veterans will always be afraid to bring back their nightmare. They need to know early on that the nightmare can be faced. All veterans fear being misunderstood. If war detox is required while people are still in uniform, the shame and fear will be faced cleanly and won't have to come out twenty years later after painful divorces, lost jobs, and alienation from society in general and their own children in particular. It wouldn't be perfect, but it would be better.

Metaphorically, veterans should be encouraged to sing. Joseph Henderson once showed me a collection of paintings in his home that were copied from pollen drawings made by a Navajo shaman. He walked me through the story of two brothers who went on a journey to find their father, the Sun. Their father armed them, and they became warriors and fought the wild monsters threatening their tribe. The paintings showed bolts of lightning and vibrant energy coming off the brothers when they returned to their village. The villagers were afraid of them and told them to leave. Sky Woman took them in and taught them to sing of their adventures. When they had made up their songs and sang them to the people, the people were no longer afraid.

This book is my song. Each and every one of us veterans must have a song to sing about our war before we can walk back into the community without everyone, including the king, quaking behind the walls. Perhaps it is drawing pictures or reciting poetry about the war. Perhaps it is getting together with a small group and telling stories. Perhaps it is dreaming about it and writing the dreams down and then telling people your dreams. But it isn't enough just to do the art in solitude and sing the song alone. You must sing it to other people. Those who are afraid or uneasy must hear it. They must see the art. They must lose their fear.

When the child asks, "What is it like to go to war?" to remain silent keeps you from coming home.

10

THE CLUB

After the warrior returns home from the initiation of combat, he becomes a member of "the Club" of combat veterans. It has always been a club with its own secrets and its own and societally imposed rules of silence. Traditionally, it has been a club tied in with the mystery of gender because being a warrior was tied in with manhood. This ancient mystery combined with the silence forms an intriguing and powerful combination for attracting future members, particularly boys. You don't join this club; you can only be initiated into it.

The warrior of the future will become a member of this club, just as have the warriors of the past, but the future warrior will have to understand that the Club's true purpose in modern society should be as an honorable guild. Like membership in all honorable organizations of craft or commerce, full membership in the guild of warriors can be an important part of the path to adulthood, but membership must no longer be considered the only path for conferring manhood. In addition, the membership requirement of silence needs to be rescinded.

I was thirteen, and we older Scouts in our troop had been learning survival skills. Now we were to be tested. We were crammed into an old crummy, the tough panel truck that hauls loggers up to the logging sites before sunrise. Its steel walls were moist with condensation from the cold outside and the breathing of the boys inside. Joe, one of our adult leaders, was a timber cruiser* and had

---

*A person who "cruises" through uncut timber estimating its potential for harvesting.

borrowed it from the large timber company he worked for. We were dropped off along a muddy logging road in pairs, without food or equipment, about half a mile apart. Before us was a series of dark fir-covered ridges cut into steep canyons by rain-filled creeks. Each succeeding ridge was increasingly obscured by the gently falling rain, the darker green of the firs getting more and more indistinct until after three ridges you could see nothing but gray.

I was paired with my best friend, Moose, and our task was to make our way to a certain rendezvous point over the next two days. If we didn't show up by dinner Saturday night, the dads would come looking for us. People didn't worry much about lawsuits in those days and the kids had a lot more freedom.

Shortly after Moose and I took off down into the first deep ravine it started to rain—hard. With no sun to guide us, we had to rely on topography, following streams up and down. This delayed us. We got soaked through, but we were wearing wool, which kept us, if not comfortable, at least protected against hypothermia. After many hours of misadventure, and some of fear, Moose and I slept the first night wrapped together for warmth in a burrow we'd dug out of a hillside, running ditches around its entrance so the water wouldn't pool where we lay curled on fir boughs laid on the clay.

Late the next afternoon we eventually found our way to the rendezvous, a lake with several lean-to shelters next to it. There we were met by our three Scout leaders, who had packed in sleeping bags and dry clothes and had waited, probably a little nervously, for the two days.

We all made it. We all were proud.

That night something important happened to me. The three leaders, all men in their late thirties or early forties, were talking around the campfire. Everyone else had long since clunked out from exhaustion, but for some reason Moose and I hadn't settled down yet, so we quietly sat with the men by the fire, hoping if we sort of sidled in no one would object. They were talking about "the war." In those days that meant World War II.

We sat very still, half expecting the glance that would send us back to the world of kids. I remember Joe pausing to look at us. The other two turned and looked at us as well. Ed worked for the railroad. Jens was a heavy equipment operator for another logging company. In the silence the fire lit their faces against the dripping black of the surrounding forest. A light mist fell on us but couldn't fight the strength of the fire. We admired these men. They gave a lot of time to us and we knew it. They taught us skills. They let us do crazy things like wander around lost. But we always knew, as scared as we were, that if we got lost they'd find us somehow.

Would they stop talking about the war? Would we be sent off to our lean-to? Joe just looked at us, it must have been for four or five seconds, and then he continued his story. We had been allowed to peek inside the Club.

Joe's story was about D-day at Normandy, Omaha Beach. Other stories came out. Ed was in the Navy in the Pacific. He talked about phosphorous glowing in the wake of the destroyer. Jens had fought in North Africa and Germany. No one talked about heroic deeds or ignoble ones. There were funny stories about military foul-ups and red tape, and there were brief vignettes of terrifying moments. I remember few particulars. Just as they were ordinary men, they had been ordinary sailors and soldiers. Moose and I knew that. No one bullshitted anyone. But we still made heroes of them. They had gone through *the experience*. What was that like?

Moose and I kept our mouths shut. The fire died down and the stories came to an end. I didn't want them to end. I remember the feeling of being "inside," and never wanting this feeling to go away.

My own father had driven trucks in the Third Army, supplying Patton's tanks, and there had been a movie just a few years earlier about this. So I said, "My dad was on the Red Ball Express," but I wasn't real sure driving a truck was a very warriorlike thing to do.

Joe looked at me and smiled. "I remember those guys. That was a hell of an operation. They drove gas and ammo up to the tanks, right up to where they'd run out, and then they'd come right back and sleep in the trucks while they were being repaired and loaded up again. You wouldn't catch me anywhere near a truckload of gas and ammo in a combat zone."

I went to sleep that night in my warm sleeping bag, rain spattering on the lean-to roof, the wet Pacific air on my face, proud of my father, proud of myself.

By passing that test of survival, and being awake at the right time, we found that the door of the Club had been opened just a little so we could see inside. Women have their clubs too. In those days they were usually based on childbirth and raising children. It's these old initiations, still with us, and these old clubs. They aren't all bad. It's just that things are changing for the reasons I talked about in the first chapter. If the initiations are changing, the clubs must change too.

In those days the club of manhood was still well intertwined with the club of warriors. It's time they separated themselves. Although both sexes today will have to incorporate some of the warrior attitude in order to enter adulthood, neither will actually have to become physical warriors or combat veterans to become men or women. Boys and girls will enter the club of manhood and womanhood by being invited in primarily by their fathers and mothers, and secondarily by other older men and women in their community, providing, of course, all these people are members themselves. Those men were inviting Moose and me, and it was valuable and good to be invited. The problem for me was simply that the clubs of manhood and combat veteran were still confused. A lot of the reason for this was that no one talked about it very much, and when anyone did talk, there were all sorts of mixed signals.

In tribal cultures when individuals successfully underwent an initiation and returned to the community they were admitted to a different club from the one to which they previously belonged. Where a person was once a member of the boys' or girls' club, he or she now became a member of the men's or women's club. Upon being made a full-fledged member of the new adult club, he or she was also asked to keep the club's secrets.*

The club of combat veterans has always had its own code of silence that wraps it in mystery just as thoroughly as the earlier initiatory clubs. Boys, in particular, read and see lots of stories about the entrance tests and exploits of club members. It doesn't seem to matter whether these stories are gruesome and horrifying or glamorous and heroic; they all have the effect of simply whetting the boy's appetite to join the club. For one reason, the boy knows that unless he experiences these things for himself, he won't understand them.† This, unfortunately, is true. But another reason the tales of horror don't dissuade a lot of boys from wanting to join the club is that the tales are too often told without

---

*There are sound psychological reasons for this, namely that if the initiation rite is demystified there will be little psychological transformation when it is undergone, and of course the whole purpose will be lost. You can't scare someone to death if he knows ahead of time that it's all a trick.

†Childbirth held much of the same mystery, terror, and transcendence for the girls. It, too, is disappearing as a means to womanhood. Women can now choose not to be mothers and large numbers will so choose. In addition, bearing children can now be done while a woman is unconscious or heavily sedated (although this choice is not generally taken), with much decreased risk of death in first-world countries.

emotion, and I mean both sides of emotions. In the horror are the pain *and* the transcendence. If the tale of horror is told without admitting the transcendence, the boy will hear it peeping through unconsciously. "I want some of that," he says, just as unconsciously. And if the horror is told without the raw emotions, the choking sobbing tears, it is abstracted and unreal.

Of course avoiding pain is one of the major reasons for the mystery and silence. Society itself would rather forget as well, and so not only colludes in this but actually enforces it with its own codes of behavior, which I'll get into shortly. The mystery that arises from all this silence simply whets the appetite to find out. People are curious, and children are very curious people. The club of warriors needs to be demystified in order to become one of many honorable clubs in which adults participate. If there is no longer any need for mystification, then there is no longer any reason for silence.

Most people seem to need a club of some kind, whether it's a secret society at Yale or a Wednesday night bowling league. We are a social species. It seems appropriate we should define ourselves as adults by being part of adult social groups. I was gradually being guided into manhood by those Scout leaders, but at the same time I was confusing the men's club with the Club, that is, the guild of the warrior. So too, probably, were they, just as many young men today confuse the men's club with the street gang, which they use as a substitute, with horrible consequences, for a more honorable warriors' guild. All this confusion is primarily a result of the silence imposed on the membership. If you can't or won't talk about it, you can't get clear about it. And one of the greatest ironies of joining the club of combat, for me, was finding out that the silence seems to be as much societally imposed as self-imposed. If you talk about what you're proud of, you're bragging. If you talk about what was painful or sad, you're whining. If you talk about the brutality, you're brutal. Society simply wants us to shut up about all of this.

My uncle, the one who was wounded in the leg in Italy, never talked about it. My father started to talk about his experiences in France and Germany only when he was in his seventies and I was in my forties, and I had to prompt him all along the way. Club members don't even talk to their sons about the club. I used to feel embarrassed, over exactly what I don't know, when I talked to my own children about the war, but I'm getting better at it.

The pressures for silence also work on the families, just as with alcoholism or any other aspect of society that is shamed. When I was first working on this book, my first wife hated to tell people that I was working on a book about war and killing.* One day while we were driving in the car she burst out in anger at me, asking me to use a pseudonym so the children wouldn't be at risk of being jeered or shamed at school over some of my less than pretty exposures. (Images of conversations in the school cafeteria: "My mom says your dad kills people when they want to surrender and he screws prostitutes.") My first wife obviously felt the same awful don't-talk-about-this stuff that I did. I still don't like it when I'm asked by people I don't know what I'm writing about, because it requires too much explanation to be sure that the questioners don't think I'm some kind of war freak who runs around in camouflage on weekends. Being interested in things military is still considered politically incorrect by a large segment of society and as a result this subject remains a virtual mystery for most people.

---

*She no longer feels this way.

There are several aspects of this code of silence. There's the stiff- upper-lip aspect. The English are particularly good at this one, having invented the phrase. One simply doesn't brag; one never complains. My experience of war is 95 percent things to complain about, 4 percent things to be ashamed of, and about 1 percent things to brag about. So if the code is don't complain, you're left with very little to talk about.

I'm reminded of the response of a much-admired older man, a don at Oxford, who I knew had been in combat in World War II. I'd asked him on several occasions about his experiences. I'd always get answers like "Oh, I just pottered around in the jungle a bit. Nothing very exciting."

We do this to ourselves, I think, because we're trying to fit back into society. Not talking about it allows this with the least disruption to all concerned. The Club is the veterans' protection against our great fear of being misunderstood. Being misunderstood means being thought bad because of having certain feelings about certain experiences, few of which were under our control at the time. It's actually not much different from being a racial or sexual minority. You have to protect yourself against the negative projections. To do this minority groups have formed their clubs too. But instead of protection through silence they use tools like "camp" or "cool."

The Club is also society's protection for those who stayed home. In war there are a lot of painful memories for nonveterans too. There is the loss of loved ones. In many countries nonveterans share much of the horror of actual warfare. Nonvets also share some of the thrill and may not want to admit it. People cheated on the black market and made lots of money working in war industries but can hardly justify talking about this. Others yearn for the sense of community, the sense of life on the edge, but can hardly justify their memories of these good feelings knowing the costs that have been paid by so many others. In short, not only are there painful memories; there are also unexamined motives and actions and, as a result, guilt. The silence of the Club suits society only too well.

There are several aspects to this societally imposed silence. First, there's the "Sunday school head lice" aspect. This I hate even more than the stiff-upper-lip and modesty games. Thou shalt not kill. Violence is bad. People who do either of the above are bad. So talking about it is going to spread the nits and infect everyone with this disturbing reminder of our human condition. This approach didn't do much good with regard to stopping venereal disease either. The United States has gone to war, actually killing people, over a dozen times since Vietnam: Cambodia (*Mayaguez*), Iran (failed hostage rescue), Lebanon, Libya (bombing Gadhafi), Panama, Grenada, Gulf I, Somalia, Bosnia, Kosovo, Afghanistan, Iraq, and Libya again. We've aided and abetted killing in the Falklands, El Salvador, Afghanistan (when the Russians were there), Angola, Cambodia, Colombia, and Israel/Palestine. We are a very aggressive and warlike nation. Denying our collective responsibility for these activities, whether they were right or wrong, is like scurrying around the house of an alcoholic hiding empty bottles and never mentioning the drinking.

If the silence continues and debate is limited solely to questions of morality and international politics without reference to our own shortcomings as humans, our own involvement in violence, and our grand illusions of power, then our sons and daughters and our next crop of political leaders will never be able to make clear judgments about entering situations where they will be asked, or ask others, to kill or be killed. We will continue to misunderstand a foundation stone, whether we like it or not, of current world society and most of human history.

Silence is a recent Club rule. It was not always so. The great Norse sagas, the epic poetry of the Greeks and Romans, all talked of war. War poetry and songs were recited and sung in the eating places. Tales were told around campfires and in the wigwams and desert tents. These epics often glorified war and warriors, with some bad consequences. But I think society has thrown a lot of nuggets out with the gravel by deciding that talking about war is taboo.

Veterans need to boast more. Everyone needs to boast more. We simply need to learn where and when it's appropriate, as opposed to what we learn now—that all boasting is inappropriate. I used to love listening to Muhammad Ali when I was in high school. He was having fun. Boasting is the same as a peacock spreading his feathers. It's a natural act. Why shame it? It can even be an art form. Listen to how Mark Twain captured the wonderful bragging of the old-time flatboat men.

"I'm the old original iron-jawed, brass-mounted, copper-bellied corpse-maker from the wilds of Arkansaw! I'm the man they call Sudden Death and General Desolation! Sired by a hurricane, dam'd by an earthquake, half-brother to the cholera, nearly related to the small-pox on the mother's side! I split the everlasting rocks with my glance and I squouch the thunder when I speak!"*

Boasting like this would be put down today as testosterone poisoning. Suppose when my daughters, Laurel, Sophia, and Devon, were young that they had gone whirling around the living room twirling their skirts, giddy with their beauty and joy and budding sexuality, and we called it estrogen poisoning. Warrior energy is fierce and wild. It upsets men who don't have it, and women who are afraid of it, primarily because the only form of

*From *Life on the Mississippi*, 1883.

it they know is the negative one that is a result of repression. And this negative side comes booming out unconsciously in the glorification of warfare and violence in books, TV, and movies, the authors of most of which aren't members of the Club themselves.

How do we bring some balance to the way the Club is perceived? What do we do when, in an honest moment, the former pilot looks right into your eyes, completely vulnerable, and says in a near whisper, "I loved it. I lit up the entire fucking valley."

One honest reaction is to be appalled. The chances are pretty good that if he lit up the entire fucking valley he probably maimed and killed a lot of innocent people along with the ones who were trying to kill him and he most certainly did vast damage to the natural habitat. But should we condemn him for speaking the truth? At one level, and one he's admitting, he certainly loved it. So did I. At another level he did what his society had asked him to do, and he did so with skill, courage, and even élan. Should that same society now cut him off at the throat or, worse, at the balls?

The appropriate response is to get him to keep talking about it. It may just be a bit shocking to find your friend has a wild and savage side that did a lot of harm. And it won't hurt him to find out that you think he did something very harmful and destructive, as long as at the same time he finds out that you won't love him any less for it. This is his great fear, that he won't be accepted back in. So he joins the conspiracy of silence. So do we all.

Society needs veterans to express all sides of their experience, the guilt and sorrow *and* the pride. Cut off one and you cut off the others. Veterans' organizations such as the VFW and the American Legion go a long way toward h\elping with the pride side and also providing a safe place for veterans to talk about experiences. These organizations are also enablers in numbing. They are filled with men drinking and smoking cigarettes. The

Department of Veterans Affairs has successfully organized groups of veterans who talk to one another about war with the help of a trained therapist. This has helped many veterans to express all sides of the war experience. The problem is simply one of numbers—too few good therapists, too few veterans willing to attend—and one of audience: it is only veterans talking with veterans. In both cases, the problem is that the veterans' experiences and feelings remain quarantined from their families and communities. They go to the dark bar at the Legion Club, where children and nonveterans are not allowed. They disappear once a week into the VA outpatient clinic to be "cured." They aren't talking to friends and family; they're talking to bar buddies and therapists.

The grief that is expressed at the Vietnam Veterans Memorial in Washington, D.C., and it is the grief that most people focus on, would not be possible if it weren't for the fact that the very building of the memorial was itself an act of recognition and pride on the part of veterans who took it upon themselves to get the project done. The memorial was not built by a grateful nation; self-respecting veterans built it and had to fight to have it placed where it is.

The combat veteran experience is still not out in the open where the whole of culture can benefit from the sorrow and the pride and society's attitude toward war and fighting can mature psychologically and spiritually. No nation will ever reach maturity, or make sensible foreign policy, until its warriors, its people, and its leaders can talk about all sides of war with equal feeling. "I lit up the whole valley" *and* "I've grieved, crying for the little ones like my own children." Without integration of the positive and negative sides of the war, the experience isn't transmitted in any practical and meaningful sense, and we will continue to seek the glory of war unchecked by wisdom about all the costs of war.

11

RELATING TO MARS

*I speak with some nervousness of relating to the war god Mars.
Who am I to suggest any human can relate to this terrifying yet
justifying god? Mars is the underlying organizing power that
creates and sustains those physical and terrible aspects of war
that seem beyond the comprehension of our small psyches. How
does one relate to Gettysburg, or Stalingrad, or Hiroshima? Yet
we must, or similar events will happen again. In the face of this
seemingly overwhelming power I am going to evoke the name of
Mars to stand for those war-making aspects of our own psyches
that love war and hate war simultaneously, aspects over which we
can exercise control. I do this because I believe that this area of
conscious control can continually increase. We waged war far less
destructively in Iraq than we did in World War II. I personally
relate to war differently today than I did when I was twenty. This
gives me hope for humanity.*

Throughout this book I have attempted to honestly share
my experiences of combat with an eye toward how I might
have managed those experiences with more wisdom and psychological, spiritual, and ethical maturity. I have argued that had I
been more conscious when I was fighting in Vietnam, I would
have contributed just as effectively, or even more effectively, to
the war aims of those in power. I would have wreaked less havoc
and less pain and still gotten the job done. In this chapter, in the

now shared context of my combat experience, I will touch on a few more general aspects of war fighting that I consider areas in which we can improve our relationship with Mars but which are more societally oriented than personally oriented.

UNDERSTANDING WARRIOR ETHICS AND PSYCHOLOGY: WAITE'S DICTUM AND THE WARRIOR'S DICTUM

Terry Waite, the special envoy for the archbishop of Canterbury, went to Lebanon in 1987 to negotiate for the release of hostages. While there, he was taken hostage as well. Day after day, for five years, he feared for his life. He was kept constantly blindfolded and chained, often for weeks at a time in a fetal position. He was tortured. If ever a person had good reasons for making an escape, Terry Waite had them.

At one point in his captivity his guard took him, blindfolded as usual, to the toilet. After Terry was let into the tiny room he removed his blindfold, and there, left accidentally on top of the toilet, was a fully loaded automatic rifle. His guard was the only guard around, just outside the door, unsuspecting. Waite walked out of the room and handed the rifle to the guard.

In an interview after his release Waite said he had no doubt that he could have killed the guard and escaped. He handed the rifle to the guard because for years he had been telling his captors and other terrorists that violence was not the way to settle disputes, and that he wasn't on one side or the other of this particular dispute. If he killed this man to escape, he felt it would have devalued everything he stood for. He said, "Other than to protect someone, I could not use that weapon."

Is Terry Waite the warrior of the future or just crazy?

He is neither. He is a brave man. Not all brave people are warriors. But in that interview Waite helped define what a warrior is when he said he would not choose sides and would not use a weapon, i.e., violence, other than to protect someone. In contrast to Waite, a warrior *does* choose sides. Choosing sides is the fundamental first choice that a warrior must make. Like Waite, a warrior is also willing to protect someone against violence, but Waite was talking about violence that is immediately being applied. The second fundamental choice of the warrior is to be willing to use violence to protect someone against even intended or implied violence. This second fundamental choice engenders an additional choice, which is accepting the risk of death and maiming that usually results from the decision to use violence against violence. To become a warrior requires making these two fundamental choices and accepting the risks entailed. Doing the above eliminates any need to use the adjective "ethical" in front of the noun "warrior." A warrior, by my definition, acts ethically. Using violence other than to protect makes a person a bully or a murderer.

The first decision, choosing sides, means taking on the warrior spirit. People who take on the warrior spirit become *metaphorical* warriors. They are *like* warriors in certain aspects, but they are not warriors. This choice is serious enough, often entailing commitments of great personal sacrifice. A prime example is a government or corporate whistle-blower. The second decision, however, choosing to use violence to protect someone else against actual and intended violence, a choice that usually also entails danger to the lives and psyches of the people who choose the violent path, moves one from being a metaphorical warrior to being a warrior in deed. Warriors are prepared to kill people.

Because warriors make these two fundamental choices that Waite does not, warriors operate under a moral code that is grounded on different principles from Waite's. At the base of Terry Waite's moral philosophy is what I call Waite's dictum: "Violence is not the way to solve problems." But Waite himself said in the same interview that he would have used a weapon to protect someone. This is the warrior's dictum: "No violence except to protect someone from violence."

These two seemingly incompatible positions invite wonderful moral philosophical debate. I can't say that Waite's position is more or less moral than the warrior's. I can say that the position of the conscious warrior will decrease the suffering of political violence in an imperfect world while the position of Terry Waite will eliminate the suffering of political violence only in a perfect world. One of *my* axioms of faith is that we don't live in a perfect world.

In order for a moral code to be of any practical value, that moral code must be applicable in the world in which we live. I unabashedly take a utilitarian stand that any moral code must help reduce suffering. This view invites the criticism that war itself causes more suffering than not going to war. The answer lies in the relative value one places on nonphysical suffering—for example, living under a dictator—and that gets us back into basic belief structures.

Although the world would definitely be less violent and therefore a better place if everyone acted like Waite, we happen to live in a world where people abandon Waite's nonviolent position regularly. When they do, they inflict injustice and suffering on innocent people. The warrior steps in and persuades them, by threatening or inflicting pain and death, to put an end to their harmful behavior.

The warrior's dictum is, however, oddly dependent philosophically on Waite's dictum. In order to adhere to the warrior's dictum the ethical warrior acts only when and if others use violence first. That is, someone else must have already abandoned Waite's position—the philosophical necessity required for the ethical application of the warrior's power. Accepting this means accepting that a moral nation's first use of its warrior power will always be defensive because preemptive strikes are immoral.

Like capital punishment, once done, a preemptive strike cannot be undone, and the nation struck could be innocent. Look at how badly the United States botched the intelligence, or botched the conclusions drawn from what intelligence it did possess, leading up to the 2003 Iraq war, namely that Iraq had weapons of mass destruction it was about to use against the United States. The United States got it wrong. Based on that justification alone, the United States was in the same position as a vigilante mob hanging an innocent man. There were more ethical justifications that should have been used and that were already well proved, namely a brutal dictator killing and torturing his own people who were powerless to stop him. The United Nations should have put a stop to it. It did not. The United States, Britain, and other states of the coalition did. Unfortunately they botched the occupation badly, setting back return to rule of law for years.

Preemptive strikes also put the nation's warriors into an untenable moral position. It's all well and good for the president to get tough and say we're going to bomb some country because he thinks it is fixing to bomb us. He, however, doesn't do the killing. Some pilot has to pickle the load on some human being, and if that human being's government never intended to strike the United States, then the pilot kills an innocent person. A warrior cannot commit to combat tentatively. Flawed as our response to Pearl Harbor was by racism and ignorance, it was not flawed by doubt about Japan's intentions. Our guys went to war with everything they had. Imagine the Roosevelt administration telling Patton he couldn't pursue the German Army south of the Loire for fear of upsetting the Vichy government.

Of course a no-preemptive-strike policy limits options and confines strategy and makes less philosophic warriors moan in frustration. Since the ethical warrior's position requires someone to break Waite's dictum, in some ultimate sense, the ethical warrior always plays defense. More traditional fighters will call this approach impractical. What they mean by "impractical" is that they are initially placed in a vulnerable position. This presents real practical problems for the warrior that should not be minimized. The point is to plan with this constraint in mind, not to abandon the principle.

We have often limited our strategic first-strike options in the past without serious harm. In many cases, by so doing, we have avoided harm not only to innocent people but also to ourselves. Take the tacit agreement between the belligerents of World War II not to use poison gas. Take the tacit agreement between the Soviet Union and the NATO powers not to use first-strike nuclear force, even though for years neither side would publicly give up this option. The strategies of mutually assured destruction, in this light, were not only practical, in that nuclear war was never waged, but moral. The problem is that a strategy of mutually assured destruction works only with opponents who have essentially the same value system. It will not work against suicidal terrorists or suicidal governments. Such people obviously value some things more highly than their own lives. This does not make these people irrational.

In the case of the suicidal opponent, there is a further problem. Deciding just when someone has broken Waite's dictum (violence is not the answer) and when to invoke the warrior's response is hardly ever a black-and-white case. Unfortunately, in terms of moral clarity, but fortunately in terms of misery, history hands us few clear-cut scenarios. Judging when to resort to violence, when to enter the warrior mode, is almost always done with limited information and under extreme duress. This means making decisions when our instinctual save-the-organism side is roaring to the fore and threatening to obliterate our feeble consciousness.

Once a decision is made, however, to commit our warriors to violence, the moral restraint of waiting for the enemy's next move should be removed. We should commit totally to the offensive, what Robert E. Lee called "taking the aggressive." The warrior should hold back force or offensive operations only when the other side stops using violence—period. The warrior stops fighting with every ethical means at his or her disposal only when one side quits. Being unclear about the warrior's dictum can get us into moral hot water with first-strike policies. Being unclear about taking the aggressive has embroiled us in the "gentle surgeons make stinking wounds" kind of fighting we have been involved in too many times since World War II. Escalation, the strategy used in Vietnam, didn't work. Just because game theory can be applied to war does not mean war is a game.

If we are unable to take sides against a clear opponent, and unable to use violence with every means at our disposal to force that opponent to stop using violence against our side, then we should not go to war. We should use other means to either encourage or coerce people to do what we want. The world community helped end apartheid in South Africa through a whole lot of pressure other than military force.

Finally, there is the very real problem that the people who make the decisions to send in the warriors often fail to adopt the warrior mode consciously themselves. It is as if they are deciding to involve someone else in a war. They "send our youth into harm's way." I do not doubt that most of our leaders take their responsibilities very seriously, but only if they see that *they* are actually doing the killing can they make a more conscious decision. Ideally, they should know ahead of time that *they* will have to face nightmares the rest of their lives over the killing. It will make for better decisions.

I have often heard, and have agreed with, people who bemoan the fact that our political leaders, once they declare war, don't get up on their horses like the chieftains of old, draw their swords, and lead the charge. That role is rightly outdated because the modern war chief must marshal and direct economic, political, and diplomatic as well as military resources and it is ineffective to do so from a horse. However, this distancing from the action should not preclude the leaders' use of their imagination so that they can get into the correct relationship with the decision to wage war. Without this leap of imagination, modern political leaders will not be prepared to think and behave like ethical warriors.

In a decision to make war, leaders must stop thinking of themselves as policy makers. The policy makers' fundamental decision is whether or not to enter the warrior mode themselves. First, they must choose sides. This is something good political leaders do or should do as a matter of course. The more problematic decision is the second step. Killing people with Marines is ethically no different from killing people with hatchets. Only the distance from the spurting blood differs. So when a politician sends in the Marines, the politician uses violence every bit as much as the Marines themselves. The decision maker must imagine that sending warriors into harm's way is the equivalent of charging the enemy with a sword with his own hide at stake. When a president or member of Congress decides to go to war, he or she must do so as a warrior, not a policy maker. It is the leaders who are choosing sides and using violence to stop violence, the very definition of a warrior. It remains a reason why the electorate should value military experience in its leadership.

THE GROWING CYNICAL "NO HOLDS BARRED" ATTITUDE

Completely taking the aggressive does not mean "no holds barred." I am constantly told, usually by people who have never been to war and who apply varying degrees of simplistic reasoning, that all is fair in love and war, that having rules of war is total nonsense. This is simply not true. To sink to the position that fair play and the impulses of good character have no place in modern war, taking some sort of tough-guy realpolitik stance, is something the ethical warrior must never do. As I have said, warriors must wage war totally, without holding back, until the enemy stops using violence. Waging war fully, committing every ounce of force at one's disposal, however, is different from waging war unethically. Entering the boxing ring with one hand tied behind your back is entirely different from agreeing not to hit below the belt. Is the veterinarian who however reluctantly kills the mad dog with sodium pentathol any less effective than the enraged man who kills it with a rifle or poisoned bait?

I can think of no finer examples of strength of character and fair play in war than those described by Hans von Luck, one of the most highly decorated of Erwin Rommel's young panzer commanders.* Luck joined the German Army in 1929 at the age of eighteen and became one of Rommel's favorite line officers. He saw action on the Eastern Front and in North Africa, France, and Germany. He was captured by the Russians in the final days of fighting before Berlin and spent five years in a Russian labor camp, returning eventually to Germany to become a coffee importer.

In North Africa Luck led an armored reconnaissance battalion. Armored reconnaissance units were constantly at the extremes of the main battle areas, screening, probing. Thus he was very often in contact with his British counterparts, the Royal Dragoons and the Eleventh Hussars. In a treeless desert, with no landmarks and no satellite fixes, it was impossible for units to find their way back to base in the dark. To light a signal would betray their position to artillery fire. So for both sides all activity ceased at evening.

One night Luck received a call from the Royal Dragoons.

> "Hallo, Royal Dragoons here. I know it's unusual to make radio contact with you, but Lieutenant Smith and his scouting party have been missing since this evening. Is he with you, and if so, how are things with him and his men?"
>
> "Yes, he is with us. All of them are unhurt and send greetings to their families and friends." Then came the brainstorm: "Can we call you, or the Eleventh Hussars, if we have anyone missing?" I asked.
>
> "Sure," he replied. "Your calls are always welcome."
>
> It was only a matter of days before we arrived at a gentleman's agreement: At 5 p.m. precisely, all hostilities

---

*Hans von Luck, "The End in North Africa," in *The Quarterly Journal of Military History* (Summer 1989).

would be suspended. We called it "tea time." At 5:05 p.m.
we would make open contact with the British to exchange
"news" about prisoners, etc. From a distance of about fifteen
kilometers, we could often see the British get out their
Primus stoves to make their tea.

One night Luck's doctor went outside the perimeter to re-
lieve himself and never came back. He was indispensable to Luck
and it was a major blow. Finally Luck called the British. Yes, they
had him. Then the British made a suggestion. They were suffering
badly from malaria. Their quinine from the Far East had been
cut off. Could they exchange the doctor for some of the German
synthetic Atabrine?

The moral issue was whether to continue to weaken the British by refusing them Atabrine or to get his doctor back. As Luck
put it, "I quickly made up my mind." He exchanged the Atabrine
for the doctor.

Once a Royal Air Force reconnaissance plane on a long-range
patrol discovered Luck's small column. There was no place to hide
on that merciless flat plain. Within an hour the fighters, Hurricanes
and Spitfires, came roaring over the horizon. They concentrated all
their fire on his antiaircraft platoon, eliminating it. They were back
within an hour and eliminated his artillery platoon. Now he was
completely defenseless, so he scattered his men away from the tanks
and reconnaissance vehicles and watched helplessly as the planes
roared in for the third time to shoot up all the tanks.

The only one to remain in his vehicle was my radio operator,
who was sending off my messages. Next to the vehicle stood
my intelligence officer, who passed on to the operator what
I shouted across to him. Then a machine—I thought I

recognized the Canadian emblem—approached for a low-flying attack on the armored radio station. At twenty yards, I could clearly see the pilot's face under his helmet. But instead of shooting, he signaled with his hand for the radio officer to clear off, and pulled his machine up into a great curve.

"Get the operator out of the vehicle," I shouted to the intelligence officer, "and take cover, the pair of you!"

The machine had turned and now came at us out of the sun for the second time. This time he fired his rockets and hit the radio car . . .

This attitude of the pilot, whether he was Canadian or British, became for me *the* example of fairness in this merciless war. I shall never forget the pilot's face or the gesture of his hand.

Small incidents like this were numerous. When the end finally came, Luck, who thought he was in a place where no one could find him, received the following letter, handed to him by a bedouin.

From C.O.
Royal Dragoons
Dear Major von Luck,

We have had other tasks and so were unable to keep in touch with you. The war in Africa has been decided, I'm glad to say, not in your favor.

I should like, therefore, to thank you and all your people, in the name of my officers and men, for the fair play with which we have fought against each other on both sides.

I and my Battalion hope that all of you will come out of the war safe and sound and that we may find the opportunity to meet again sometime, in more favorable circumstances.

With greatest respect.

I'm not trying to say that throughout the Second World War the Germans and the British didn't do horrible things to each other. They did. But there were these incidents when they did not. As Luck puts it, "The prevailing atmosphere was one of respect: We 'understood' each other." The word *respect* is notable. For some reason, these particular men did not pseudospeciate each other. They remembered their common humanity and controlled the beast that lies within us all. Remembering our common humanity and controlling the beast that wants to obliterate that memory is the task for all conscious warriors of the future.

Basic training is oriented toward eliminating the enemy's humanity. I am well aware that this presents us with a very difficult question. Will our young people carry out our war policies if they can't overcome the fact that they are killing a person just like themselves? Will increased consciousness decrease effectiveness?

I think not.

If a young warrior falls into killing from a rage or killing while thinking of the enemy as less than human, then, with some prior warning, some prior understanding, there is the chance for quick recognition of what is happening when the killing stops. It's like catching cancer early. There's a better chance for a cure if it isn't allowed to grow unnoticed. I do not doubt that warriors will invariably switch into and out of consciousness and on occasion kill from rage. Warriors will almost always kill with the conviction, at the time of killing, that the enemy is not human. Our goal should be to strive not to do so and, when we do, to get back to consciousness as soon as we are out of immediate danger. Training for such a goal will not be likely to perfect us, but it will move us forward.

BESTIAL NATURES, CONTROL, AGGRESSION, AND COMPASSION

I shall probably never be as thrilled as I was that one moment I left a safe position to join my old platoon in the assault where I ended up trying to pull Utter from underneath the machine gun. I ran toward the fighting with the same excitement, trembling, and thrill as a lover rushing to the beloved in the spiritual love poetry of the mystics. Perhaps these are identical transcendent psychological states. But I don't ever want to do it again. It is also a dangerous inflated state of being.

The transcendent state is a major reason warfare is an intractable human problem and so difficult to put a stop to. It offers us raw life: vibrant, terrifying, and full blast. We are lifted into something larger than ourselves. If it were all bad, there would be much less of it, but war simply isn't all bad. Why do kids play war games? Why do adults enter professions such as ambulance driver, search and rescue, firefighter? Because these activities lift you from your limited world.

To teach the children who will become the warriors of the future about the dangers of this kind of power, each of us must know it and be able to draw on this energy when appropriate.

I was in Germany with my friends Albert and Hilde and their four children. Hilde is from the Prussian aristocracy. We

were visiting a large fortress and castle that had been in the keeping of Hilde's family for many generations. As I walked down
the corridors in the castle, I couldn't help noticing that many of
the portraits of the old warriors hanging side by side, generation
by generation, on the walls, looked remarkably similar to Hilde.

Hilde wandered off with the three girls, and Albert and I
ended up with his son, Wilhelm, or "Vim," on top of the wide and
exposed castle walls. The fortress was high on a hill in the center
of a small city. A large valley with gentle rolling hills stretched
out below us. You could see tidy farms and villages out to the
green horizon.

Vim, who had barely turned four, was far too young to know
anything about the castle or the portraits on its walls. He left us
and walked over to the wall's edge. There was no parapet, no safety
fence, nothing between him and the scene stretched before him
and death below him. Albert and I stopped talking, frozen.

Vim spread his legs wide apart. Standing only inches from
the edge, he put his small fists on his hips, thrust out his chest,
and lifted his chin defiantly. In a clear piping voice, suddenly
strangely powerful, he called out to that empty space and rolling valley, "Ich bin Deutscher."* Something had taken over Vim
and it gave me shivers. The ghosts of the ancestors were here.
The fierce Germanic god Wotan, the leader of the Wild Hunt,
had come.

Albert, who had lost his own father in the Second World
War, gently walked over to Vim, knelt beside him, and put his
arms around him. Albert is a wonderful man whose respect for
traditional values doesn't stop him from actively supporting the
Greens. He looked out at the scene with Vim for a moment. I

*I am a German.

can't translate verbatim, but the words and the tone conveyed something like "Yes, you are a German. It's beautiful, isn't it." He brought Vim back to safety and said quietly to me in English, "The smartest thing you Americans ever did was split us in half."

Wotan exists. I think Wotan is closer to the surface in some cultures than in others. I think Wotan is closer to the surface in boys than in girls. I know that within me, or all around me, are very fierce and wild forces. These forces have to be channeled and guided. They are too big to dam or damn. These forces, which can come through all of us, are not created in childhood. However, the strength of character required to guide these forces is greatly helped, or greatly damaged, by how we parent our children, particularly when this force appears. Without such character the ego simply abandons ship when it faces this situation. There's no ego strength left to control the unconscious forces that come ripping through the abandoned channels of the body and mind. The loss of this "I" is, according to most mystical traditions, the way to ecstasy, but it can also be the way to horror.

Homer spoke of the warrior energy nearly three thousand years ago through the voice of Odysseus.

> great Ares* and Athena
> gave me valor and man-breaking power,
> whenever I made choice of men-at-arms
> to set a trap with me for my enemies.
> Never, as I am a man, did I fear Death
> ahead, but went in foremost in the charge,
> putting a spear through any man whose legs
> were not as fast as mine. That was my element,
> war and battle. Farming I never cared for,

*Ares is the Greek god of war. Mars is the Roman equivalent.

nor life at home, nor fathering fair children.
I reveled in long ships with oars; I loved
polished lances, arrows in the skirmish,
the shapes of doom that others shake to see.
Carnage suited me; heaven put those things
*in me somehow.**

The great mothers—Mother Teresa—and the great
fighters—Chesty Puller—are simply people who have dedicated their lives to the power that "heaven put into them." Such
people, however, are on an extreme end of a spectrum most of us
only share in varying degrees. Women can briefly enter the realm
of the Great Mother whenever they give birth. I entered the realm
of Mars for a time in Vietnam. Some of us get swallowed alive by
these energies or archetypes and some of us reemerge to carry
on with other activities. Recognizing that we share these energies,
but need not dedicate our lives to them, allows us all to use them,
but not be used by them, or be manipulated by society into being
used by them. To try to kill these energies through repression and
shame is not only impossible but very damaging to individuals and
society. A lot of current societal forces and politics try to do just
this. But to be used by these energies also damages individuals.
Women can more easily be manipulated and consumed by the
Mother and men by the Warrior. To strike a healthy relationship
we need to first see that "heaven put these things in us somehow."

Given that this responsibility rests on our individual shoulders, how are we to bear this load? How are we to recognize and
acknowledge the evil within, yet not give in to it and act it out?
How are we to be warriors who essentially perform violent acts
yet still maintain our humanity? Our only hope is to see this Mars

*Homer, *The Odyssey*, trans. Robert Fitzgerald, 1963.

energy clearly so we can be aware of ourselves as distinct from it yet a part of it. There is no hope for limiting the tragedy of warfare and violence if we don't see it. It will take us over, obliterate our egos, turn us all into people overwhelmed by our dark sides. "Command yourself" is the second great principle of the ethical conscious warrior.

Our response to the problem of keeping the beast in check while we are still waging frightful war has been the typical flip-flop of extremes that people usually adopt when faced with seemingly irreconcilable demands. At the one extreme we say things like "War is hell," excusing ourselves as we ride the beast over Tokyo, firing paper houses and burning civilians, or ride it a quarter century later, doing the same things with napalm in Vietnam. At the other extreme we make extraordinary efforts to keep the warrior leashed, mistakenly hoping that somehow if we leash the warrior the beast will also remain leashed. But at this extreme all we can do is wring our hands and point fingers while all the things we hold dear, our children, our ideals, our values, are ground into the mud by the beast unleashed by the opposing side. It seems an impossible situation. How can we kill to protect without releasing the dark warriors of pseudospeciation, racism, hatred, and slaughter?

This dilemma isn't a new one.

Our greatest protection against falling into the thrall of the beast is children raised without shame and suppressed rage. This will ultimately demand a revolution of respect in child rearing.*

To deal consciously with the warrior aspect of small children, our task as parents is to recognize that aggression and the warrior energy are as natural and as problematic as sexuality.

---

*I refer the reader to the works of authors such as Alice Miller, John Bradshaw, Gershen Kaufman, Adele Faber, and Elaine Mazlish.

There is a biological base to them, the strength of which varies from individual to individual. Just as some people like to make love more often than others, some people are naturally more aggressive than others. Just as virtually all people like to express sexuality, so too with aggression. Natural aggression, like sexuality, can either be repressed, to eventually emerge ugly and out of control, or it can be guided into healthy and productive uses.

One day our son Alex, when he was three, got accidentally locked out of the house. My wife and I were upstairs cleaning his brother's and sisters' bedrooms. We could hear him pounding on the door, shouting for us to open up, but we were in the middle of trying to reverse the laws of entropy with the toys and decided he could wait a minute or two.

We heard a shattering of glass.

I ran down the stairs. Alex was standing in the living room with glass all around him, door wide open, a large stick in his hand. He was radiating. He had smashed the window in the door to unlock it from the inside.

I gently took the stick from his hand and carried him up to his room for a quiet talk. I was so dumbfounded I couldn't think of what to say. I suppose I should have told him how frustrated he must have felt when he couldn't get in and how strong he must have felt to solve his problem all by himself by smashing in the window. Then I should have told him that his strength needs to be used for different sorts of occasions, for instance if he were really endangered, or a friend were endangered. At least I didn't go into a rage and make him feel ashamed of his natural, albeit misplaced, vitality.

One of the results of repressing natural aggression in children is that aggression gets blocked permanently and is replaced by passivity. This has traditionally happened to women. We've actually gotten ourselves into such a state with repression of natural aggression in women that many women are now going to classes to unlearn the shutdown imposed on them by society. They can't even draw on this natural energy that the gods put in them to save their own lives. I worry that the same thing is now happening to men. It's the wrong response to the problem of violence. Repressing natural aggression until it becomes passivity works only temporarily; the aggression will be released as unconscious rage years later, through either physical violence or ugly, damaging verbal aggression.

The first time the child smashes the window to get inside the locked door you must recognize and check your own fear of the violence that act invokes in you. Then you must recognize, and help the child recognize, how good and strong that must have felt. Never cut the child off from his or her warrior feelings, particularly by statements such as "You don't really feel that way." Once you affirm that the feelings are honest, you then immediately say how that strength and those feelings should be used for something better than smashing windows.

When a child grabs a playmate's toy, or defends himself violently against someone else who is grabbing the toy from him, you show both children what warrior energy is used for by immediately protecting the victim of the aggression, innocent or guilty. Then you help the little warriors see clearly what happened and how they feel. "That made you mad. That anger helped you feel strong. You may need that strength someday when there is nobody else to help. But you didn't need it here. You can get your toy back without hurting someone."

Preschool teachers constantly repeat the convenient shorthand "Use your words" when a child gets aggressive. The overriding message is that aggression is bad. It doesn't recognize the healthy aspects of aggression. Unrecognized, the healthy drive frequently goes over to the dark side. There are times when physical aggression is an appropriate response. When you meet the serial killer on the jogging path, words are going to fail you.

At home, parents should wrestle with their children, showing them physical aggression under control. It's fun to wrestle. It's fun to pin Dad (or Mom). It's fun to cause him a little pain. And Dad has some fun pinning the kids too. But the kids learn that the fun stops at painful chokeholds or arm bars. They learn that little brother starts crying if his three older siblings pile on top of him.

Roughhousing often ends up with someone crying at some point. This is because crying is a child's sign that things have gone too far. Children are learning. They have to push to this point to find out when enough is enough. A normal reaction to games that evoke crying is to ban them because they hurt people. What should be banned is not the rough games but continuing beyond the point where the child signals that things have gone too far. Young children will understand what going beyond that point means only when they have pushed to the point where they see, hear, or feel the consequences for themselves. And they will push to that point time and time again.

What needs to be taught is that the aggressor must stop when the opponent asks for the fighting to stop. Parents must attempt to link the feelings of the child being hurt to the memory of similar feelings on the part of the aggressor child. The best way to do this is to continue the game, because, sooner or later, everyone ends up on the bottom of the pile. The bottom of the pile is the best place to learn empathy.

Empathy can be taught and learned. Traditionally we learn it the hard way. When I was in grade school, I never got into a fight thinking I was going to inflict pain on someone. I especially never got into a fight thinking I'd have the pain inflicted on me. I just got into a fight. Pain was the last thing on my mind.

Along with teaching empathy we also need to teach the difference between empathy and sentiment. Warriors need empathy, but a warrior must not fall into mushy sympathy. My great-uncle Charlie raised cattle. The summer I was seven I got the job of feeding a little bull calf who'd been rejected by his mother. I imaginatively named him Ferdinand. I remember petting the hot coarse hair on his bony spine and talking to him, looking at his broad white face, noticing how his eyes rolled white when he tried to see me coming up behind him. I used to tag around with him, dodging mother cows and cow pies. I'd feed him from a bottle. I brought Ferdinand anything I could think of, flowers, candy, hay, rolled oats from my great-aunt Sandra's cupboards.

One already hot morning Ferdinand was gone. I went back to the house. "Aunt Sandra, where's Ferdinand?" She looked at me, flour on her hands from making bread. "Go talk to Kalle Sita." So I found Uncle Charlie, who was on the John Deere 40 haying, and asked him the same question. He asked me if I'd like to ride the pickup into town for a milkshake. There at the counter, beneath the paper straw sleeves hanging down from the ceiling where kids had blown them with gum attached to the ends, he explained the economics of ranching, including where the spending money came from to buy my milkshake.

I cried. Charlie just put his hand on my shoulder. When we got back, he said something to his daughter, my aunt Lydia, in Finnish, and she took me over to my cousins' farm to go swimming in the river. There was no mystery. I knew Ferdinand had been turned into meat. And I knew why. Money sends kids to college, not sentiment. If the air support comes loaded with napalm, you burn your enemy and save your recon team.

INCORPORATING SPIRITUAL AND PSYCHOLOGICAL
SOPHISTICATION INTO THE CONDUCT OF WAR

Raising our children to come to terms with natural aggression will bring us more mature and psychologically balanced warriors. Changes still remain to be done by the military. The first change will have to be in how it approaches spirituality. The second will be in how it incorporates the explosion of knowledge about psychology and brain chemistry into its training programs.

Eighteen-year-olds haven't lived long enough to be much aware of the spiritual and individualizing part of their personal development. They are in phase one, the societal-role part. Odysseus had been working on phase two for twenty years, and he still nearly lost it when tested defending his father's farm against the revengeful relatives of the slain suitors. These kids will need a lot of spiritual guidance once they are in the military, and I don't mean the battalion chaplain handing out cheer at Christmas.

I would leave a great deal of the particulars of spiritual training up to the individuals themselves. I worry about the military's natural tendency to do everything by the numbers, which, ipso facto, destroys the individual character of the training. But the military should provide the structure and the tools for individuals to successfully engage in personalized training. To begin with I'd make each advance in rank a time for reflection and instruction. By the time soldiers are old enough and have had enough experience to reach ranks such as staff sergeant or company commander, they should have to go through several weeks of intensive inner work, particularly dealing with their own rage on the psychological level. On the spiritual level they need to come to terms with the fact that their job will probably require them to lead anywhere from forty to several hundred soldiers whose job it will be to kill other warriors and, because we are not perfect fighters with perfect weapons, innocent people. I can think of few other professions that require as much leavening in their leadership and ranks of phase-two leaders for the well-being of society. I can think of no other profession, save perhaps psychotherapy, which should have more psychological training than these warrior professions. When I got promoted I got drunk.

Men and women should have significant parts of this inner training separately. You can't relate well to the opposite sex until you come to terms with your own sex and sexuality—and your unconscious contrasexuality. In the immediate future, many heterosexuals are going to have difficulties with homosexuals. Women choosing the military as a profession are going to have an immense struggle not to become pseudomen. It's not just a woman's problem, however. There are a lot of male pseudomen in the world, still behaving like forty-year-old frat boys. A pseudoman, whether male or female, can be an effective killer but cannot be a conscious warrior.

The old Women's Army Corps, like the other women's services, had already made a good start, perhaps unconsciously, on much of what I'm talking about. The women's branches had their own traditions, rituals, and standards, which were separate from those of the men. Unfortunately, these were eliminated when the military integrated.

Young soldiers will also need help from the older men and women they work with. Today, however, we have lost almost all old soldiers down in the ranks. Many poor and illiterate men found permanent homes in the armies and navies of the previous centuries. The all-volunteer military has moved a considerable distance from that former economic role. Today our military consists of educated working-class or middle-class personnel, and people who aren't capable of advancing are usually encouraged to leave.

This has left the military with mostly young people in low ranks. There are no more old peasant soldiers with pipes dispensing hard-won wisdom. Older, and therefore higher-ranking, people now need to actively get down into the ranks to be more involved with younger military people's personal development. When I promoted a fire team leader to squad leader, I never once asked the usually teenage kid how he felt about the added responsibility or the moral burden. Even though I was only three years older, I was older and should have. Had someone ever asked me such questions, it probably would have been sufficient to prompt me to ask them similar questions, because I would have seen the value.

We were being resupplied on an operation north of Khe Sanh when out of the resupply bird came a sweating, cursing caricature of an overweight top sergeant. But this top sergeant had been busted back to gunnery sergeant and sent to Vietnam for using Marine Corps equipment to build a secret swimming hole for the kids in his company back in the barren hills behind Camp Pendleton.

Ex–first sergeant Michaels, or "Gunny Mike," as he came to be known all over the regiment, was close to retirement. He drank too much. He ate too much. His heart was bad. We could hear him wheezing and gasping whenever we stopped, his face florid, refusing to sit down for fear he'd never get up again. He never complained. When asked if he was all right, he would snap back, "I'll-goddamnit-get-in-shape-now-leave-me-the-fuck-alone." Old Corps—to the core.

He was with us in the bush around a week when he finally faltered and fell on a very steep ridge on a very hot day. The corpsman passed the word up the column to the skipper. The gunny's blood pressure had skyrocketed. We'd kill him if we didn't get him out of the bush. That night the skipper ordered Gunny Mike back to the regimental staging area at Vandegrift Combat Base. He told the gunny we needed someone back at VCB to make sure we got supplies sent out to us in the bush and to clean up the company's supply tent, which was always in notoriously bad shape because no one was back there to look after it. This was all true, but Gunny Mike knew the real reason. I watched his lips tense, holding back what emotions I don't know. He saluted. No one salutes in the bush.

From that day on we had an institution. All the kids in the company —passing through sick, passing through on R&R, coming in-country, going home—all went through Gunny Mike. He'd walk them to the LZ when they were too scared to walk there themselves. He'd sit them down with cold beers and let them talk off the most recent horror when they came back. He'd help them write letters home.

Once, at three in the morning, I came to crash in the tent on my way back into the mountains after a one-night drunk. There was Gunny Mike playing cards with a lone new guy. A candle was guttering on the steel supply table, throwing wavering shadows against the dark canvas walls that luffed slightly in the damp night air. He was listening to the kid nervously telling him what must have been his entire life story before he would have to sky up with me two hours later for the unknown terrors waiting for him in the bush.

When we would come off an operation there would be ice cream. We'd burn out machine-gun barrels, and there to replace them would be barrels stolen at great risk from Army helicopters. One time he had two hours of porn movies and popcorn waiting for us. He was no saint. And we never asked questions he'd have to lie about.

Gunny Mike was twenty or twenty-five years older than the oldest of the rest of us, which would have put him somewhere in his forties. He seemed like an elder uncle or even a grandfather. His value was inestimable. What he did won him no medals and what appeared on his military file would never come close to describing what he did in our supply tent. He counseled. He performed communion with a cup that held Wild Turkey and a host of freeze-dried trail food, also stolen from the Army. He made room for soul.

What Gunny Mike was doing is nothing more or less than what therapists call co-counseling. He happened to be a gifted natural at it. But this sort of thing can be taught. I would have everyone trained in it at least a little bit and NCOs and officers trained in it a lot. It would save money and lives in the long run and improve efficiency and motivation in the short run.

I envision a system where each unit, maybe as far down as platoon level, could elect somebody to help conduct ceremonies of significance. Another way might be to provide combat corpsmen and medics with some of this training. They often act as platoon psychologists in any case. Such a person would do this in addition to his or her normal duties. It would be wrong to set someone up as a specialist exempted from the dirty work, wrong for that person and the unit. Our kids talked with Gunny Mike because he'd been there in Korea. They hardly ever talked to the chaplain.

The only difference between unit spiritual helpers and the other fighters would be that the helpers receive some extra training in addition to their basic killing skills. This would be something that chaplains could do well, along with some co-counseling techniques and consultation on particularly knotty problems. The unit spiritual leader would conduct simple ceremonies, with no particular religious heritage, mourn dead friends, bury dead enemies, and help people come to terms with the fact that they've just killed someone who was probably as innocent as they were in this whole mess. They could conduct small ceremonies before going into battle or going on ambushes or patrol where battle might suddenly erupt. These people and their ceremonies would help line other people up with the right reasons for what they are about to do. They would help detoxify others from the contaminants of rage, shadow, and the occasional missions devoid of meaning. They would help release, gradually and steadily, as close to the actual time of combat as possible, the overwhelming emotions and psychic pressures of war. I think if more of this was done, atrocities would be less likely to occur. Infantry platoons have medics for the body. Why not for the soul?

MYTHOLOGY: COMING TO A NEW UNDERSTANDING OF MARS

Beyond fundamental changes in child rearing and military training, we need, finally, a new mythology about war itself. We must recognize that even the mythologies of the past don't always bring sufficient wisdom to our situation today. We are presently being asked to move beyond the old myths, even as we still struggle to grasp their deep wisdom.

This is not a new situation in history. Many an old religion has disappeared to be replaced by something "better" or more true. The Odysseus of Homer was different from the Odysseus of Sophocles. Odysseus grew and changed as the consciousness of the poets grew and changed. We must take from an epic mythology such as the Bhagavad Gita what we can, but we must apply to it our own expanded knowledge of other cultures and other myths. In the Bhagavad Gita, Krishna says to the despairing

Arjuna, "A wise man never weeps." The Bible verse all Christian kids love to memorize, John 11:35, says, "Jesus wept." We are no longer limited to one tribal myth. We can choose.

Joseph Campbell has said that the new world mythologies yet to come must transcend national boundaries. So too must civilization's use of warriors. When you put the primary duties of the warrior into a global perspective, rather than simply a national one, the warrior comes out looking more like a police officer. This is because at last we have come back full circle, back to the mythologies of the original warrior gods.

The warrior gods in prehistorical times were gods of justice as well as war. In my view, this seems to be in large part because early people almost invariably considered themselves the *only* people. In their eyes, they constituted everything that was human. Subsequently their mythologies and religions were themselves global, explaining all.* If you were never confronted with an enemy, and particularly an enemy with a totally different religious system, you didn't need a war god on your side, because, in effect, you were the only side. The god of war could easily be a god of justice, putting to rights differences between people of essentially the same beliefs.

As populations increased, however, territories got abandoned and invaded. Mass migrations confronted these early people with alien religious forms and understandings of the world. "Us" became "them and us." People began to need a war god more than they did a god of justice. The war god split off from the god of justice as communities came into conflict. As the world is reunited

---

*This is one reason why the advent of science so shook most religions. Science proved that what was in fact global didn't fit the old mythologies based on a false sense of what was global.

and made smaller through advanced communications and technology, once again we become the only people. The war gods will have to shift back as well.

For people of European, Persian, and Indian ancestry all the war gods evolved from the Indo-European god Deus. The name means "shining heaven" or "light of day." Deus was probably the supreme sky god of these early people as well as their god of battle.* *Deus* is the root word for Zeus, the supreme god of the Greeks. It is also the root for Dyaus pita, which means father Deus and was shortened to Jupiter, the supreme god of the Romans. The Indo-European source word for the sky god still exists in words like *deity* and *day*.

The early Germanic tribes, long before they split into the tribes of history such as the Norsemen, Goths, and Vandals, also worshipped a god with a variation on this name. This god was called Tiwaz, another variant of Deus or Zeus, the original form of the Tyr in the story of the binding of the Fenris wolf and, as Hilda Ellis Davidson, a distinguished researcher of pre-Christian northern Europe, says, this god was "no mere crude deity of slaughter."

Early Roman travelers associated Tiwaz with their god Mars, calling him Mars Thingsus. The Thing was the assembly of free men where disputes were settled. The Thing is not only one of the earliest known forerunners of the jury, a fundamental institution of our current judicial system, but also a precursor of Western legislative systems.

Tiwaz was the god of the justice system as well as of battle. He was the protector of law and order in the community. Davidson quotes Tacitus, the early Roman historian who wrote about the

*H. R. Ellis Davidson, *Gods and Myths of Northern Europe*, 1984.

Germanic tribes. "No man might be flogged, imprisoned, or put to death among the Germans save by their priests, 'in obedience to the god which they believe to preside over battle.' If the god of battle punished criminals, then he must surely have been regarded as the supporter of order and justice."

This shouldn't surprise those of us from a Judeo-Christian heritage. Our Jehovah basically started out as a war god, the Lord of Hosts. It was this same Lord of Hosts who gave Moses the tablets of the law. Tiwaz was one-handed, another reflection of the sacrificed hand of Tyr or of Nuada Argetlam (He of the Silver Hand)—all gods who sacrificed a limb for the good of others. He also wielded a sword. The statue of blind Justice in our courtrooms shows her wielding a sword as well as scales.

Over time, Tiwaz disappeared. Eventually Tiwaz turned into Wotan for the early Germans and, later, Odin for the Norse Vikings. Davidson writes, "As time went on the emphasis seems to change from that of a supreme ruler holding in his hand victory or defeat, who taught men the value of law and order among themselves, to that of a more capricious power who bestowed madness on his followers, and who meted out victory or defeat with the arrogance of an earthly tyrant." These splits in our culture become representations in our own psyches. As our psyches split, so too did our images of our gods, and today we are left with a war god split off from an earlier, more whole figure.

By Greek and Roman times the combined war and justice god had become a god of battle, the terrible Ares or Mars. Robert Graves comes down pretty hard on him: "Thracian Ares loves battle for its own sake. All his fellow-immortals hate him, from Zeus and Hera downwards, except Eris, his sister, and Aphrodite who nurses a perverse passion for him, and greedy Hades who welcomes the bold young fighting-men slain in cruel wars."*

My reading of Graves is that of a man who himself never came to terms with Mars. When you read of his terrible experiences during the First World War and the years he spent afterward with painful physical and untreated psychic wounds, it is obvious that he suffered terribly from post-traumatic stress disorder. His unhealed wounds influenced greatly his view of the war god, and it is such a point of view that many in today's culture hold. This is because so many people in today's culture need the same healing. Despite Graves's description, and our own one-sided view of Mars, it is clear that the ancient Greeks had still retained much of the earlier, more whole form of Mars, or Ares, as they called him. The connection between the war god and god of justice is evident in the hill in the midst of Athens called the Areopagus, the Hill of Ares. The Areopagus is where the Athenians had their principal court of justice. Judges were called areopagitae.

What all this says to us today is that it is time to return Mars to his lost connection with justice. The "them and us" perspective we've gone through for the past several thousand years is coming to an end. It isn't over yet, however. Many in America, including many of our leaders, still cast their dark shadows on a so-called evil empire, an "axis of evil," or Muslim countries in general, and they on us and on one another. I will never forget the image of burning oil fields during the Iran-Iraq War, two great nations futilely destroying what was dragging them into the modern world. What happens in Uganda is instantly known in Siberia. People all over the world view the same soccer game at the same time. My

*Robert Graves, *The Greek Myths,* 1955.

Italian soccer shoes have leather uppers from Argentina and soles from Malaysia; they are assembled in China, marketed through an American retail chain, and advertised on Japanese televisions whose components are made in Singapore. The smith that Cúchulainn defends today is everywhere. Once again we are forming into the only tribe there is, the only people.* Mythologically speaking, this is turning the pure war gods, such as Mars, back toward the gods of war and justice, such as Tiwaz.

It is important, however, to remember that information technology and international commerce change far more rapidly than culture and religion. We are moving toward a world that sees itself as one people, but we aren't there yet. During this period of transition, we will find ourselves increasingly embroiled in wars where the primary goal is to restore, or even establish for the first time, civil order and a workable system of justice, not to defeat a clearly defined enemy who is trying to harm us. It behooves us to recognize the difference in order to make it clear whether troops are acting in the role of warriors or the role of police. As I said at the start of this chapter, warriors choose sides. Police cannot choose sides; they must be on the side of the law.

We cannot expect young men, particularly teenagers, who are trained to take sides as warriors, trained to fight the enemy with all the hotheaded passion and lack of introspection and, let's face it, lack of mature judgment that makes them ideal weapons of the state, to do the job of the police, who need to be extremely mature and the very opposite of hotheaded. Even more problematical, we cannot place even mature policemen in situations where there is no agreed-upon law with which they can side. If you go to

*Perhaps with the same myopia. Someday people may be amazed that we didn't think of trees as "people."

any penitentiary in this nation and ask its inmates if it is wrong to murder or commit armed robbery, virtually all of them will agree that it is. Yet in Afghanistan there is fundamental disagreement on whether or not it is wrong to cut off the ears and nose of a woman who disgraces her abusive husband by trying to run away. Which law do our mature police side with there: sharia law, tribal law, or the law of modern democracies? Forces acting as police must act with the legitimacy provided by law that is recognized as being impartial. If foreign troops are placed in situations where they are expected to act in the role of police but where the legitimizing law is not agreed upon and not supported by the local population, then troops trying to act like police will fail and should not be committed. If national policy is to force compliance with a view of the law other than what already exists in the location in question, then this requires warriors. Committing troops as warriors, however, requires a sober assessment of whether or not using coercive violence to accomplish a change in commonly accepted law is moral, particularly if those who don't agree with us aren't threatening us. It also requires ascertaining just how long it will take before forced compliance turns into nonforced acceptance. In societies where currently accepted law is approximately ten centuries behind the accepted law of modern democracies, it could be decades. If we are unwilling to commit warriors for decades we should stay put, relying instead on nonmilitary forms of pressure to bring about the required change. Again, South Africa is exemplary; the law did change there.

In addition to moving back toward justice as well as war, the war gods are also changing in another important way. This change has long been part of our mythology. The offspring of Ares and Aphrodite is Harmonia, harmony. As Graves puts it, "Harmonia is, at first sight, a strange name for a daughter borne by Aphrodite to

Ares; but, then as now, more than usual affection and harmony pre-
vailed in a state which was at war." This is certainly true. My parents
often talked with affection about the war years, when "we all were
pulling together." There is also the fact of incredibly deep bonds of
affection among soldiers. Graves, however, stops short. What I think
the mythology is telling us is that inner harmony, personal harmony,
is the result of the union of Aphrodite and Ares, the integration of
love, sex, justice, and war. Without this union, there is no harmony.
The relationship between Ares and Aphrodite is far from perverse,
as Graves has it; it is a step in human consciousness, and the sooner
we take that step, the less we will suffer. There is evidence that this
is occurring, at long last. On the personal level, men and women
are integrating their contrasexual sides. Gender roles are far more
flexible. This has thrown both sexes into turmoil, or at least it sure
threw me into turmoil, but I have hope that eventually harmony
will prevail and we'll have females who are integrated and healthy
women and males who are integrated and healthy men.

Militaries of true democracies now take great pains to minimize the deaths of innocent people. In that same war in which my
parents found affection and harmony on the home front, both sides
were killing civilians by the hundreds of thousands, in horrible
ways, and not even thinking about it much. Many of the people
who fought in that war are still among us. This is incredibly rapid
change. Military forces are often employed on missions of mercy.
The militaries of most democracies have successfully integrated
women into all specialties except those involving close physical
combat. Ares and Aphrodite have formed a union, but, like all
unions, it isn't without its difficulties and it takes a lot of work.

AFTERWORD

I have tried to explain what it was like for me to go to war: why I went in the first place, what happened while I was there, and how it was when I came home.

What got me into the temple of Mars was a contradictory mixture of patriotism, genetic imperative, the draft, a yearning for transcendence and escape from the humdrum, a need to prove my manhood, and just plain self-testing and curiosity. Inside the temple I experienced a surprising love for those who entered with me. There I prayed for deliverance from horror, carnage, and death. Never have I felt closer to God and more baffled by the problem of evil. In that temple, I experienced transcendence and, momentarily, ecstasy. I also experienced flawed humanity and raw savagery, my own and that of others, beyond comprehension for most people. I've never approached the intensity of these feelings after returning home. I do, however, find disturbing reminders of the bad ones when I read the newspapers, hear jingoistic claptrap, awake from nightmares, or see unbidden images welling up from my memory at the most awkward times. I have learned to find gentle reminders of the good ones when I write fiction, play the piano, share holidays with my family, see old comrades, and make love. I still long for the stronger feelings of war's transcendence and ecstasy, but, like the recovering alcoholic, I also know their destructive and dangerous aspects.

We must be honest and open about both sides of war. The more aware we are of war's costs, not just in death and dollars, but also in shattered minds, souls, and families, the less likely we will be to waste our most precious asset and our best weapon: our young. The more we recognize the feelings of transcendence and the psychological and spiritual intensity of war, the easier it will be to prevent their appeal from clouding our judgment about going to war the next time. What ultimately will save us from the appeal of war is achieving this transcendence and intensity through other means. The substitute for war is not peace; peace is a seldom-achieved political state of being. The substitutes are spirituality, love, art, and creativity, all achievable through individual hard work.

As long as there are people who will kill for gain and power, or who are simply insane, we will need people called warriors who are willing to kill to stop them. I've done my part. I can only pass on what I've learned in the hope that some current or future warrior will be more conscious of the conflicting forces I've touched on in this book in order to better control them and be a better warrior than I was. Warriors must always know the people they are protecting and why. They must undertake the personal responsibility for deciding when to kill and for what higher cause. This implies a commitment to a cause beyond self-interests, or even national interest alone. The split-off war god Mars must be brought back together with Tiwaz as protector of order and justice, no longer solely for the local tribe, but for all humanity.

ACKNOWLEDGMENTS

I would like to thank my wife, Anne; my children, Peter, Laurel, Sophia, Alexander, and Devon; and my first wife, Gisèle, for their wonderful support. Anne and Gisèle helped greatly with suggestions on early drafts. I am grateful for Julia Karpeisky, whose fine mind untangled many of my self-tied logical knots. I would like to thank my friend and spiritual guide, David Bona, and those VA psychologists, psychiatrists, and counselors who made such a difference in my life: Larry Decker, Sharon Rapp, Emmett Early, Lorry Kaye, and Ellen Li. I would like to thank the members of the Three A. M. Shopping Club, combat veterans all; you know who you are, why we keep running into each other at deserted twenty-four-hour supermarkets, and how much you mean to me. Finally, I would like to thank my editor, John Flicker, whose skill in shaping and cutting greatly improved the book; the people at Grove/Atlantic, particularly Morgan Entrekin, Deb Seager, Jodie Hockensmith, Sue Cole, and Peter Blackstock; Don Kennison, for the much appreciated and fine job of copyediting; Susan Gamer for her careful and thoughtful proofreading, and the people at International Creative Management, particularly my agent Sloan Harris, for their support, skill, and hard work.

RONALD RIGGS

Karl Marlantes, Vietnam, 1969